WADE HAMPTON
AND THE NEGRO

WADE HAMPTON

WADE HAMPTON AND THE NEGRO

The Road Not Taken

By

HAMPTON M. JARRELL

University of South Carolina Press - Columbia
1949

For my wife, who listened patiently,
and for my daughter, who did not.

CONTENTS

CONTENTS

FOREWORD

THIS book concerns a thirty-year cycle of revolution and counter-revolution in South Carolina, a cycle that ran its course between 1865 and 1895. The revolution lifted the Negro to political supremacy in the state for almost a decade; the counter-revolution first curbed his power and then eliminated him from politics. This futile and costly sequence of events illustrates with startling clarity the tragic results that may follow political conflict between irreconcilable extremists, particularly when emotion and propaganda supplant reason and knowledge.

Now, more than eighty years after the events here told began, there is again a dangerous increase in tension between extremists, North and South, again about the Negro. In the North, again, the propaganda mills are working: political speeches, plays, novels, sermons, stories, and heavily slanted articles in newspapers and magazines, all pointing towards federal action against the *status quo* in the South. In the South, again, extreme meets extreme with an upsurge of anti-Negro sentiment long quiescent, with the election of anti-Negro political leaders, with an increase in anti-Negro organizations, with—worst of all—the discrediting of those forces in the South, Negro and white, which are working toward more social justice for the Negro.

Eighty years ago wise and moderate men like Presidents Lincoln and Johnson in the North and like Wade Hampton of South Carolina and L. Q. C. Lamar of Mississippi sought a middle way whereby they could, without hatred and strife, solve the difficult social problem of two races living side by side in almost equal numbers; but the outraged screams of the extremists of both sections made their efforts vain. This study, therefore, is not only a record of the past, but also a plea for moderation now and in the future.

ix

Conflict between extremists can never lead to stability or balance. As a matter of sober fact, the North cannot shape the social and political structure of the South, even though it may destroy our traditional pattern of constitutional government in the effort. Such an attempt failed disastrously for all concerned during Reconstruction in spite of every advantage of force on the side of the reformers. A brief summary indicates how formidable their power was: a twelve-year military occupation of a beaten and bankrupt land; political control of a tightly organized Negro majority; control of all governmental agencies, local and national, including the army and the courts; federal election laws so stringent that, as *The Nation* observed, for a Southern white man even to talk politics with a Negro was construed as "intimidation," a federal offense; the firm support of the large majority of Northern people, who were blinded by carefully nurtured war hate and by a generation of abolitionist propaganda; almost no political representation in Washington for the white South; and a determined administration with the power to pass and implement any "force acts" it could devise. With such a preponderance of force the North, acting through the federal government, could punish the South (as it did), but could not determine the pattern of the South's social order. It could increase hatred and suspicion between the races, largely to the detriment of the Negro; but it could effect no permanent increment of justice or friendship. Such power will probably never again be available to remold the South as the reformer would have it; any true friend of the Negro should seek another way.

As a matter of equally sober fact, the South cannot ignore the moral sentiment of the nation, and indeed of many Southerners, in its treatment of the Negro, as thoughtful Southerners have long been aware. Southern extremists, if they love their section more than they do their phobia, should assist rather than resist a new search for a middle way. Moderate men of both sections (and there are many such in each) must work together on this problem if the nation is to avoid another tragic cycle of action and reaction, wherein, again, all but a few shrewd opportunists will lose and wherein the Negro will lose most of all.

I have confined my study to South Carolina because there the various conflicting forces are clearly differentiated; but during this thirty-year cycle similar forces were at work throughout the South. In South Carolina, too, one can most clearly discern the social changes that resulted as political power shifted from Northern moderates like Lincoln and Johnson to Northern extremists and Negroes — then to

Southern moderates under the leadership of Wade Hampton and finally to Southern extremists led by Ben Tillman.

I have shaped my story around the personality of Wade Hampton because throughout the period he was at the center of the conflict and also because he embodied the best tradition of Southern friendship for the Negro. To Southern men like him the nation must look for any substantial improvement of race relations in the South.

An understanding of the thirty-year cycle of revolution and counter-revolution in the race struggle in South Carolina is made more difficult by the complications of a simultaneous class struggle to determine whether white political control would remain with the ante-bellum ruling class or would go to the increasingly assertive common man. Many complexities and apparent contradictions are explained by the facts that in every crisis the class struggle was completely subordinated to the race struggle and that, as the Marxists would *not* have it, egalitarians in the class struggle were most extreme in their opposition to Negro participation in politics. Tillmanism completed the triumph both of white over black and of the common man over the old leadership. This study is primarily concerned with the race struggle rather than with the class struggle.

I wish to express my sincere thanks to the librarians of Winthrop College, the University of South Carolina, Duke University, Emory University, and the Hayes Memorial Library. Dr. Austin Venable kindly read parts of my manuscript, and my wife gave careful help in the tedious job of reading proof.

HAMPTON M. JARRELL

Winthrop College
Rock Hill, S. C.
June, 1949.

WADE HAMPTON
AND THE NEGRO

Chapter One

PRELUDE TO NEGRO SUPREMACY
1865-1867

THE extreme phase of the revolution that put the Negro in political control of South Carolina for nearly a decade did not immediately follow the close of the Civil War. For about two years after Lee's surrender the plan of reconstruction devised by President Lincoln and implemented by President Johnson determined the political complexion of the state. This was the brief period during which moderate Northern sentiment was a dominant factor in the South, though from the start the intent of the President was effectively thwarted by an extremist faction in Congress that was called Radical Republican.

In its essence the Presidential policy for reconstruction was to let each Southern state work out its own destiny under Presidential supervision. Each state would become again a working part of the nation as soon as it organized a government loyal to the national Constitution and adopted a state constitution acceptable to the President. Regarding "war criminals," too, the President's purpose was one of reconciliation rather than retribution.

As for the Negroes, the Presidential policy provided for the protection of their newly gained freedom, but did not grant them the right to vote. The existence of large Negro majorities in some Southern states, particularly in South Carolina, made this issue of Negro suffrage the crucial one, for to give an unrestricted ballot to the blacks, not five per cent of whom could read and almost none of whom had had the least political experience, would impose a heavy burden on a society already shaken by war and defeat. The President's position on suffrage, moreover, had at first the backing of the mass of Northern people of both parties. Even Oliver P. Morton, who was later to be a rabid leader of the Radical Republicans, found it "impossible to

3

conceive of instantly admitting this mass of ignorance to the ballot."[1]

On the other hand, the question of Negro suffrage was equally crucial to the ambitions of many Radical leaders. If the Southern states could be made and kept Radical Republican, Radical control of the nation, they thought, would be perpetuated. As Thad Stevens put it, the restoration of Southern states to the Union would be considered only when the federal Constitution had been so amended as "to secure perpetual ascendancy" of Radical Republicanism.[2] The enfranchisement of Negroes in the South was an absolute prerequisite. Not the least of the many ironies of Reconstruction — the very term is ironic — is the fact that within ten years Stevens' policy had created the solid Democratic South.[3]

Thus, while President Johnson was trying to bind up the wounds of civil strife, powerful forces within his own party were at work against him both in the South and in the North. During the spring of 1865 Chief Justice Salmon P. Chase of the Supreme Court toured the South, assuring the Negroes that they would soon have the vote and winning Negro support for the Radicals. At the same time representatives of the Union League were herding blacks by the thousands into political clubs with impressive ceremonies including an oath always to vote Republican. Moreover, agents of the Treasury and of the Freedmen's Bureau, along with various other political adventurers, all later to be known as carpetbaggers, were diligent in the good cause and in feathering their own future political nests.[4]

---

[1]William D. Foulke, *Life of Oliver P. Morton* (Indianapolis, 1899), I, 444ff., quoted by Claude G. Bowers, *The Tragic Era* (Boston, 1929), p. 16.

[2]Stevens reiterated this sentiment in various speeches before the House from December, 1865, until his purpose was accomplished. For *The Nation's* matured judgment on this use of the "brute vote," see XXIII (October 19, 1876), 238. See also D. H. Chamberlain, "Reconstruction in S. C.," *Atlantic Monthly,* LXXXVII (April, 1901), 437f.

[3]For example, according to his biographer, Bernard Baruch remained an "almost fanatical hater of the Republican label" because of his childhood memories of Reconstruction in South Carolina, this in spite of early removal to the North and in spite of sometimes violent objection to Democratic policies or candidates. Carter Field, *Bernard Baruch* (New York, 1944), pp. 89ff. See also Woodrow Wilson, "The Reconstruction of the Southern States," *Atlantic Monthly,* LXXXVII (January, 1901), 11.

[4]John W. De Forest, novelist, army officer, Republican, and official of the Freedmen's Bureau, recorded his observations in South Carolina during 1866 and 1867. Of such officials he said, "One wonders that the South did not rebel anew when one considers the miserable vermin who were sent down there as government officials." Croushore and Potter (eds.), *A Union Officer in the Reconstruction* (New Haven, 1948), p. 44. For harm to Negroes from political leagues, see *ibid.,* pp. 99f.

In the North, too, the Radical extremists were stoking their fires and bringing the old abolition fervor and the sectional hatreds of the war back to a boiling point. "Waving the bloody shirt," as this propaganda technique was called, became the mainstay of the Radicals, who founded their power on continued hatred and suspicion towards the white South — and the fires that they kindled have not yet entirely cooled. Perhaps President Lincoln could have withstood this clamorous pressure of Northern extremists, but President Johnson could not. The moderate Northern policy towards the Negro in the South was never given a fair chance.

1

In South Carolina the spring of 1865 was a time of despair and bitterness for the past and of blackest fear for the future. The state had staked its wealth, almost the highest per capita wealth in the nation, on a Southern victory; and defeat entailed economic desolation.[5] Graver than bitterness over the past, however, was dread of what might lie ahead. That the federal government would take some sort of punitive action against the South seemed certain; that South Carolina, as a leader in the secession movement, would be a principal victim seemed equally sure.

By June, however, there was a bright gleam of hope. Already the moderate Presidential reconstruction policy had indicated a road to union that the South could follow without humiliation. As General Grant reported to the President, ". . . the mass of thinking men of the South accept the present situation of affairs in good faith. The questions which have heretofore divided the sentiments of the people of the two sections — slavery and state rights, or the right of a state to secede from the Union — they regard as having been settled forever. . . . I was pleased to learn from the leading men whom I met that they not only accepted the decision arrived at as final, but that now the smoke of battle has cleared away and time has been given for reflection, that this decision has been a fortunate one for the whole country. . . ."[6] An influential Charleston minister, A. Toomer Porter, voiced

---

[5] De Forest served as an official of the Freedmen's Bureau in charge of a district in the Piedmont section, or Up-country, of South Carolina for fifteen months from October 1, 1866. Although his district was one least touched by war, he states, "In Naples and Syria I have seen more beggarly communities than I found in the South, but never one more bankrupt." *Ibid.*, p. 199.

[6] Letter from General Grant to President Johnson submitted by the President to the Senate on December 19, 1865.

the opinion of many moderate South Carolinians when he said, "The victorious arms of the Federal Government abolished slavery, and I, for one, thank God it is done. I would not have done it so suddenly; it means suffering, and wholesale death to the poor blacks. . . . But it is done, and now, if we have any sense left, let us make the most and the best of it."[7]

Henry W. Ravenel, distinguished South Carolina botanist and slave-owning planter, was writing in his journal late in May his acceptance of the fact that emancipation will be the settled policy, but whether immediate or gradual will be decided by Congress. . . . Both policy and humanity would dictate that it should be gradual, so that both parties at the South may accommodate themselves to so radical a change in social and political economy."[8]

By June 12 he had accepted emancipation and was reflecting on the political future of the Negro race:

> Now that he has received his freedom as soon as he is qualified to become a citizen and to exercise the rights of a citizen, consistency would require that he should have all the rights. God forbid that I should wish to keep him back from any privileges with which his maker may endow him. At present I believe the negro is too ignorant to be intrusted with the right of voting. If, in the course of time his freedom is so used as to improve his condition, both physical and mental, I would be glad to see them elevated in the scale of life.[9]

John W. De Forest, an official of the Freedmen's Bureau, observed this general acquiescence: ". . . I found a surprisingly general satisfaction over the accomplished fact of abolition, mixed with much natural wrath at the manner of accomplishment."[10]

On June 30, 1865, President Johnson appointed as provisional governor of South Carolina Benjamin F. Perry, a man who had vigorously opposed secession but who had supported the Confederacy after that decision had been made. During July Perry conferred with General Wade Hampton and other leaders of the state and convinced them that President Johnson had instituted a conciliatory policy towards the South. In September he assembled a convention to write for the state a new constitution that would be acceptable to President Johnson. Hampton, after his conferences with Perry, had retired to his

---

[7]A. Toomer Porter, *Led on! Step by Step* (New York, 1899), pp. 199f.
[8]Arney R. Childs, (ed.), *The Private Journal of Henry William Ravenel: 1859-1887* (Columbia, 1947), p. 238.
[9]*Ibid.*, p. 244.
[10]De Forest, *op. cit.*, p. 195.

home in the mountains of North Carolina and therefore had received notice of election too late to attend the convention.

The primary task of this state constitutional convention and of the state government that it created was to make a clear definition of the new social, legal, and political status of the Negro imposed by emancipation.

As early as the fall of 1865 a few South Carolinians, with Wade Hampton as their recognized leader, sought some means whereby the newly freed slaves could be given a chance to become voting citizens without allowing their three-to-two majority to dominate the state. The plan generally proposed was bi-racial suffrage with an educational and property qualification applicable alike to black and white.

Although no such demand had come from the federal government, Provisional Governor Perry seriously considered making such a proposal in his inaugural address to the state constitutional convention in the fall of 1865.[11] Joseph LeConte, later to be a distinguished scientist, wrote in his autobiography, "I insisted that the convention should adopt a franchise *without distinction of color,* but with small educational and property qualification. My friends admitted the wisdom of the suggestion but said that it was impossible, as the leaders had not 'backbone' enough to propose it and the people were not ready to endorse it."[12] Similarly A. Toomer Porter declared in a sermon in Charleston that "as free men" the Negroes "would surely be given the ballot, and we should offer it to them when they could read, write, and cipher, and owned five hundred dollars of freehold property."[13] An ex-governor of the state commented on this sermon, "If this is the way our public men are going to speak, there is hope for the old land yet; we shall live and not die."[14]

The prevalence of this sympathetic attitude towards the Negro as a citizen, as well as the bitter opposition to it — the line of cleavage that was later to split the leadership of the state — is indicated in the testimony of Dr. A. P. Wylie of Chester before the joint Congressional committee in 1871.   Dr. Wylie had favored Negro suffrage at the

---

[11]Benjamin F. Perry, *Reminiscences of Public Men* (Greenville, S. C., 1889), p. 275. See also p. 312: "I, myself, thought that colored men who could read and write and paid a tax on five hundred dollars worth of property should be allowed to vote. The Republican authorities at Washington thought differently at that time. But a sudden change came over them when they found that all the Southern States had gone Democratic...."

[12]Joseph LeConte, *Autobiography,* ed. W. D. Armes (New York, 1903), p. 236.

[13]Porter, *op. cit.,* p. 199.

[14]*Ibid.*

state constitutional convention of 1865. "I thought it might be best to have some qualification in regard to education for both blacks and whites. Judge Darling and others expressed themselves so, but they had not seen their constituents. On account of my votes, some extreme men cursed me, and called me an abolitionist, but not the respectable part of the people. They appeared to approve it."[15]

This small but influential group of moderate South Carolinians increased in number and influence until, in 1876, they controlled the state under the leadership of Wade Hampton. They were strongly opposed, however, by South Carolina extremists led by General Martin W. Gary. In 1865 this line of division was indicated by divergent attitudes towards the freedmen, but was not clearly drawn. In 1874, in a bitter speech before the Taxpayers' convention, General Gary focused attention on the schism by a scathing attack on all South Carolina white men who had sought to "harmonize" with the Negro, particularly on Hampton for his early advocacy of qualified Negro suffrage. After the white victory of 1876, this division became an open break; but Gary's faction was decisively defeated. The Tillman movement of 1890 was in part a new and successful bid for control by the Gary faction, now under the leadership of Ben Tillman; and it marked the political extinction of Hampton and his moderate supporters as well as the end of their policy. That Hampton and his much-maligned fellow "Bourbons," many of them ante-bellum leaders, were the moderate men who sought a middle road was a fact too little understood, both North and South. It was their fate to be damned with equal enthusiasm by the extremists of both sections.

In the state constitutional convention of 1865 the entire problem of Negro suffrage was simply avoided in public debate since it was a subject of uncompromisable difference of opinion and since white unity was essential if the convention were to do its job quickly and effectively. As the *Charleston Daily Courier* remarked, "It cannot but be the earnest desire of all members that the matter be ignored *in toto* during the session."[16] None the less, the prevailing tone of the convention was definitely moderate, and the nomination for governor was offered to Hampton. When Hampton refused because his high rank in the Confederate Army made him an object of suspicion in the North, the nomination and election went to another moderate,

---

[15] *Ku Klux Conspiracy, S. C.* (Washington, 1872), V, 1434.

[16] September 26, 1865. Quoted by Frances Butler Simkins and Robert Hilliard Woody, *South Carolina during Reconstruction* (Chapel Hill, 1932), p. 41.

James L. Orr, at one time speaker of the national House of Representatives, who later during Reconstruction went over to the Radical Republicans. If the promise of this beginning could have been kept, if moderate men of both sections could have continued to preside over the reconstruction of the South, one of the ugliest chapters in American history would never have been written.

2

The constitutional convention called by Provisional Governor Perry and the first legislature under Governor Orr faced two different and, in many respects, conflicting sets of realities. One they totally misunderstood; the other they understood thoroughly.

The reality that they did not grasp was the attitude of many Northerners towards the social, economic, and political "rights" of the freedman. Even before the Radical press began its all-out propaganda campaign, there was a considerable amount of suspicion in the North as to the good faith of the South in regard to the new status of the Negro, though there was little demand at first for Negro suffrage. This suspicion was scarcely justified. De Forest, for example, who had expected to find blind racial prejudice in South Carolina courts, concluded after several months of diversified experience, "Of the fifty or sixty magistrates in my district I had occasion to indicate but one as being unfit for office by reason of political partialities and prejudices of race." He added, "New York City would be fortunate if it could have justice dealt to it as honestly and fairly...."[17] Both the convention and the legislature of South Carolina made an honest, though perhaps not entirely enlightened, effort to adjust the state machinery to the new order.[18] They did not, however, make any effort whatsoever to placate Northern feelings. The common failure to heed warning voices from the North is indicated by a comment in the *Charleston Daily Courier*: "It may be safely said that the views and opinions of Sumner, Thad Stevens, Wilson and some other Northern Radicals have been considered too unworthy to be seriously commented upon

---

[17]De Forest, *op. cit.*, p. 31. See also *ibid.*, p. 74, "... The Southerner was not hostile towards the Negro as a Negro, but only as a possible office-holder, as a juror, as a voter...." See also *ibid.*, p. 97, Negroes who did their work "seldom suffered injustice."

[18]See Lillian A. Kibler, *Benjamin F. Perry* (Durham, 1946), pp. 414f. and note, and pp. 422ff.

by members of the convention. It is well known that the sentiments of those gentlemen are extremely unpopular in the North."[19]

It seems likely that nothing South Carolina could have done would have prevented the Radical drive for control. What was done, however — the hard and fast definition of a separate status in the community for the Negro — provided adequate material for both righteous and unrighteous indignation north of the Mason and Dixon line.

The problem that the legislators did understand, the social and economic *needs* of the freedmen, was treated with more decisiveness than tact. A clear-cut distinction between white and black was a part of the accepted folkways of the state, and legal distinctions on the basis of color that shocked some Northerners were accepted as a matter of course by both races in South Carolina. At any rate, the new laws made this distinction with utmost frankness. Then, as now, much Northern indignation was aroused, not so much by what Southerners did about the Negro, which differed little from Northern practice in many communities, but by the public avowal of legal distinctions on the basis of race.

Besides the general question of racial distinctions, there were many special problems relating to the newly freed labor. Whatever may have been the cause, it was a sad fact that Negroes had their own well-recognized attitudes toward work, toward truth, and toward private property. Testimony on this point is abundant and typical results of first-hand experience may be found in comments from the private correspondence of some of the New England abolitionists who in 1862 had come to the sea islands of South Carolina to help care for the abandoned slaves and to produce cotton on the abandoned plantations, thus admirably combining service with profit.

One writes in December of 1865, "There is a universal feeling of dissatisfaction, not to say disgust, with our colored brethren here at the present time, on account of the extraordinary development of some of their well-known characteristics. They are stealing cotton at a fearful rate. . . . We none of us feel secure against these depredations."[20] Another notes, "Dr. Oliver and Captain Ward, who have bought 'Pine Grove,' have taken the usual disgust for the people. They have got it bad; say they would not have bought here had they imagined half the reality. . . . I say the same when I say anything about

---

[19]September 26, 1865. Quoted by Simkins and Woody, *op. cit.*, p. 42. See also Kibler, *op. cit.*, pp. 425f.

[20]Elizabeth W. Pearson, (ed.), *Letters from Port Royal* (Boston, 1906), p. 322.

it."[21] Another comments, "We had a call from Dennett (a correspondent of *The Nation*) on his Southern tour, a few weeks ago. He said he was disappointed in not getting better reports of the negroes here on these islands, for he had been looking forward to this place, feeling sure he should find something good to offset the many evil reports he had heard of them all the way down through the country."[22]

One of the leaders, "an older man, a teacher, a person of great loveliness of character and justice of mind," writes on October 9, 1865, "I have no reason to complain of my people for any extraordinary delinquencies, for they have worked as well as we shall probably ever be able to get these negroes to work; but I have frequently had occasion to be vexed at their slow, shiftless habits and at their general stupidity. It is a very great trial to any Northern man to have to deal with such a set of people, and I am satisfied that if Northerners emigrate to the South and undertake agriculture or anything else here, they will be compelled to import white laborers."[23] By December, though, we learn that this same gentleman's cotton had been stolen, that he would be "glad to get away from this 'Sodom'," that "he is too good a man to be worn out by the barbarians of this latitude," and that the correspondent of *The Nation* thinks him "very much demoralized on the negro question."[24]

These are the comments of the best (those who "stuck" for several years) of "a party of men and women who were almost without exception inspired purely by the desire to help those who had been slaves."

Most people in the North could not imagine "half of the reality," though they knew exactly what ought to be done. But members of the first state convention and legislature very well knew the facts.

---

[21] *Ibid.*, p. 328. Indeed, writing many years later, Governor Chamberlain, the last and best of the carpetbagger governors, asserted, "I find myself forced by my experience and observation to say that [we should undo] what we have heretofore done for the negro since his emancipation, namely, the inspiring in him the hope or dream of sharing with the white race a social or political equality; for whoever will lay aside wishes and fancies and look at realities, will see that these things are impossible...." Quoted by Henry T. Thompson, *Ousting the Carpetbagger from S. C.* (Columbia, 1926), p. 175.

[22] Pearson, *op. cit.*, pp. 320f. Stephen Powers, a mustered-out Northern army officer who in 1868 walked through much of the South, in *Afoot and Alone* (Hartford, Conn., 1872), p. 96, quotes a successful Negro planter, "... perhaps half my race have the will to make an honest living. But not one-third of them have judgment enough to keep land, if they had any."

[23] Pearson, *op. cit.*, pp. 315f.

[24] *Ibid.*, pp. 321ff. See also Simkins and Woody, *op. cit.*, pp. 332ff.

They formulated strict laws to check vagrancy, to keep the laborer on the farm until a crop was harvested, and to prevent petty theft, particularly the theft of crops.[25]   The Radical press dubbed these laws the "Black Code" and screamed that slavery was being reinstituted under another name.   As a matter of fact, the vagrancy laws were no more severe than those in many Northern states (Massachusetts, for example), and the general tenor of the code was sincerely believed to be in the best interests of the Negro as well as the white community.   These laws were, however, needlessly strict in some particulars and foolishly tactless in the use of such terms as "servant" and "master," though they were notably less severe than the measures employed by many federal officers to meet these same conditions in districts under their command.[26] Above all, they frankly differentiated between black and white.

The "Black Code," had it been continued, would, with a few modifications, have provided a much-needed period of transition from slavery to citizenship.   The course that was followed under Radical Reconstruction, on the other hand, left a child-like and undisciplined

[25]Conditions in the Low-country indicating need for something like the "Black Code" are described by Henry Ravenel from information given by his half brother, Rene (August 23, 1865): "He gives a deplorable account of the condition of affairs in the country [around St. Johns].   Robberies are of daily occurrence.   Ebough, Markly and Esterling and others are buying all the cotton the negroes can steal and carry to them.   Everybody is losing cotton, cattle, hogs, and sheep.   William had his cotton removed into his dwelling house at Woodlawn, and it has been stolen.   But little provisions will be made, not enough to serve the negroes but a small portion of next year.   The planters will only make from their share of the crop enough for their own support, and of course will not be able to engage laborers next year for want of provisions.   The prospect is that they will barely get a support, and even that will probably be stolen from the field or the barns as soon as it is ready for harvest."   Childs, *op. cit.*, pp 250, 256.   "The negroes seem indisposed to work in the country, and are flocking to the towns and cities.   Where they have been under contract during the past season, they have in most cases disregarded their contracts, and have made but little provision for the coming year. . . . There must also be stringent laws to control the negroes, and require them to fulfill their contracts of labor on the farms.   No one will venture to engage in agricultural operations without some guarantee that his labour is to be controlled and continued under penalties and forfeitures. Without these, there would be certainty of loss."   See also *ibid.*, pp. 258, 262ff.

[26]See, for example, *ibid.*, pp. 283f.   "As a punishment for theft an eighteen-year-old negro boy had his head shaved and was required by the military authorities to stand exposed in the sun from 6 a.m. to 6 p.m. for a week and then hard work for one month with ball and chain."   See also William W. Ball, *The State that Forgot* (Indianapolis, 1932), p. 128.   Since flogging was prohibited, the military authorities hung two Negroes by their thumbs.   "The Negroes begged to be flogged instead."

people without checks or controls, and confirmed them in many of those ways of thought and action that are still the curse of the race.[27] "What judgment shall we pass upon abrupt emancipation, considered merely with reference to the Negro?" asked De Forest. He answered his own question, "It was a mighty experiment, fraught with as much menace as hope. To the white race alone it was a certain and precious boon."[28] But De Forest did not know that the whites were about to be subjected to ten years of Negro rule.

One evidence of the baleful effect of Radical Reconstruction is to be found in the increase in the Negro death rate. De Forest noted that "a large part of the colored race was incapable of self-support and without natural guardians.... But for the pity of former owners, themselves perhaps bankrupt... multitudes of aged, infirm, and infantile blacks would have suffered greatly or perished outright."[29] Dependable figures are available only for Charleston; but they are representative of the entire state and agree with many individual observations. So many Negroes, particularly children, died during Reconstruction, and venereal and other social diseases increased at such a rate, that some observers even predicted that the race would die out within a few generations. Up to 1865 the proportion of Negroes to whites in the state had steadily increased, reaching 50-50 in 1820 and about 66 to 33 per cent in 1865. Since the Civil War, however, the proportion has steadily decreased, though the Negro birth rate has considerably exceeded that of the white people. For the thirty-six years before the war the Negroes' death rate per thousand in Charleston had averaged almost the same as that for whites, 26.45 and 25.60 respectively. For thirty-nine years after the war, however, the Negro rate increased 69 per cent to 43.33; the white death rate dropped to 24.04.[30] During the same periods, too, Negro deaths from tuberculosis increased nearly 400 per cent. Many Southern friends of the race like Hampton deeply regretted the senseless state of affairs that was bringing about this physical as well as social demoralization of a kindly people.

[27] See Simkins and Woody, *op. cit.*, pp. 329ff. See also Laura J. Webster, *The Operation of the Freedmen's Bureau in S. C.* (Northampton, Mass., 1916), pp. 103f.
[28] De Forest, *op. cit.*, p. 134. See also *ibid.*, p. 46, "... living Heaven alone knows how and growing up to be merely vicious and indolent."
[29] *Ibid.*, p. 58.
[30] Figures quoted by Simkins and Woody, *op. cit.*, pp. 336f., from Fredrick L. Hoffman, *Race Traits and Tendencies of the American Negro*, pp. 53f., and *Handbook of S. C.*, 1883, pp. 675f. See also Alrutheus A. Taylor, *The Negro in S. C. during Reconstruction* (Washington, 1924), pp. 12ff.

Never since 1865 has the Negro death rate even approached the ante-bellum ratio to white deaths.

Good or bad, wise or unwise, the "Black Code" was passed in September, 1865, giving the employer, who was frequently the former master, considerable control over the lives of the former slaves. The general authority and supervision of the Freedmen's Bureau, as well as state law, would have prevented anything like reenslavement if that course had been contemplated, but the employer was given certain much-needed authority after the labor contract was voluntarily signed. The abrogation of this provision led many Negroes to desert their crops before the harvest. Consequently white owners were forced to plant smaller crops the following year, and thousands of Negroes were thus thrown out of work and had to be fed by the Freedmen's Bureau.[31] The share-crop system, which ties the laborer to the crop, was the ultimate solution of this problem.[32]

On January 1, 1866, General Sickles, a federal officer whose duty it was to preserve order in the state, declared the entire code null and void; for all laws, he asserted, must be applicable alike to all inhabitants. In the fall of 1866 the legislature revised the legal aspects of the code but refused to institute those social reforms, such as legalizing interracial marriage, that were being demanded by the Radicals. It also refused, by a vote of ninety-five to one in the house, to ratify the Fourteenth Amendment, which not only enfranchised the Negro but disfranchised several thousand white men in the state. Nevertheless, by October General Sickles turned legal processes back to the civil authorities, and the state functioned normally, except that it was unrepresented in Congress.

3

Meanwhile the political leaders of the state, as of the entire South, had come to realize that President Johnson was their real friend in Washington. Since he was being repudiated by the Republican Party, the principles that he stood for needed some sort of party

---

[31]See note 25 above. See also Webster, *op. cit.*, pp. 108f., 116f.

[32]For descriptions of approaches to the share-crop system, see Childs, *op. cit.*, pp. 303f. (in January, 1867). In November 1869, a state labor convention under the presidency of Negro R. B. Elliott recommended for agricultural laborers "one-half the share of the crop or a minimum daily wage of seventy cents to one dollar." Simkins and Woody, *op. cit.*, p. 235. See also Webster, *op. cit.*, p. 106, and De Forest, *op. cit.*, pp. 28ff.

backing. That backing was provided by the National Union Club, which called a convention in Philadelphia for August 14, 1866. The South Carolina state convention of the club met in Columbia on July 31. Governor Orr was the president, and Hampton was one of the four vice-presidents. The theme of these conventions was national harmony and support of President Johnson; they had, if any influence, an adverse one on the Congressional elections of 1866, which increased the power of the Radicals.

During the fall of 1866 most South Carolinians were convinced that the Lincoln-Johnson policy would survive the attacks of the Radicals. Believing that the relations between the two races would be determined by the whites, Hampton made every effort to promote justice and kindness. In a speech delivered at Walhalla in September to an audience consisting of many of his old soldiers, the General urged good treatment of the freedman:

> As a slave he was faithful to us; as a freeman let us treat him
> as a friend. Deal with him frankly, justly, kindly, and my word
> for it he will reciprocate your kindness, clinging to his old home,
> his own country, and his former master.[33]

A feeling of genuine responsibility for the Negro was characteristic of the leading elements of Southern white society, and a curious sort of mutual trust and affection survived even Reconstruction and persists to this day.[34] As a Radical wryly observed in 1871, the Negro went to his old master for advice on every subject except how to vote.[35] Hampton hoped to build a harmonious political relationship between the two races on that foundation.

Duncan Clinch Heyward gives, in *Seed from Madagascar*, an indication of Hampton's status with both races in 1866:

> Conditions, too, in Richland County, in which Goodwill [plan-
> tation] lay, were greatly disturbed. Columbia was still occupied

---

[33]Quoted from the Charleston *Daily Courier*, October 10, 1866, by John P. Hollis, *The Early Period of Reconstruction in South Carolina* (Baltimore, 1905), p. 57.

[34]Ravenel writes, "I feel nothing but sympathy for them [Negroes] as a poor, homeless and unprotected, proscribed race." Childs, *op. cit.*, p. 278. He comments on a Negro riot in Charleston during June, 1866, "The feeling of indignation at these outrages is intense, but I believe, with reflecting men, more directed against the authors and instigators of this spirit than [against] the poor ignorant and deluded negro." *Ibid.*, p. 287. Such expressions occur throughout the Reconstruction years in Ravenel's diary, as in many Southern records.

[35]*Ku Klux Conspiracy, S. C.*, p. 14. See also "Letter of William Henry Trescot on Reconstruction in S. C., 1867," *American Historical Review*, XV (April, 1910), 578. "... negroes who will trust their white employers in all their personal affairs are entirely beyond advice or influence upon all political issues."

by Federal troops, and throughout the county there was great unrest among the Negro population. With the consent of the military authorities, a local company of young white men, of which my father was made captain, was organized in the neighborhood of Goodwill. The purpose of this company was to suppress any conflicts that might occur between whites and blacks; to reassure the whites of safety; and also to protect the blacks should such a necessity arise. This purpose Barnwell Heyward set forth in a long letter to General Wade Hampton, who had, at the close of the war, returned to his home near Columbia. In this letter there was also a request that the General come to that section of the county and make an address to both races. The Negro population of the state, regardless of the fact that he had been a large slaveholder, had great confidence in Hampton, which they showed ten years later when many of them voted to elect him governor, and in addition to this he was the idol of the whites. Barnwell Heyward felt that Hampton could do more than anyone else to pour oil on the troubled waters of those critical times.[36]

During 1866 Hampton had appealed primarily to the white men of the state for kind treatment of the Negro; but during the winter the Radical victories in the Congressional elections completely reversed the balance of power. By March of 1867 the General realized that the power of decision in the state as to harmony or strife between the races had passed to the Negro. Although he had already received his pardon from the President, he was again disfranchised by the Reconstruction acts and, later, by the Fourteenth Amendment. Nevertheless, he sought with all his influence to persuade the blacks to join with the white men of the state in shaping its political structure. At a mass meeting of Negroes held in Columbia in March he made a plea to the blacks similar to that he had made to the whites during the preceding fall:

> Why should we not be friends? Are you not Southern men, as we are? Is this not your home as well as ours? Does not the glorious Southern sun above us shine alike for both of us? Did not this soil give birth to all of us? And will not all alike, when our troubles and trials are over, sleep in that same soil on which we first drew breath?[37]

At this time, too, he explained to the Negroes that he approved a restricted ballot, but not the universal suffrage granted by the Radicals.

---

[36]Duncan Clinch Heyward, *Seed from Madagascar* (Chapel Hill, 1937), p. 151.
[37]Quoted by Hollis, *op. cit.*, p. 57.

From March through July a vigorous campaign was conducted by Hampton and those who agreed with him as to the best way for the state to react to the imposed new order. Processions and free barbecues were held for the Negroes, who were addressed by speakers of both races. The *New York Herald* gave a not too friendly summary of the position taken:

> He appeals to the blacks, lately his slaves, as his political superiors to try the political experiment of harmonizing with their late white masters before going into the political service of strangers. . . . The broad fact that the two races in the South must henceforth harmonize on a political basis to avoid bloody conflict is the ground covered by Wade Hampton.[38]

A more typical Radical reaction to Hampton's efforts to achieve racial harmony in the state is seen in a cartoon in *Harper's Weekly*, where Hampton is shown on his knees, polishing the shoes of a well-dressed Negro. The Radical accusation that white leaders did not attempt to achieve racial harmony was not advanced until Reconstruction was a palpable failure. Then the blame was placed on the shoulders of those perennial whipping boys, the ante-bellum leaders.

The General failed in his efforts to win Negro support for moderate white leaders, and the Negroes did go "into the political service of strangers." They *were* exploited and then abandoned by their new-found friends, and new barriers *were* thus erected between them and the white people among whom their future lay, exactly as Hampton and his friends had warned them would be the case. Hampton and his fellow moderates failed; but even the unsuccessful effort was honorable. If harmonious race relations could have developed in South Carolina in spite of the Reconstruction acts, Hampton pointed out the only possible road and urged the blacks to follow it. The fact was, of course, that harmony between the races in the South was exactly what the Radicals in Washington and their numerous field representatives did not want. The kind of fishing that they planned to do required muddy water. It is a simple fact that, since their continuation in power depended on a solid Radical vote in the South, they deliberately hammered wedges between the races in every way that a powerful organization made possible, from quartering undisciplined Negro troops on Southern communities to endlessly reiterating to the Negroes that their former masters would reenslave them if Southern whites ever got back into power.

---

[38]Quoted by Simkins and Woody, *op. cit.*, p. 84. See also Kibler, *op. cit.*, pp. 449f. and note.

Southern irreconcilables, too, attacked Hampton's policy, thus making a little clearer the line of division already indicated in 1865. Even ex-Governor Perry asserted, truly enough, "General Hampton and his friends had just as well try to control a herd of wild buffaloes ... as the Negro vote."[39] Major Tom Woodward, later prominent in his objection to Hampton's conciliatory racial policies after his election as governor, asked eloquently why "Southern nigger worshippers" did not stop their efforts at harmony and let the Negroes do their work in the fields.[40] Perry and Woodward acted on the assumption that the Supreme Court would invalidate the Reconstruction acts; their hope, of course, was as futile as Hampton's. The Radicals in Washington were dealing all the cards, and they were not doing much trusting to luck.

By August of 1867 Hampton was convinced of the utter futility of his efforts towards political harmony with the Negroes. He was thus impelled to join with South Carolina extremists in urging the white voters of the state to try to prevent a majority vote for the new constitutional convention required by Congress to end military rule. Thus the two white factions reached agreement on the point that continuation of military government would be preferable to Negro supremacy under the Reconstruction acts — and the next decade of Negro government proved them right. As had happened during the abolition movement and as would happen too often again, the pressure of Northern extremists on the Negro question forced moderate Southern friends of the black man into the camp of the Southern extremists.[41] And, as usual, the deluded Negro sacrificed the substantial support of responsible men in his own community for the transitory enthusiasm of ardent champions from above the line, a process to this day very much in evidence.

An exchange of correspondence during August of 1867 marks the end of Hampton's effort at political unity between the races under the Reconstruction acts. About sixty prominent men of the state who had been supporting Hampton's policy addressed an open letter to the General, pointing out the complete failure of their efforts to win Negro support for moderate Southern white leaders and asking what

---

[39]Letter from Perry to *Daily Phoenix* (Columbia), July 31, 1867, quoted by Lillian A. Kibler, *op. cit.*, p. 455.

[40]Simkins and Woody, *op. cit.*, p. 85.

[41]*Ibid.*, pp. 85f.

they should do about the coming registration and election under the
Reconstruction acts.[42]

Hampton replied in a very long letter dated Columbia, August 7,
1867, urging that every man not disfranchised should register and
vote against the proposed convention, since it would, in his opinion,
be better for South Carolina to remain under military rule than to
give its sanction to measures "which we believe to be illegal, unconstitutional, and ruinous." He repeated his advocacy of friendliness
and fair dealing towards the Negroes, pointing out that they were
not in any way responsible for the condition of affairs in the state.
As for Negro suffrage, he repeated the stand he had previously taken:

> On a late public occasion [probably speech to Negroes in Co-
> lumbia on March 18, 1867], where many of you were present, I
> expressed my perfect willingness to see impartial suffrage estab-
> lished at the South, and I believe that this opinion is entertained,
> not only by a large majority of the intelligent and reflecting
> whites, but also of the same class of blacks. . . . The states . . . are
> competent to confer citizenship on the negro, and I think it is the
> part of wisdom that such action should be taken by the Southern
> states. We have recognized the freedom of the blacks, and have
> placed that fact beyond all probability of doubt, denial, or recall.
> Let us recognize in the same frank manner, and as fully, their
> political rights also. For myself, I confess that I am perfectly
> willing to see a constitution adopted by our state, conferring the
> elective franchise on the negro, on precisely the same terms as it
> is to be exercised by the white man . . . a slight educational and
> property qualification *for all classes*.[43]

4

Meanwhile the registration of all voters not disfranchised by Congress was going on under the supervision of the military. By the end
of September it was completed. The *New York Herald* for September
24 described the process:

> Many of our new found brethren [the freedmen], in fact nearly
> all of them, had no idea what registering meant, and as a natural
> consequence the most ludicrous scene transpired. Quite a num-
> ber brought along bags and baskets "to put it in," and in nearly
> every instance there was a great rush for fear we would not have
> registration "enough to go round." Some thought it was some-
> thing to eat; others thought it was something to wear; and quite a
> number thought it was the distribution of confiscated lands under

[42]*Daily Phoenix*, August 28, 1867, and Hollis, *op. cit.*, p. 76, who quotes at
length. This letter is dated July 31, 1867.
[43]*Daily Phoenix*, August 28, 1867. See also Kibler, *op. cit.*, pp. 459f.

a new name. . . . All were sworn and several on being asked what was done when they were registered said that "De gemblin wid de big whisker make me swar to deport de laws of United Souf Calina."

The Negroes were bewildered, but those managing the registration, Radicals all, knew very well what they were doing and did their job thoroughly indeed. The result was the registration of 46,346 whites and 78,982 Negroes, with black majorities in twenty-one out of thirty-one districts in the state.[44] Hampton, of course, was legally barred from registration since a Congressional act of July 19 declared that no citizen should be entitled to be registered by any previous executive pardon.[45]

The election "for" or "against" a convention was called for November 19 and 20. A week before that time Conservative Democrats met in Columbia with a moderate, General Chesnut, presiding and with Hampton and Perry among the vice-presidents. The only action of this meeting was to issue an address to the people of South Carolina, denouncing the Congressional imposition on the state of "not negro equality merely, but negro supremacy." "The people of the South are powerless to avert the impending ruin," the address concluded. "We have been overborne; and the responsibility to posterity and to the world has passed into other hands."[46]

The election, too, was well managed. There are various figures given for the results, but according to John S. Reynolds, *Reconstruction in South Carolina*, 68,876 Negroes voted for the constitutional convention, though few had any idea what it was, calling it the "invention" and the "inspection." Not a single Negro vote was registered against it. As for the whites, only 130 voted for the convention.[47] One group of disappointed blacks told a white friend that they didn't

---

[44] John S. Reynolds, *Reconstruction in South Carolina* (Columbia, 1905), pp. 73f. Simkins and Woody, *op. cit.*, p. 89, quoting from Rhodes, *History of the U. S.*, VI, pp. 83ff, gives 46,882 and 80,550 for whites and blacks, respectively.

[45] Trescot, *op. cit.*, p. 575, stated, "Now in the Country Districts, there is not a neighborhood in which the most respectable citizens . . . are not disfranchised." Alfred B. Williams, *Hampton and His Red Shirts* (Charleston, 1935), p. 22, estimated 8,000 whites in S. C. disfranchised.

[46] This address quoted in full by Reynolds, *op. cit.*, pp. 75f. For a full report of the proceedings of this meeting see Charleston *Daily News*, November 1 and 9, 1867. Trescot, *op. cit.*, pp. 578f., warned that the Republican policy was politically dividing the state on the color line and that "Negro supremacy is one of those inventions which will surely return to plague the inventor."

[47] Reynolds, *op. cit.*, p. 74. Simkins and Woody, *op. cit.*, p. 89, gives whites voting "for" as 2,350; Negroes "for," 66,418. No Negro voted against; "All were led to believe that they had no choice but to vote 'For a Convention.'"

get to vote. The white gentlemen, they said, fixed up some papers for them to put in a little box, but they never did get to vote. That describes the election. The white gentlemen "fixed up" everything. They continued to do so until about 1870, by which time the Negroes learned to do more of the "fixing."[48]

De Forest stated that in his district, where "the Negroes had lived nearer to the whites than on the great plantations of the low country and were proportionately intelligent," they voted quietly and fairly intelligently, "obedient to the instructions of their judicious managers." Elsewhere the story was different:

> With a Bureau officer who was stationed in the lowlands of South Carolina, I compared impressions as to the political qualifications and future of the Negro. "In my district," he said, "the election was a farce. Very few of the freedmen had any idea of what they were doing or even of how they could do it. They would vote into the post office or any hole they could find. Some of them carried home their ballots, greatly smitten with the red lettering and the head of Lincoln or supposing that they could use them as warrants for land. Others would give them to the first white man who offered to take care of them. One old fellow said to me, 'Lord, mars'r! do for Lord's sake tell me what dis yere's all about.'
>
> "I explained to him that the election was to put the state back into the Union and make it stay there in peace.
>
> "'Lord bless you, mars'r! I'se might' glad to un'erstan' it,' he answered. 'I'se the only nigger in this yere districk now that knows what he's up ter.'"[49]

By the end of 1867 the stage was set for a drama of misrule such as seldom has been seen in a civilized community. In spite of the fact that his disintegrating plantations in Mississippi demanded his attention, Hampton lent his influence to minimize violence and ill will. So well did he do his part that in 1876, when he ran for governor, he still enjoyed the respect of both races, but he had failed in his effort to persuade the Negroes to accept political cooperation with the white men among whom they lived, rather than political opposition. South Carolina has fully acknowledged its debt to Hampton for the liberation of 1876, but the state has been too little aware of his wise policy of conciliation throughout the bitter preceding years.

---

[48]*The Nation*, XI (August 11, 1870), 83, comments that in South Carolina the Negro will no longer "take a back seat." See also [Belton O'Neal Townsend], "The Political Condition of S. C.," *Atlantic Monthly*, XXXIX (February, 1877) 193f.

[49]De Forest, *op. cit.*, p. 126.

Chapter Two

NEGRO SUPREMACY
1868-1876

THROUGHOUT the nation 1868 was a year of political agitation. For the federal government it brought the election of General Grant as President, and it consolidated the power of the Radicals in Congress. In South Carolina it firmly established Negro and carpetbagger rule. Hampton was politically active in both the state and the nation. His efforts to achieve harmony between the races having failed, the General hoped to prevent Negro political domination of the state.

1

The state constitutional convention which the voters had approved during the preceding November met in Charleston in January, under the supervision of the military governor. Of 124 delegates, seventy-six were Negroes. They behaved well and voted as they were told, not yet having learned to assert themselves.[1] Of the forty-eight white men, twenty-seven were Southerners, most of them the type of collaborationists that were known as "scalawags." As the *New York Times* noted, "There is scarcely a southern white man in the body whose character would keep him out of the penitentiary."[2] The remaining twenty-one white men, seven from Massachusetts, were petty federal officials and political adventurers. This was the type known as "carpetbaggers," described by Horace Greeley, as "fellows who crawled down South in the track of our armies, generally at a very safe distance in the rear. . . . And they stand, right in the public eye, stealing and plundering, many with both arms around negroes, and

[1]Simkins and Woody, *op. cit.*, pp. 91f.
[2]*Ibid.*, p. 93.

22

their hands in their rear pockets. . . ."[3] This class, at least, profited from Reconstruction. The irresponsibility of this convention is further evidenced by the small amount of taxes paid by its members, twenty-three of the whites and fifty-nine of the Negroes paying none whatsoever.

While the white people of the state looked helplessly on, this convention drew up a constitution. This instrument had some good features copied from constitutions of other states, but it placed no limit on the amount of debt the legislature could contract or on the purposes for which such money might be used.[4] Having made these provisions for future profit, members of the constitutional assembly joined a convention of the state Republican Party and nominated congressmen and state officers, largely from among themselves. The constitutional assembly finished its work and adjourned about the middle of March; the military governor called an election to approve the resulting constitution and to elect state officers, the election to be held on April 14, 15, and 16.

The white men of the state were helpless but not entirely idle. Their best chance of avoiding Negro and carpetbag rule seemed to lie in defeating the constitution to be submitted at the April elections, though such action would mean the continuation of military government. With this in mind a convention of the state Democratic Party met in Columbia on April 2. Having pledged allegiance to the national Democratic Party and having elected delegates to the national Democratic convention, they not very hopefully attacked the local problem. Their slight chance lay in a large white vote against the constitution and in persuading several thousand Negroes either not to vote or to vote with the whites.

With the futile hope of weaning colored voters away from their new friends, this Democratic convention took the position on Negro suffrage that had been held by Hampton and his supporters three years before, promising "that as citizens of South Carolina, we declare our willingness, when we have the power, to grant them, under proper qualifications as to property and intelligence, the right to suffrage."[5]

---

[3]Quoted in *Committee Reports, Ku Klux Conspiracy,* S. C., pp. 522f. See also Powers, *op. cit.,* p. 43, ". . . utterly worthless and accursed political adventurers from the North, Bureau leeches . . . fattening on the humility of the South and the credulity of the freedmen."

[4]Simkins and Woody, *op. cit.,* pp. 102f.

[5]*Ibid.,* p. 108. *Ku Klux Conspiracy,* S. C., p. 1222, quoted from *Daily Phoenix,* April 4, 1868.

This assertion must have sounded tame indeed to black men who had been listening to the shining promises of the scalawags and carpet-baggers.

Though Hampton did not attend this convention, a State Central Executive Committee was elected with him as chairman. In a forth-right "address to the colored people of South Carolina," Hampton's committee issued what subsequent events proved to be a fairly accurate analysis of the situation:

> Your present power must surely and soon pass from you. Nothing that it builds will stand and nothing will remain of it but the prejudices it may create. It is therefore a most dangerous tool that you are handling. Your leaders, both white and black, are using your votes for nothing but their individual gain. Many of them you have known heretofore to despise and distrust, until commanded by your leagues to vote for them. Offices and salaries for themselves are the heights of their ambition, and so that they make hay while the sun shines they care not who is caught in the storm that follows. Already they have driven away all capital from the South; and while they draw $11 a day thousands among you are thrown out of employment and starve for lack of work. What few enterprises are carried on are only the work of Southern men who have faith that the present state of affairs is but temporary. The world does not offer better opportunities for the employment of capital than are to be found in the South; but will your Radical friends send their money here to invest? Not one dollar. They would just as soon venture on investments in Hayti or Liberia as commit their money to the influence of your legislation. Capital has learned to shun it as a deadly plague.
>
> We therefore urge and warn you, by all the ties of our former relations still strong and binding in thousands of cases, by a common Christianity and by the mutual welfare of our two races, whom Providence has thrown together, to beware of the course on which your leaders are urging you in a blind folly that will surely ruin both you and them.
>
> We do not pretend to be better friends to your race than we are to ourselves, and we only speak when we are not invited because your welfare concerns ours. If you destroy yourselves you injure us, and though but little as compared with the harm you will do yourselves we would if we could avert the whole danger.
>
> We are not in any condition to make you any promises or to propose to you any compromises. We can do nothing but await the course of events — but this we do without the slightest apprehension or misgiving for ourselves. We shall not give up our country, and time will soon restore our control of it. But we earnestly caution you and beg you in the meanwhile to beware of the use you make of your temporary power. Remember that

your race has nothing to gain and everything to lose if you invoke
that prejudice of race which since the world was made has ever
driven the weaker tribe to the wall. Forsake, then, the wicked
and stupid men who would involve you in this folly, and make to
yourselves friends and not enemies of the white citizens of South
Carolina.[6]

This protest, of course, went unheeded. As the blacks loved to
chant, "De bottom rail's on de top now, and we's gwine to keep it
dar." The constitution was ratified by a large majority, and the entire
Radical ticket was elected. In the legislature there were eighty-four
Negroes and seventy-two whites, all Radicals except seven white men
in the senate and sixteen in the house. Whatever government emerged
from this noble experiment in democracy, an experiment implemented
by Northern religious, humanitarian, and political enthusiasm, the
responsibility lay with Congress and with the Negro voters of the
state, not, as many Radicals were later to insist, with the white citizens
of South Carolina.[7]

Hampton's committee made one last futile effort to avert the calamity of Negro rule. Appeals were carried by a sub-committee to both
houses of Congress, petitioning those bodies not to accept the new
constitution. The petition concluded:

> The Constitution was the work of Northern adventurers, South-
> ern renegades, and ignorant negroes. Not one per cent of the
> white population of the State approves it, and not two per cent of
> the negroes who voted for its adoption understood what this act
> of voting implied. . . . And think you there can be any just, lasting
> reconstructon on this basis? . . . We do not mean to threaten re-
> sistance by arms, but the people of our State will never quietly
> submit to negro rule. We may have to pass under the yoke you

[6]Reynolds, op. cit., pp. 90f. As early as January 30, 1868, The Nation, a
Radical but not hysterical publication, had foreseen the ultimate return of
Southern whites to political power: "It is as certain as anything in politics can
be . . . that before very long the whites will reassume their old ascendency. The
worst enemies of the blacks are those who deceive themselves on this point."
XI, 85. By March 9, 1871, The Nation was convinced that the "proper men
to legislate for the South are those in whom the community has most confidence. . . ." XII, 150. See also ibid., pp. 192f. (March 23, 1871). For a
schedule of objections to the new constitution listed by the Democrats, see
Reynolds, op. cit., pp. 91ff. The truth of the prophecy in the Executive Committee's address is testified to by The Nation eight years later: "We believe that
any one who is cognizant of the working of negro suffrage in the South, and who
has watched the transition from political apathy to a determined effort for
supremacy on the part of the whites, must admit that Republican legislation in
Congress, and particularly the Civil Rights bills, have made the color line iden-
tical with the party line. . . ." XXIII (September 28, 1876), 188.
[7]See below, pp. 35ff. and 43n.

have authorized, but by moral agencies, by political organization, by every peaceful means left us, we will keep up this contest until we have regained the political control handed down to us by an honored ancestry. . . .[8]

After the constitution had been accepted by the House, a new plea was addressed to the Senate, backed by a statistical argument. Pointing out the very small proportion of the members of the constitutional convention who were taxpayers, the committee submitted figures to show that the rate of taxation under the new constitution would be, in effect, about twenty times that which had prevailed before the war, this burden to be imposed on a people already nearly bankrupt. "Taxation without representation," the petition continued, "is combined with representation without taxation." In this connection the appeal noted that of the eight major state officials elected, six paid no taxes whatever; as for the other two, the Lieutenant Governor paid $15.99 and the Adjutant Inspector General paid one dollar.[9] In spite of these appeals and over President Johnson's veto, the new constitution was approved, and South Carolina was readmitted to the Union on June 25, 1868.

Since many Northern states had refused to ratify the Fourteenth Amendment to the federal Constitution, a condition to readmittance of South Carolina, as of other Southern states, was the ratification of this amendment. The Fourteenth Amendment, therefore, has this peculiarity: it was ratified by the vote of those Negroes to whom, by an odd retroactive twist, it granted citizenship; Southern leaders like Hampton (about eight thousand in South Carolina alone), whom it disfranchised, were not allowed to vote on it at all. Can it be wondered that Southern white men have not been notably loyal to the spirit of the Fourteenth and Fifteenth Amendments? Let citizens of the North who evaded the Prohibition Amendment, which was ratified by an honest vote, think twice before they feel holier-than-thou towards Southerners who have evaded the Fourteenth and Fifteenth Amendments, which were imposed by political jobbery.

2

By the first of June Southern white men clearly realized that the only hope for them lay in ending Radical control in Washington. Thus the coming national election assumed an importance to the South rarely equaled.

---

[8]Reynolds, *op. cit.*, pp. 93f.
[9]*Ibid.*, pp. 95f.

The die-hard element in South Carolina, epitomized by General Martin W. Gary, had viewed with extreme distaste the faltering effort of the April Democratic convention to find common political ground with the Negro. W. D. Porter, for example, who had been nominated for governor on the Democratic ticket, had refused to accept the nomination from a convention that approved even limited Negro suffrage.[10] The failure of the Democratic convention's effort to attract any perceptible colored vote, too, added strength to the dissenters. Again Hampton and the moderates had completely failed, and the conviction was driven home to many minds that no political middle ground could be found. The issue, they believed, would always be Negro supremacy or white supremacy. Justly or not, that conviction was to be strengthened many times during the nine years that followed. Justly or not, it has never been forgotten.

Because of this dissatisfaction the Democratic citizens of Edgefield District, home of General Gary, called for a new Democratic convention. This convention met in Columbia during June and adopted a resolution calling for "a white man's government."[11] Hampton attended and effected a reconciliation between the two factions. Although no specific declaration was made, the opinion was probably general that the Democrats of the state had abandoned the position on Negro suffrage taken by the April convention,[12] though, it should be added, this declaration was reaffirmed by Hampton's executive committee in October.[13] Again the pressure of events had forced the moderates towards the camp of the extremists so as to preserve the white unity deemed essential under the circumstances, but the line between moderates and extremists on the Negro question became clearer than in 1865. Hampton remained chairman of the central committee and was elected delegate for the state at large to the national Democratic convention to be held in New York on July 4.

In retrospect the part in the national election of 1868 played by the South, and by South Carolina in particular, seems pitiable in the extreme. In the first place, the electoral vote of the state was already neatly wrapped, tied, and delivered to the Radicals. In the second

---

[10]Simkins and Woody, op. cit., p. 110.

[11]Reynolds, op. cit., pp. 100f. For Gary's leadership in opposition to Hampton's progressive stand on the Negro, see Kibler, op. cit., pp. 468f.

[12]Simkins and Woody, op. cit., p. 110.

[13]Ku Klux Conspiracy, S. C., pp. 1249f., quoted from Columbia Daily Phoenix, October 18, 1868. See also Hampton's statement in his letter to G. L. Park, Appendix A.

place, not only were Southern delegates unable to deliver the votes of their own states, but their activity in the national Democratic Party made plausible a Radical Republican campaign of violent war hate which swept the North in November.[14] The sad truth is that complete political apathy on the part of the South would have produced more Democratic votes than did the vigorous campaigning that occupied the months before the election, for the participation of prominent Southerners in the national Democratic campaign greatly strengthened the Republican Party in the North.

In prospect, however, there seemed to be some hope that the South would be saved from Negro domination by a national triumph of the Democratic Party. Hampton entered ardently into the convention proceedings. He served on the platform committee and made a speech seconding Blair's nomination as vice-president. After the convention he made addresses before mass meetings in New York and Baltimore. All was harmony and good fellowship. Even *The Nation,* then ardently Radical, noted during the convention that Hampton behaved properly.[15]

When he returned to Charleston, he was suffering from a severe cold and could barely speak. Nevertheless, he made a few remarks there, in the course of which he referred to a clause in the Democratic platform, "And we declare that the reconstruction acts are unconstitutional, revolutionary and void" as "my plank in the platform" meaning, as he explained later, "the plank to which I, as well as any other southern man, clung for safety."[16]

Ironically enough, the Radical press picked up the phrase and presented the General to the nation as the archetype of the unreconstructed, fire-eating rebel who threatened to start the war all over again. It painted a lurid picture of Hampton dominating a cowed

---

[14]*Harper's Weekly,* for example, began an active campaign a month before the Democratic convention opened (see XII, 355, June 6, 1868). On June 13 it stated that the Democratic Party "fights as furiously for the corpse of slavery as it did for slavery living and powerful" (p. 370). On June 20 it described the Democrats as "a party whose Southern wing rebelled and whose Northern wing did what it could, short of fighting, to make rebellion successful" (p. 387). After the convention the line became more violent. Various Southern delegates to the convention were described as coming to the convention "dripping in blood shed in rebellion to perpetuate slavery" (p. 450). After that there was no limit except the ingenuity of the writer.

[15]*The Nation,* VII (July 9, 1868), 21.

[16]See Appendix A. See also *Ku Klux Conspiracy,* S. C., pp. 1260ff., quoted from *Daily Phoenix,* July 26, 1868, which quoted from Charleston *Mercury,* July 25, 1868.

committee and "dictating" the party platform. *Harper's Weekly* discovered that the election was to "decide whether General Grant or Wade Hampton represents the national conviction and purpose. . . ."[17] "Wade Hampton, the rebel," this periodical declared, "and Vanlandingham, the copperhead, combined and ruled the convention."[18] Furthermore, Hampton, it asserted, "would like nothing better than to see the country again in arms . . . revenge is sweet."[19] Therefore, according to *Harper's Weekly*, Hampton advocated that Seymour and Blair be carried into the White House "at the point of the bayonet."[20] Even *The Nation*, much more restrained than some Radical papers, began to talk about Hampton's advocating the use "of the bayonet"[21] and threatening war.[22]

These charges, in all conscience, were ridiculous enough, since the Southern delegates approached the convention hat in hand; but they were clever party propaganda of the "lose-the-peace" variety, and they were reiterated throughout the North until squeezed of their last drop of effectiveness.[23] So strong was their impact that Tilden opposed Hampton's nomination as governor of South Carolina eight years later for fear that his national reputation would hurt the Democratic Party in the North.[24]

The irony of the situation lay in the fact that Hampton, whose record as a moderate man was consistent and unassailable, should have been chosen as the "fire-eater." Before secession he had been well known in the state as a Union man, though that sentiment was unpopular.[25] In 1852 he had spoken vigorously in the state senate against the secession movement that then had a flurry, and he had later

---

[17]*Harper's Weekly*, XII (August 1, 1868), 482.

[18]*Ibid.*, (August 15, 1868), p. 514.

[19]*Ibid.*, (August 8, 1868), p. 498.

[20]*Ibid.*

[21]*The Nation*, VII (July 23, 1868), 63.

[22]*Ibid.*, (August 6, 1868), p. 101.

[23]As late as May 6, 1871, *Harper's Weekly* was indignantly reminding its readers of the election of 1868, when the national Democratic Party was "helpless in the grasp of Wade Hampton and his Southern friends. . . ." XV, 402.

[24]William A. Sheppard, *Red Shirts Remembered* (Spartanburg, S. C., 1940), pp. 112f., who cites the Augusta, Georgia, *Chronicle and Sentinel* for January 10, 1877. See also Hampton's speech before the nominating convention, quoted by Reynolds, *op. cit.*, pp. 350f. For more detail, see pp. 51f.

[25]Benjamin F. Perry, *Biographical Sketches of Eminent American Statesmen* (Philadelphia, 1887), p. 566. Perry was the leader of the Unionists in South Carolina.

strongly opposed the reopening of the slave trade.[26] During the winter
of 1860-1861 he had been bitterly attacked in the state because he
did not favor secession.[27]   His record after the surrender, too, had
consistently been one of attempted reconciliation between the races
and between the sections. So closely was he identified with the policy
of conciliation in the state that General Gary charged before the Taxpayers' convention of 1874 that Hampton's advocacy of qualified suffrage for Negroes was "the entering wedge" for universal suffrage.[28]
Yet when uncomplimentary words about General Grant in Gary's
fiery speech were shown to the President, Grant wanted to know,
"Who made that speech? Wade Hampton?"[29]

The Radicals wanted a villain, and Hampton could be made to fit
their picture of the unregenerate aristocrat. Regardless of the record,
they manufactured their bogey man.

In a letter from a friend in Wisconsin, written September 28, 1868,
Hampton was asked to make a public statement of his views because
of the "importance attached to everything spoken by you, and the
great efforts made to present you as still adhering to and anticipating
a renewal of the 'lost cause' in a struggle with the Government, and
because I believe you are greatly misrepresented, and therefore you,
and through you the mass of the southern people, are wronged. . . ."
This correspondent wanted "a statement as to the real opinions you entertain upon the issues of the war, its results and consequences, and
also those of the people at large, whom you, to a great extent, represent."[30]

Hampton answered in a long letter (see Appendix A), giving his
account of what actually happened while formulating the plank in

---

[26]J. H. Easterby, "Wade Hampton," *Dictionary of American Biography*, VIII,
214. See also *Ku Klux Conspiracy*, S. C., pp. 1218f.

[27]Easterby, *loc. cit.* See also Edward L. Wells, *Hampton and Reconstruction*
(Columbia, 1907), pp. 33f. According to the Charleston *Courier*, November
26, 1860, however, Hampton had spoken in favor of secession. The explanation seems to be, as Wells says, that Hampton believed in the state's right to
secede, but did not believe that Lincoln's election gave due cause. For Hampton's own testimony on his record as a moderate man, that he opposed secession
and did not return to South Carolina until after the attack on Fort Sumter; also
that some were bitter towards him on that account and "found great fault with
me for my lukewarmness," see *Ku Klux Conspiracy*, S. C., pp. 1218f.

[28]Sheppard, *op. cit.*, p. 15.

[29]*Ibid.*, p. 21, quoting Alvin F. Sanborn, *Reminiscences of Richard Lathers*
(New York, 1907), pp. 323f.

[30]See Appendix A.

question, which was introduced by a delegate from Connecticut. In this letter Hampton described the attitude of the Southern delegates:

> So anxious were the southern delegates to promote harmony — so solicitous were they to avoid any action that might endanger the success of that party, to which alone they could look for relief, that every one of them who had offered resolutions withdrew their resolutions at once. In withdrawing those I had the honor to submit, (and which, by the by, looked to the Supreme Court for the solution of this question of reconstruction,) I said the introduction of those three words [unconstitutional, revolutionary and void] into the platform would satisfy us entirely, and that we would trust to the Democratic party to relieve us from measures that we know must ruin our country.[31]

Throughout the summer and fall of 1868 Hampton sought to promote national harmony. In Massachusetts John Quincy Adams II had attracted Southern attention by his denunciation of the policies being followed by Congress. In October Hampton invited Adams to Charleston for "a consultation upon the living principles of our free institutions," since "it is no longer a question of party, but of social life."[32] During his visit Adams made an address in Charleston, with Hampton presiding. "If he is a rebel," said Adams after several days of intimate association with Hampton, "he is just such a rebel as I am and no more."[33] As Bowers pointed out in *The Tragic Era*, however, Hampton's "gesture of conciliation toward the reasoning element in the North met only with jeers."[34] National harmony, of course, was the last thing desired by the Radicals, whose power depended on continuing Northern hatred for "traitors and rebels."

Hampton's efforts to lead his party to victory in the state were equally fruitless. The Democrats were defeated in the electoral vote by what came to be recognized as the conventional Negro majority. Two Democratic congressmen were elected, but both were unseated by the Radical majority in Congress, who felt, perhaps, that all their efforts in South Carolina entitled them to exclusive representation. No other all-out Democratic political effort would be made in the state until the successful one in 1876, though various reform and fusion movements were tried in unsuccessful attempts to split the Negro vote.

---

[31]*Ibid.*
[32]Bowers, *op. cit.*, p. 233.
[33]*Ibid.*
[34]*Ibid.* For a jeering account of this effort at conciliation see *Harper's Weekly*, XII (October 31, 1868), 690.

3

Meanwhile the new Radical legislature had begun its first session in July. The number of officeholders had been extravagantly increased, and these Radical officials (state, county, and township) were giving alarming evidence of their incompetence and dishonesty. In the legislature, too, votes were already being openly bought. Even the Republican newspapers of the state were complaining of "corruption,"[35] and the Democratic press was making accusations that in a sane political world would have seemed maniacal. [36] Yet, as Simkins and Woody assert in *South Carolina during Reconstruction*:

> Practically all the charges made by the Conservative press were later substantiated by an investigating committee appointed by the Democratic legislature in 1877. The chairman of this committee was a Republican who had been a member of the Reconstruction legislature. The report of the committee was based on documents, official papers, and letters, diaries, and the sworn testimony of many who had participated in the frauds. The evidence is incontrovertible. . . ."[37]

Louis F. Post, who came to Columbia in 1870 and for a time served in a minor clerical position, wrote:

> The body as a whole was in a legislative atmosphere so saturated with corruption that the honest and honorable members of either race had no more influence on it than an orchid might have on a mustard patch. . . . The capital atmosphere seemed to produce a peculiar intoxicating effect. Just to breathe it made one feel like going out and picking a pocket.[38]

This atmosphere of corruption, which characterized Radical Republican government in South Carolina throughout its existence, was

---

[35]The Charleston *Daily Republican*, for example, listed five "evils from which the state has been suffering:"
"1. In our state the superiority of numbers threw the government almost absolutely into the hands of the colored citizens. . . . This was a calamity. . . .
"2. The evil will be seen to be greater if we look at the real condition of the colored people as they emerged from slavery. . . . They too often trusted the veriest scoundrels simply because they pretended to bear the dear name of Republican. . . . They were not fitted to do everything in ruling South Carolina.
"3. Corrupt and incompetent officers.
"4. Heavy taxation.
"5. The militia, so organized, as claimed, the whites have not the same advantages as the colored people."
Quoted by *The Nation*, XII (March 30, 1871), 213.
[36]Simkins and Woody, *op. cit.*, pp. 134ff.
[37]*Ibid.*, p. 135.
[38]"A 'Carpetbagger' in South Carolina," *Journal of Negro History*, X (January, 1925), 17, 35.

particularly infuriating to the white men of the state in 1870, as Governor Scott's first two-year term of office came to a close and he was nominated for a second term.

In March of 1870 *The Nation* was observing, ". . . the Legislature which has just adjourned in South Carolina was one of the most corrupt assemblages of men that ever legislated for a State, and one of the most contemptible in point of ability."[39] By May this paper remarked that South Carolina "seems to be almost completely at the mercy of the white and black corruptionists who have been plundering it for some years past . . . and nothing is surer than that the rescue of South Carolina from her present rulers is a thing for which decent men everywhere — Democrats and Republicans, especially Republicans — should pray with fervor."[40] In March of 1871 even the Charleston *Daily Republican* was mournfully listing the "evils from which the state has been suffering," all of them palpably the result of the Congressional policy of reconstruction.[41]

Many white citizens were outraged by this open and unpunished dishonesty as well as mortified by their own political impotence. Moreover, in many instances the whites were angered and, particularly the women, terrorized by the increasing rowdiness of the Negroes, whose mob action was incited rather than checked by the authorities. These general causes greatly increased the tension created by the political activity leading to the state elections held in November of 1870. As a result, during September and October there were several outbreaks of violence, the far-famed Ku Klux Klan outrages, in three instances leading to the murder of Radicals, one of them a white man.

Hampton, as chairman of the Democratic Executive Committee, issued an address to the people of South Carolina on October 23. "We beg you to unite with us in reprobating these recent acts of violence," the address said, "by which a few lawless and reckless men have brought discredit on the character of our people. . . . No cause can prosper that calls murder to its assistance, or which looks to assassination for success." Referring to the practice of many Radical speakers who deliberately incited Negro hatred of Southern whites, however, he added, "We ask those who are opposed to us, politically, to unite with us to check and discountenance all incendiary language,

---

[39]*The Nation*, X (March, 1870), 200.
[40]*Ibid.* (May 12, 1870), 295.
[41]See note 35 above.

whether uttered in public or in private, and to join us in the effort we are making for the preservation of peace, the supremacy of law, and the maintenance of order."[42]

This plea to the people of the state was effective, and, on the whole, the election was a quiet one. In another address to the people Governor Scott answered, "It is now my pleasing duty to congratulate you upon the beneficial results that have ensued from the admirable and well-timed address of General Hampton and the executive committee to the democratic party."[43]   Again as was his principle and his practice Hampton had promoted conciliation and had prevented violence; but *Harper's Weekly* took the news of Hampton's successful plea against violence as evidence that "he is himself a ringleader in the disorders. . . ."[44]

4

The national election of 1868 had ended Hampton's active participation in the political affairs of South Carolina until 1876. His disfranchisement had made him ineligible for office and the increased power of the Radicals in Washington left the white men of the state no recourse except time. Moreover, Hampton's affairs in Mississippi were demanding his attention. He had already neglected them too much during the summer and fall.

Throughout the following eight years the General appeared in his native state from time to time, but never as a political leader. In 1870 he remonstrated with Governor Scott because of the wide-spread practice of arming undisciplined bands of Negro militia while at the same time refusing to accept white companies in the militia at all.[45] The suave reassurances of the Governor on that subject were about as reliable as his financial reports, which were designed to conceal the debt of the state until after his reelection.

In 1870, too, Hampton assisted to some extent in a "fusion" campaign directed by General M. C. Butler. This election marked the last all-out attempt in the state at real political cooperation between the races. Every possible concession was made to the Negroes. A carpetbagger Republican more honest than his fellows was run for

[42]*Ku Klux Conspiracy*, S. C., pp. 1248f., quoted from *Daily Phoenix*, October 23, 1868.

[43]*Committee Reports, Ku Klux Conspiracy*, S. C., p. 580.

[44]*Harper's Weekly*, XII (November 14, 1868), 722.

[45]*Ku Klux Conspiracy*, S. C., p. 1219.

governor, Negroes were included on the ticket, and all connection with the Democratic Party was avoided. The only major issues introduced were economy and honesty in government, and the candidates vigorously stumped every county in the state. The blacks listened tolerantly to white speakers, but they violently resented any Negro participation.[46] Hampton was on the platform in Charleston when a colored man was assaulted by a Negro mob for associating politically with Conservative white men.[47]

The Republican campaign speeches were designed to arouse all possible enmity towards the whites.[48] Judge Carpenter, the carpetbagger candidate for governor on the fusion ticket, told the investigating committee that the "most serious charges made against me by the colored population ... were, first, that ... I would reduce them again to slavery; and second ... would not allow their wives and daughters to wear hoop skirts."[49] As the minority report of the Congressional committee observed:

> The elections pretended to be held were mere farces; all the registrars, judges, ballot counters, police, militia and other machinery were in their [the Radicals'] own hands ... where the negroes could not be inspired with sufficient hatred ... to vote for these loyal leaguers and carpet-baggers they were forced to do so ... and the recusant negro who dared to disobey was ostracized, denounced, and often beaten to compel obedience. The testimony taken is full of incontrovertible proof of all these things.[50]

The election, too, showed the usual Negro majorities for all Radical candidates. This election is significant in that it gave finality to the growing conviction in the state that political harmony between white and black would never be possible.

In 1871, Hampton testified at length before a senate investigating committee in Columbia on the subject of various outbreaks of violence in the state, which were popularly lumped together under the term "Ku Klux Klan outrages." Not even the Radicals on the committee implied any direct association between the General and these "outrages." The majority report did, however, use a carefully selected

---

[46]Simkins and Woody, *op. cit.*, p. 454. See also *Committee Reports, Ku Klux Conspiracy*, S. C., pp. 302ff.

[47]*Ku Klux Conspiracy*, S. C., p. 1228.

[48]See, for example, *ibid.*, p. 146, testimony by Suber; and by Judge Carpenter, *ibid.*, p. 241.

[49]*Ibid.*, p. 238.

[50]*Committee Reports, Ku Klux Conspiracy*, S. C., pp. 302f.

part of Hampton's testimony to illustrate its thesis: While these Radicals admitted the utter failure of Reconstruction government in the state, the responsibility, they asserted, lay with the white leadership, which had refused to assist the poor, ignorant Negroes in forming a government and had thus left that duty to outsiders, some of them unworthy.[51] *Harper's Weekly* had foreshadowed such a line of reasoning as early as January 1, 1870: "The old masters were, so to speak, the natural leaders of the freedmen. But they cursed the new citizens, who were obliged to seek leadership elsewhere, and they turned to the Northern settlers, many of whom were educated.... But others were ... mere adventurers who would stop at nothing that might secure their selfish advantage."[52]

By June of 1870, however, *The Nation,* at first ardently in favor of the Congressional plan of reconstruction, had repeatedly noted the utter failure of this plan in the South, particularly in South Carolina.[53] It had asserted, too, that the chief cause of intolerably corrupt conditions was the giving of an unrestricted ballot to the Negro. As for where the blame lay, *The Nation* solemnly confessed, "Those who advocated, as we did, the extension of suffrage to the blacks as an essential feature of reconstruction have naturally more to answer for in this matter than anybody else, and it would be wrong even if it were not futile to try to escape the responsibility.... We wish sincerely it had been coupled with an educational test, imposed on all colors

---

[51]*Ibid.,* p. 51.

[52]*Harper's Weekly,* XIV (January 1, 1870), 2.

[53]Edwin L. Godkin, one of the greatest American editors, was editor of *The Nation* during Reconstruction. His education in regard to the facts of life in the South makes an interesting sequence. In July of 1868 *Harper's Weekly* (XII, 435) praised *The Nation* for staunch Republicanism. At that time *The Nation* was confident of the wisdom and virtue of Congressional Reconstruction with Negro suffrage. It repeatedly chided the Associated Press for the alleged anti-Negro flavor of its press reports from the South (IX, July 7, 1869, 1, and IX, January 14, 1869, 22), and accepted at face value Radical accounts of Southern "outrages." By March 1, 1870, however, it was questioning such tales, pointing to the self-interest of those who propagated them (X, 199). In May of the same year it called attention to the unanimous vote of a Senate committee that tales of "outrages" in Georgia were actually "prepared to order, like boots or dinners furnished to them [Governor Bullock and his friends] and paid for..." (X, 328); and a month later it remarked, "Now, it is about time that we ceased helping rogues make fortunes out of 'the cruelty of rebels'." (X, 378). On May 4, 1871, *The Nation* pointed to the political motives behind lurid tales of K. K. K. "outrages" in South Carolina (XII, 314f.). (De Forest, *op. cit.,* p. 108, said generally no outrages.)

Meanwhile *The Nation's* education was progressing in other directions. As early as August 20, 1868, it gently warned the South Carolina Radical legislature against trying to force social equality by law (VII, 142, 203, 304); and on

equally."[54] Such a test, of course, was exactly what Hampton and his friends, the very ones blamed for current conditions by the majority report, had recommended from the first.

As for the outbreaks of violence, it was obvious that these were largely the work of the poor whites. The majority report insisted, nevertheless, that influential men like Hampton were responsible since they denounced the corruption in the state government. "With the intelligence which enables one class to appreciate evils, and to know that denunciation in a particular vein will lead another class to violence, the country will not hesitate long in determining which class should be held most rigidly responsible for the violence thus wilfully incited."[55] South Carolina leaders, it seems, not only had to "take" Reconstruction, but ought to pretend to like it. As early as December, 1869, however, *The Nation* had remarked, "The fact is that the state of things we established at the South . . . has probably been one of the worst witnessed. . . . That the disorders of every kind that afflict Southern society should be great is no wonder; the wonder is that they are not greater. . . .[56]

The minority report of the Congressional committee answered this Radical charge and was a closely reasoned and documented attack on the entire Congressional policy. This report quotes, for example, the findings of a state Radical committee of both races elected to investigate the finances of the state when the legislature was in a rare mood of moral indignation, having been denied its slice of the pie.

December 10, 1868, it began to show faint suspicion of that state's financial doings (VII, 471). In February of 1869 it called attention to the poor quality of Radical Congressmen from the South (VIII, 81f.); on July 1, 1869, it began to question the character of many Northern Radicals in Southern States (IX, 4), and four weeks later it was expressing complete disillusionment with Radical leadership in South Carolina (IX, 81). After July of 1869 *The Nation* opposed the whole idea of Congressional Reconstruction because of its manifest corruption, injustice, and ineptitude. The time had come for Congress to quit trying to govern the Southern States. (X, March 17, 1870, 165f.)

[54]*The Nation*, X (June, 1870), 378. Years later Chamberlain, in his article in the *Atlantic Monthly*, *op. cit.*, p. 476, stated, "But it is not true that Stevens or Morton counted on such cooperation of the whites or cared for it. It was an afterthought to claim it; a retort to those who uttered reproaches as the scheme of reconstruction gradually showed its vanity and impossibility."

[55]*Committee Reports, Ku Klux Conspiracy, S. C.*, p. 51.

[56]*The Nation*, IX (December 2, 1869), 476. See also *The Nation's* comments on Governor Scott's account of the Ku Klux outrages: "This is all horrible, but we have no hesitation in saying that it is the not unnatural consequence of the caricature on government which has been kept up in that state for the last four years." XII (March 9, 1871), 150.

This state legislative committee could get nothing but conflicting financial reports from various state officials, but it finally found a basis to work on by determining how many blank bonds had been bought by the state from The American Bank Note Company. It never did uncover the entire state debt, but it did learn that during the period from July, 1868, to October, 1871, the debt of the state government alone had increased from about five million dollars to more than twenty-nine million, about six million dollars worth of bonds having been fraudulently issued.[57]

A resolution to impeach the Governor and the Treasurer of the state was introduced in the legislature, but by using $48,645 of his militia fund to bribe members of the legislature ($15,000 to Speaker Moses, the next governor) Scott stopped the proceedings.[58] In spite of all the robbery, state and county, during Reconstruction, the guilty were almost never punished.

This kind of stealing continued in the state until South Carolina bonds could no longer be sold or hypothecated. State bonds issued before 1868 had sold for as high as ninety-five cents on the dollar. By November of 1868 the price in New York was still eighty-five. Shortly after the legislature began to show its real nature, however, the bonds began to drop. By 1873 their price was fifteen cents.[59] The credit of the state had been wiped out, and for a long time South Carolina had to pay a high price for whatever money it borrowed and was burdened by the Reconstruction debt, which was not entirely repaid until 1943.[60]

Bonds were not the only source of revenue. As the flesh of the state diminished, the bones were picked cleaner and cleaner. Taxes were just about what Hampton's committee had anticipated.[61] Throughout this period the burden of taxation and the arbitrary fixing of tax values by insolent petty officials were a constant reminder to

[57]*Committee Reports, Ku Klux Conspiracy*, S. C., pp. 533ff. See also *ibid.*, pp. 411ff.

[58]Reynolds, *op. cit.*, pp. 172f.

[59]Simkins and Woody, *op. cit.*, p. 166.

[60]A sinking fund was provided for the final payment of this debt, Act 21, *Acts of the General Assembly*, 1943.

[61]See *Committee Reports, Ku Klux Conspiracy*, S. C., pp. 532ff. "No such rate of taxation, upon the same basis of property valuation has ever occurred in the history of the world." See also *Ku Klux Conspiracy*, S. C., p. 238. Judge Carpenter quoted Beverly Nash as saying in a public speech, "The reformers complain of taxes being too high. I tell you they are not high enough. I want them taxed until they put these lands back where they belong, into the hands of those who worked for them." "That," added Judge Carpenter, "was the key-note of the whole stumping from the seacoast to the mountains."

the property owners of the state that they were a subjugated people. Payment of taxes became a major strain on an economy already at the breaking point. In the year 1874 alone more than a half million acres of land were forfeited to the state for nonpayment of taxes, a state of affairs rather pleasing than otherwise to the landless legislators.[62]

In spite of this exploitation of every source of revenue, no public work was done during the period, not even on roads and bridges. Even the established institutions of the state, particularly the schools, went without minimum support.[63] More than half a million dollars were appropriated in a worthy and ambitious scheme to buy land for settling would-be Negro farmers; but the money was stolen or squandered, and the needy blacks profited not at all.[64] As fast as money was collected, it was stolen or wasted in extravagance. Meanwhile, the people of the state, white and black, suffered in the resulting economic stagnation. Yet — and this is a fact that white men of the South cannot forget about the Negro vote — the black vote of the state would not refuse to return a man to office because of his record. No amount of manifest dishonesty or incompetence seemed to have the slightest effect on the Negro majority. Even convicted criminals were promptly returned to office.[65] The moral tone of the last legislature was no scruple higher than that of the first, nor was its political judgment. By large majorities this body gleefully elected as circuit

---

[62]Reynolds, op. cit., p. 269. See also [Belton O'Neal Townsend], "South Carolina Morals," Atlantic Monthly, XXXIX (April, 1877), 473.

[63]Said Chamberlain in the Atlantic Monthly, op. cit., p. 477, "For all this increase [of debt] the state had not a single public improvement of any sort to show. . . ." The state constitution of 1868 set up a very advanced school system on paper, one that would have required an annual expenditure of nearly a million dollars a year, but "no law restrained the irresponsible legislative and executive authorities from using the school funds as they saw fit." "The legislature . . . was either indifferent, ignorant or culpably insincere in its dealing with the public school interest during the entire period of Reconstruction." See Simkins and Woody, op. cit., pp. 434ff.

[64]See Committee Reports, Ku Klux Conspiracy, S. C., pp. 406, 412f., quoting a South Carolina Radical legislative committee that investigated frauds in the state. This committee found "as far as known" an expenditure of $746,724.07 by the Land Commission. It states that the commission had been an "outrageous and enormous swindle," but no prosecutions followed.

[65]See [Townsend], "South Carolina Morals," op. cit., p. 475. For example: C. C. Bowen, ex-gambler, in jail for murder, released by federal troops, two terms in Congress, convicted on federal charges, pardoned by President Grant, promptly elected sheriff of Charleston County as well as a member of the state general assembly. Simkins and Woody, op. cit., p. 118. In 1878 he was leader of the state Republican Party. Also B. E. Whittemore, Massachusetts Methodist preacher, elected to Congress, expelled for selling a cadetship, promptly reelected, refused a seat, elected to state senate. Ibid., pp. 117f.

judges W. J. Whipper and "Robber Governor" Moses, two men notoriously among the worst rascals of the state, men without public or private honor. A few carpetbaggers were eliminated, it is true, as black leaders took their places. But from the carpetbaggers the Negroes had learned how to rob, not how to rule.

An account of the social, economic, and political evils of Reconstruction could be continued indefinitely. It was after 1865 that the bitterness of hate entered the Southern heart.[66] For nine years South Carolina saw the plunderers of the state protected by federal courts and federal soldiers, and for nine years they saw the dignified protest of their best citizens rejected with scornful jeers by the President and Congress. In 1876, when Hampton ran for governor, the white people of the state were desperate. They were ready for counter-revolution, whatever the cost. They were determined to win political control of the state or to force another invasion by federal armies.

---

[66]Commented *The Nation*, XI (August 4, 1870), 66, "The Northern people are beginning to understand the carpetbagger tolerably well ... and it is to be hoped that ... there may not be a man in the Republican Party who does not justify the South in its hatred of him, and see why the South is to be partly excused for hating us."

Chapter Three

DESIGN FOR COUNTER-REVOLUTION
1876

BECAUSE of his leadership in the Red Shirt Campaign of 1876, Wade Hampton holds first place in the hearts of South Carolinians. That campaign is best understood, not as an election, but as a counter-revolution. From the time of the American Revolution to 1868 the sovereign power of the state had been vested in the white citizenry. The Radical program of 1868, which was devised by Congress and imposed on the state by military force, shifted this power to the newly freed Negro majority, which forthwith decreed Negro supremacy and consistently voted as a bloc. For almost a decade this revolutionary government was bad, proving its inability to provide prosperity, security, or justice and demonstrating, too, its unwillingness to correct itself. The counter-revolution of 1876 returned the sovereign power to the white citizenry of the state, where it has since resided.

1

Many of the events leading up to the Red Shirt Campaign revolve around the personal qualities of Radical Governor Daniel Henry Chamberlain, one of the most able and, in some respects, most admirable men produced in the South by Radical Republicanism.[1] He was

---

[1]For a defense of Chamberlain see Walter Allen's *Governor Chamberlain's Administration in South Carolina* (New York, 1888). This defense, however, barely touches the years from 1868 to 1872, when Chamberlain's crimes, if any, were committed, and gives in great detail the years from 1874 to 1876, when Chamberlain won the strong support of the reform element in the state. For another favorable appraisal, see *Dictionary of American Biography*. For a less favorable sketch, see Simkins and Woody, *op. cit.*, pp. 115ff., and *passim*. For a contemporary view, see *The Nation*, XXIV (April 19, 1877), 230.

a native of Massachusetts and a graduate of Yale. In the fall of 1863, after about a year in the Harvard Law School, he joined the army.

From early adolescence he had been an ardent abolitionist of the Garrison-Phillips persuasion. In 1866 he came to South Carolina, and for two years tried to grow cotton so as to repay money that he owed for his college education. Like many others of his kind, however, he found the Negro more easy to glorify than to work with; and, unable to make a profit, he gave up planting cotton and in 1868 began to cultivate Negro votes, with more remunerative results. He was very active in the Radical Republican constitutional convention, after which his zeal and ability led to his election as attorney general of South Carolina. Although he had had but one year's legal training and had never practiced law, he was probably, all things considered, the best-qualified man for his job on the Republican state ticket.

He served as attorney general throughout the four years of Scott's two terms as governor. During this period he was closely associated with the worst robbers of a thievish administration. When he was nominated as governor in 1874, he insisted that the charges then current against him were "each and all, false in every particular and in every sense."[2] Yet he was strongly opposed by the small reform element in his own party and elected by the corruptionists. When, much to the surprise of friend and foe alike, he actually tried to implement the reforms promised in his campaign, he was bitterly denounced, by those who had elected him, as a renegade and traitor.[3]

However honorable his subsequent career as governor, Chamberlain was gravely implicated in some of the most profitable thefts of the very administration that bilked the state of most of its negotiable resources. He was a member of the "printing ring," along with the notable corruptionists, Governor Scott and Niles G. Parker; and large sums spent on printing constituted one of the notorious frauds of the

---

[2]Allen, op. cit., p. 496. Allen's defense of Chamberlain's "integrity and honor" consists largely of reprinting a long letter by Chamberlain published in the Columbia Union Herald, dated August 19, 1874. Concerning this letter, Niles G. Parker, state treasurer during the Scott administration, testified under oath as follows: ". . . and just before Chamberlain addressed his communication to the public in the summer of 1874 concerning the charges made against him with reference to the public debt and other matters connected with Governor Scott's administration, he promised me by the side of his sick bed in his own house that if I would permit that letter which he had prepared to go before the public without contradiction and he should be nominated and elected as Governor I should be paid my share [of the fraudulent settlement with Kimpton]." Report of the Joint Investigating Committee on Public Frauds (Columbia, 1878), p. 9.

[3]Kibler, op. cit., p. 482. See also Allen, op. cit., pp. 31ff.

administration. He was also party, along with "Honest" John Patterson, to a transaction that relieved the state of one of its few valuable assets, the Greenville and Columbia Railroad. In a letter to the South Carolina Financial Agent, H. H. Kimpton, dated January 5, 1870, Chamberlain outlined this plan and asserted gleefully, "There is a mint of money in this or I am a fool."[4] Moreover, he was one of four members of the financial board which did some very remarkable things with state bonds, pumping dry the credit of the state in three years. He was also one of the five-man Land Commission which managed to spend nearly a million dollars of the state's money in acquiring land worth a quarter million, in transactions which even a Radical Republican committee branded as fraudulent. It is worth noting, too, that though he did a great deal of denouncing in general terms during the time he was governor, he did not bring to justice a single malefactor; yet the men were in the state, and the evidence was in records as available to him as to later investigators. Noteworthy, too, is the fact that the diary of Josephus Woodruff, corrupt clerk of the senate, describes Chamberlain in 1874 as a "bloated bond-holder" and comments on his "slippery tactics and hypocrisy."[5] It is indeed difficult to give him a clean record at this stage in his career, and certainly he was far from penniless when he left the state in 1877.

Nevertheless, his courageous fight for reform after his election as governor in 1874 won him the respect of many honest men in the state.[6] It seems probable that he genuinely preferred virtue to corruption,

---

[4]Letter dated January 5, 1870, and signed D. H. Chamberlain. This letter outlines a plan that cost the state "a cool six million dollars, with nothing to show for it." See Henry T. Thompson, *Ousting the Carpetbagger from South Carolina* (Columbia, 1926), p. 36. See also Columbia *Daily Register* (hereafter cited as *Register*), March 24, 1878, quoting the New York *Sun*. The *Sun* quotes the entire letter and states that when it was shown to Chamberlain, written in his own handwriting, he refused to affirm or deny authorship.

[5]R. H. Woody, "Diary of Josephus Woodruff," *Journal of Southern History*, II (February, 1936), 92, 95.

[6]See Allen, *op. cit.*, pp. 31ff. and *passim*. In spite of his record Governor Chamberlain won the cordial and enthusiastic cooperation of the Democrats of the state as soon as he showed evidence of sincerity in his demands for reform. This fact should be taken into consideration in evaluating Radical claims that the white men of the state refused to help in the government. Chamberlain's own assertion to that effect is to be found in an interview with the editor of the *News and Courier* immediately following the election of Whipper and Moses as judges: ". . . and it was also my fondest hope . . . to have worked out, through the Republican party, the solution of the most difficult and one of the most interesting political and social problems which this century has presented. If these results shall not be reached, the responsibility for the failure will not rest upon me, nor upon the Conservative citizens of South Carolina, who have hitherto

would rather do right than wrong. He liked gentlemen and, as he later confessed, did not like the Negroes with whom he was forced to associate.[7] Moreover, he sought the approbation of good men and was deeply pained by the notoriety that he had won. But, more than any of these, he craved wealth and power.

About 1873 "Honest" John Patterson, whom Chamberlain had rescued from a trial for bribery and with whom he had been associated in the railroad steal, made his famous prognostication, "There are still five years of good stealing in South Carolina."[8] Chamberlain, a shrewder man, knew better. In the first place, any future robbery would have to be in trickles since there were no more pools to drain. Even more important, though, was a new spirit abroad in the nation, a cry for reform that would not be stilled.[9] Chamberlain realized that the time had come when Radical thieves in the South could no longer depend on the aid of honest Northerners by merely crying, "Rebels and traitors are persecuting loyal men." As early as June of 1870 *The Nation* had concluded, "Now, it is about time that we ceased helping rogues to make fortunes out of 'the cruelty of the rebels.'..."[10] After his election as governor, therefore, Chamberlain made a statement of policy that gave a faint glimmer of hope to the white men of the state but that seemed, to say the least, inadvisable to his associates.[11]

During the legislative session of 1875 he fought a continuous battle with the Radical majority, handing down in all eighteen vetoes, which could not be overridden because the Conservatives and the few reform Republicans combined to back the governor. He capped his program by refusing to sign the supply bill, into which various attempts on the treasury previously vetoed were slyly inserted. Moreover, equally incredible in a Radical governor, he sold no pardons and granted none for political purposes.

---

with unvarying fidelity and generosity, stood by me in my work; but upon those, and all like them, who dealt the cause of good government so deadly a blow on Thursday [Negro legislators who voted for Whipper and Moses]." Quoted by Allen, *op. cit.*, p. 196.

[7]Daniel H. Chamberlain, "Present Phases of our So-called Negro Problem," *News and Courier*, August 1, 1904. He spoke of such repulsion as "a feeling so deeply implanted ... that it is simply quixotic to attempt to preach it down...."

[8]Thompson, *op. cit.*, p. 36.

[9]The files of *The Nation*, for example, abound in cries for reform. The Republican Party almost lost—or did it lose?—the election of 1876 primarily on that issue.

[10]*The Nation*, X (June 16, 1870), 378.

[11]Allen, *op. cit.*, pp. 32f. See also Thompson, *op. cit.*, pp. 98f.

Meanwhile, more and more of the Conservative newspapers in the state, particularly the influential Charleston *News and Courier,* were giving him warm support.[12] What must have been even more gratifying, he and his lovely wife were being accepted socially, and he was being invited to attend and address many affairs in the state to which his political position as such gave him no entré.[13] He almost succeeded in traveling on both sides of the fence at once. For a while it seemed as though in the campaign of 1876 he would achieve his aim, the backing of the Republican Party combined with the support of the reputable white men in the state.

2

Two factors in the situation defeated Chamberlain's purpose: First, the majority of his party, particularly in the legislature, violently objected both to his friendship with the whites and to his curb on their own rapacity.[14] Second, many determined white men in the state were unwilling to submit to Negro supremacy even though its ill effects were modified by honest leadership.[15] These two factors led, in turn, to two events which profoundly affected the political climate in South Carolina.

Throughout 1875 the Radical majority in the legislature sought to thwart the Governor's reforms, and he was bitterly attacked in both chambers. On December 16, 1875, the legislature took advantage of the Governor's one-day absence from Columbia to elect as judges of the Charleston and Sumter judicial circuits Whipper and Moses, men whose names were synonymous with rascality even throughout the North.[16] Chamberlain at once perceived the danger both to himself

[12]Simkins and Woody, *op. cit.,* p. 482. See also Thompson, *op. cit.,* pp. 97f., and Sheppard, *op. cit.,* pp. 32ff., and Allen, *op. cit., passim.*
[13]Simkins and Woody, *op. cit.,* p. 479.
[14]Allen, *op. cit.,* pp. 38ff.
[15]Thompson, *op. cit.,* p. 98. See also Alfred B. Williams, *op. cit.,* pp. 32, 41f. Gary had come into prominence as irreconcilable to any cooperation or fusion with Republicans or Negroes when he made his speech before the Taxpayers' Convention of 1874 (see above p. 8). He and General M. C. Butler led a "red-hot, straight-out" movement in 1876 while a majority of the white men in the state still favored cooperation with Chamberlain. For an ardently pro-Gary account of this movement, see W. A. Sheppard, *op. cit., passim,* particularly pp. 44ff.
[16]*The Nation,* XXII (January 27, 1876), 54 sardonically commented on a speech by Whipper. In a later issue it quoted from a letter by Chamberlain, "...unless the belief among all classes of people in the state is mistaken, he [Moses] is as infamous a character as ever in any age disgraced and prostituted

and to his hopes for a reputable Republican Party in the state. Commenting on the election for publication, he said, "I look upon their election as a horrible disaster — a disaster equally great to the state and to the Republican party.... This calamity is infinitely greater, in my judgment, than any which has yet fallen on this state...."[17]

Although he did what he could to correct the situation, he was right in his fear for his party. Many Conservatives were rudely jerked from the fools' paradise that they had been lulled into building, in which good government could be achieved by a good governor in spite of a corrupt majority in the legislature. Public indignation meetings were held throughout the state.[18] Speaking before such a meeting in Charleston, General James Conner expressed the general sentiment:

> Since 1868 the Conservative citizens of this State have put aside party obligations and the hope of party ascendancy; have put no party ticket in the field, but have sought and hoped for peace, stability, and pure government through the Republican party. They have striven not to antagonize, but to harmonize, conflicting races, interests, and opinions, patiently waiting to obtain, as the fruit of their forbearance, the blessings of good government.
>
> In every form in which the effort could be made it has been tried, and when, through the wise, firm, and patriotic Administration of Governor Chamberlain, the end seemed about to be obtained, a Republican Legislature repudiates the honest efforts of a Republican Governor, impatiently resents his control, and with a recklessness born of ignorance and hate, commits the State to a career destructive of its peace and fatal to its prosperity. The failure to obtain relief through the Republican party of the State is utter and hopeless.[19]

As a result of these meetings, active Democratic Clubs soon were organized throughout the state for the first time since 1868.[20] By June

---

public position.... [Whipper is] ignorant of law ... ignorant of morals, a gambler by open practice and an embezzler." XXII (February 3, 1876), 71. For this entire letter to Senator Morton see Allen, *op. cit.*, pp. 229ff. For numerous quotations from the press of the country on the Moses-Whipper affair, see *ibid.*, pp. 237ff.

[17]Allen, *op. cit.*, p. 195. Writing twenty-five years later, Chamberlain asserted that the Whipper-Moses election was the cause of his losing Democratic support. He did not explain the effect of his making political capital of the Hamburg affair. (For other opinions as to the turning point, see note 26 below). *Atlantic Monthly*, LXXXVII (April, 1901), 479ff. It seems likely that Chamberlain's reaction to this election for a time actually strengthened his personal popularity with the white men of the state.

[18]Allen *op. cit.*, pp. 201ff.

[19]*Ibid.*, pp. 202f.

[20]*Ibid.*, pp. 209ff. Ironically these plans to organize were at first designed to provide backing for Chamberlain.

of 1876 the Democrats were well organized, but they had not yet decided on a program. A very active minority, ably led by Generals Martin W. Gary and M. C. Butler, wanted a "Straight-out" Democratic ticket "from governor to coroner."[21] A more moderate majority, actively stimulated by the *News and Courier,* wanted the Democrats to support Chamberlain if he should be nominated by the Republicans.[22] They pointed to the Negro majority of nearly thirty thousand in the state as an insuperable obstacle to the ambitions of the Straightouts. As late as the May convention of the state Democrats, assembled to elect delegates to the national convention, this "watch and wait" wing of the party won on a test vote, in spite of strong pleas by Gary and Butler.[23] Governor Chamberlain, whose stock was very high, might still receive the backing of the Conservatives, but he would have to bargain with an organized party, not merely accept the help of grateful citizens.

Late in June Wade Hampton briefly appeared on the scene, though with no expectation of entering into politics. In December he had been placed on the "Democratic State Central Committee," a body that apparently had no authorized status, but not being in the state, he had not attended its meeting early in January. The committee had recommended only that Democrats in the state should organize.[24] Hampton visited Charleston in June to attend the Fort Moultrie Centennial and to ride at the head of a magnificent parade. At an elegant banquet in Hibernian Hall he sat on the toastmaster's right with Chamberlain on the left. These two men faced each other through an evening devoted to "unity and peace," little dreaming of the bitter struggle soon to follow.

Gary and Hampton happened to leave Charleston on the same train and fell into a discussion of the political affairs of the state. There

---

[21]Edward J. Maxwell in a well-informed, well-written account of the election that ran through seven issues (February through August, 1878) of a short-lived magazine *The South Atlantic,* states that the newspapers backing the Straightout movement as early as May, 1876, were Greenville *News,* Abbeville *Medium,* Newberry *Herald,* and Edgefield *Advertiser.* The *South Atlantic,* I (February, 1878), 333.

[22]See notes 12 and 13 above. As the *News and Courier* stated, however, "What divides the two wings of the party is simply the conflict of opinion upon the question whether it is wiser to nominate state officers, from Lieutenant Governor down, or a full ticket, including Governor." Quoted by Maxwell, *op. cit.,* p. 335.

[23]Williams, *op. cit.,* pp. 31f.

[24]Sheppard, *op. cit.,* pp. 52f. Gary objected to this implied support of Chamberlain as he had consistently opposed all approaches to compromise or fusion with the Negro voters of the state throughout Reconstruction.

had been antagonism between these two generals — their tempera-
ments were diametrically opposed — since early in the Civil War,
antagonism that had been increased by Gary's scornful objection to
Hampton's efforts at conciliation during the early stages of Reconstruction.   Nevertheless, both men were actuated by too deep a love
for their state to be misled by personal antipathy.   Gary learned that
Hampton strongly favored the Straightout program.   He realized that
Hampton's name, fame, and personal qualities made him the ideal
Democratic candidate for governor.   Perhaps he thought that Hampton would be a figurehead; therefore, in spite of personal animosity,
he asked if Hampton would accept the nomination if it were offered.
Hampton would.[25]

Immediately following this conversation, Hampton went to the
North Carolina mountains for the summer.   Shortly afterwards the
second event occurred which, in conjunction with the election of Whip-
per and Moses, cost Governor Chamberlain the backing of white
South Carolinians in his campaign for reelection, and thus ended
Negro supremacy in South Carolina.[26]

This second event was what the Radical press, quoting Governor
Chamberlain, immediately called "The Hamburg Massacre," the very
name carrying an unjust implication.   To sift the mass of evidence
and testimony on the Hamburg riot is too lengthy a task for this study.
The basic cause lay in the fact that eight years of Reconstruction had
developed, particularly in Edgefield and Aiken Counties (in which
Hamburg was situated), a condition that made violent reaction inevitable.   Since these counties had Negro majorities, legal redress of
wrongs had proved extremely difficult for whites, if not impossible.

---

[25]As told by Sheppard, op. cit., pp. 83ff.   But, according to Simkins and Woody,
op. cit., p. 490 note, "On June 28 M. W. Gary had gone to Charleston to broach
the nomination of Butler in the Charleston Journal of Commerce.   On the way,
he met Hampton and told him that his friends had decided to nominate him on
the Straightout ticket.   On July 8 Butler published a letter withdrawing his
name and nominating Hampton."   Simkins and Woody do not explain the contradiction of Gary's bearing such a message from Hampton's friends while Gary
was on his way to "broach the nomination of Butler."   According to Thompson,
op. cit., p. 104, "From the time in 1875 that the Straightout movement started,
Wade Hampton had been prominently mentioned as the Democratic candidate
for Governor. . . ."

[26]See Williams, op. cit., p. 27.   "It was a strange, almost fearful, coincidence,
noted by nobody then, that the real beginning of the revolution of 1876 was
on the fourth of July, precisely a hundred years after the signing of the declaration. . . ."   See also, Allen, op. cit., p. 312, ". . . the turning point in the course of
political affairs. . . ."

Judge T. J. Mackey, a Radical Republican who had been dispatched by Governor Chamberlain to Edgefield a year before to investigate complaints, had commented, "No such iniquity as the county government of Edgefield has been inflicted upon any portion of the English-speaking race since the Saxon wore the iron collar of the Norman. . . . The condition of Edgefield presents a problem that demands an instant solution in the interest of public peace and the due preservation of life and property."[27]   Mackey later added, "The government of Edgefield has been for eight years a festering ulcer upon our body politic, and a diligent attempt is now being made to hide with the 'bloody shirt' the appalling wrongs committed by the Republican party on the white population of that section."[28]

Moreover, the affair could hardly be called a massacre since of the company of Negro militia, which was barricaded in a brick building and armed with army Springfield rifles, only six were killed. Five of the six, however, were killed after they were captured.

The real political significance of the riot lay in Governor Chamberlain's reaction. An objective judicial inquiry with a resulting correction of causes and punishment of malefactors of both races would have proved him a man worthy of white support.[29] The pressure on him, however, was too strong, particularly from national party headquarters, where a few juicy "outrages" were badly needed in the impending national election and where Chamberlain's stock was getting dangerously low.[30] As a realistic Radical politician is reported

[27]Thompson, op. cit., pp. 85f.

[28]Ibid., p. 86. Chamberlain's awareness of such conditions in the section is shown in a letter rebuking Judge Carpenter, dated June 24, 1875. "I must say that I fear not a little for the peace of that county during the present summer. . . ." He listed a comprehensive schedule of complaints that he had received from whites there who were unable to get justice in Carpenter's Negro-dominated court. Allen, op. cit., pp. 310f.

[29]At first the press of the state, particularly the News and Courier, showed itself ready to back Chamberlain in a thorough investigation of the affair and a stern punishment of guilty men of both races. See Williams, op. cit., pp. 32f. See also Simkins and Woody, op. cit., p. 488, "The generality of the press very frankly condemned the Hamburg affair, but Chamberlain was censured for giving the matter a political twist. . . ." The Nation shrewdly objected to ". . . the unnecessary and somewhat heated letter of Governor Chamberlain to the President about the Hamburg matter, and the President's extravagant answer. . . . It is impossible not to wish that Governor Chamberlain would quietly and vigorously push the prosecution of the Hamburg murderers." XXIII (August 10, 1876), 81.

[30]See Allen, op. cit., pp. 225ff. ". . . Senators Morton and Conkling were seeking and obtaining support for themselves upon the ground that his [Grant's] administration had been wise and successful, especially in its Southern policy. . . ." These men began an attack on Chamberlain for flirting with the Democratic

to have remarked, "A kilt nigger is worth twenty thousand votes north of the Potomac!"[31]

Chamberlain bombarded the North with lurid accounts of the affair based on the excited claims of Negro participants. His chief conclusion was that this act of "atrocity and barbarism" was designed to prevent Negroes from voting, though, as a matter of fact, the riot occurred five months before the election, and Chamberlain knew that it was largely due to local conditions — indeed had predicted something of the sort in a letter prodding Judge Carpenter: "I must say that I fear not a little for the peace of that county during the present summer." He thus put himself "right" with his party chiefs, who, particularly Senator Morton, had been looking on his reform efforts with deep suspicion;[32] but he forfeited forever the chance for strong white support in South Carolina.

The coroner's jury that acted on the riot consisted of twelve Negroes, the foreman a participant and nine of them unable to sign their names. Most of the white men whom they "bound over" for complicity voluntarily surrendered to the authorities (except one who had been dead for six months before the riot), yet Chamberlain used the affair to excuse a cry for more federal troops, always an effective prelude to a Radical Republican election in South Carolina. No Negroes were bound over, though the riot started with their protecting one of their number from legal processes and though it was at least probable that they fired the first shot — certainly they killed the first man. Sixty-one white men were bound over, but never tried

---

vote, most particularly, for confessing Republican sins in the South, which they were busy denying as "the prejudiced and vindictive misrepresentations of men who were lately rebels." An extract from the *National Republican* indicates how precarious Chamberlain's position had become with his party chiefs, whose support was essential to his plans: "Governor Chamberlain has been inveigled into a path of political turpitude, which must eventually end in his political destruction. By a shrewd and carefully prepared scheme the Democrats have succeeded in . . . securing his gubernatorial influence to further their efforts in overthrowing the Republican power in the state." *Ibid.*, p. 240. This party reaction to his attack on Whipper and Moses made it essential that he "get right" with the bosses. The Hamburg riot provided an opportunity.

[31]Williams, *op. cit.*, p. 33.

[32]Just how worried Chamberlain was about his status in the national party is indicated by the frantic tone of his letters to Senator Morton and Grant about Whipper and Moses. Allen, *op. cit.*, pp. 228ff. *The Nation* chided Republican Party leaders for the obvious glee with which they received Chamberlain's lurid, *ex parte* accounts of the Hamburg affair. "Some of them talk . . . as if one more good, substantial slaughter of negroes would make Hayes' election sure." XXIII (July 27, 1876), 52.

since later Negro testimony, as well as that of the whites, showed how far the first accounts had deviated from the truth.[33]

One immediate result of Chamberlain's use of this unfortunate affair for Radical political advantage was a tremendous surge forward of the Straightout movement. Within four days the Democratic Executive Committee called a convention of the party for August 15, by which time the Straightout minority had grown to a majority and the organization of Democratic Clubs had gone forward rapidly. Even Chamberlain's ardent champion, the *News and Courier,* had begun to refer to him a bit coolly. Thirty-three years later "Pitchfork" Ben Tillman, who participated in the riot, spoke of it as the crucial event of the campaign.[34]

3

Hampton's active participation in the campaign began with the August convention, which he attended as a delegate from Richland County. Although he had been generally discussed as a possible candidate from the very beginning of the Straightout movement, he had been outside the state; therefore the general affection and respect felt towards him had not been marred by the factional quarrels that had marked the spring and summer. His first public statement on the issue had appeared in the Columbia *Daily Register* for August 9 in answer to a letter from General M. C. Butler, who had withdrawn from the race and had nominated Hampton. Hampton asserted that the Democrats "should enter into no compromise or form no fusion with the Radical party." He wanted a full ticket of "tried and trusted sons ... for whom our people can vote without the sacrifice of principle."

Pre-convention talk was strong against Hampton as a candidate because Samuel J. Tilden, the national Democratic candidate for the presidency, was afraid of Hampton's political reputation as a "fire-eater," unjustly gained in 1868, and was decidedly cool towards the Straightout movement altogether. John F. Coyle, representative of the National Democratic Committee, was in Columbia agitating against the Straightouts and particularly against Hampton, whose name on

---

[33]For the report to Chamberlain from the state Attorney General, see Allen, *op. cit.,* pp. 313ff. For Chamberlain's letters to Senator T. J. Robertson and to Grant, see *ibid.,* pp. 318ff. For B. R. Tillman's sensational account, see B. R. Tillman, *The Struggles of '76.* See also Simkins and Woody, *op. cit.,* pp. 486f. and note, and Williams, *op. cit.,* pp. 29ff., and Reynolds, *op. cit.,* pp. 344ff.

[34]Tillman, *op. cit.,* pp. 15, 27.

the ticket, he asserted, would injure the party in the North.[35]   Nevertheless, after a close debate for seven hours, the Straightouts won by a
narrow margin.

General M. C. Butler then nominated Hampton for governor, and
the nomination was seconded by Robert Aldrich of Barnwell.   In a
few earnest words Hampton referred to the statement of his principles
published a few days before in the Columbia *Daily Register* and then
called attention to the two objections to his candidacy: vilification of
him by the Radical press in 1868 might still make his name a liability to
the national party; his high rank and war record also might make him
unacceptable.   Before retiring from the hall, he begged the convention
"to look over the whole field."[36]   Two men who were nominated after
Hampton had left the hall withdrew in favor of the General, who then
was unanimously chosen by acclamation.

After the rest of the ticket had been filled, Hampton made a short
address.   He did not minimize the difficulties before them in "this hour
of gloom and peril."

> You are struggling for the highest stake for which a people
> ever contended, for you are striving to bring back to your pros-
> trate State the inestimable blessings which can only follow orderly
> and regulated liberty under free and good government.... For
> myself, should I be elevated to the high position for which you
> have nominated me ... I shall be Governor of the whole people,
> knowing no party, making no vindictive discriminations, holding
> the scales of justice with firm and impartial hand, seeing, as far
> as in me lies, that the laws are enforced in justice tempered with
> mercy, protecting all classes alike....[37]

The nomination of Hampton put an end to vacillation and division
of purpose among the white men of the state.   Once the decision was
made, Democrats united in a desperate determination not to fail.[38]

---

[35]See Sheppard, *op. cit.*, pp. 112ff.   *The Nation* reveals even liberal reaction
in the North to Hampton's nomination: "The South Carolina Democrats...
have shown that they possess their full share of the party capacity for blunder-
ing.... He [Hampton] is neither a statesman nor a politician, nor a man of
conciliatory disposition, nor anything but a Southern gentleman of the old School,
to whom niggers, Yankees, schools, roads, free labor, and free speech are almost
as hateful as to the Pope himself."   XXIII (August 24, 1876), 11.   During the
following month *The Nation* was to change greatly its estimate of Hampton.
[36]For entire speech, see Reynolds, *op. cit.*, pp. 350f.
[37]*Ibid.*, pp. 352f.
[38]John A. Leland, *A Voice from South Carolina* (Charleston, 1879), pp. 160ff.
See also Williams, *op. cit.*, *passim* and Thompson, *op. cit.*, pp. 112ff. and Ball,
op. cit., p. 178.

They were not blind to the obstacles before them, nor did they shut their eyes to the fact that the struggle ahead was no normal election. As early as May the *News and Courier* had summed up the difficulties in urging against the Straightout movement. The editorial predicted that Chamberlain would be the Republican candidate and that there would "be no bolt." The overwhelming difficulty, of course, was a Negro Republican majority of twenty to thirty thousand. "Add to the solid Republican vote," the editorial continued, "the power to obtain Federal troops as they may be needed, the Executive appointment of Commissioners of Election, the broad and undefined powers of the Board of State Canvassers, and what prospect is there that he should be defeated? It could be done in only one way: *by armed force.*"[39] This schedule left out the Negro militia, which throughout the state was well armed and organized.

In the seven-hour secret session that preceded the decision, the price of victory and the cost of defeat must have been squarely faced. The Democrats had only one trump card, a card which fortunately they did not have to play: They preferred forcing the reimposition of military government to continuing under Negro rule.

Hampton did not agree with the *News and Courier* that victory could be won only "by armed force." He and the men chosen as a State Executive Committee, particularly the chairman, Colonel A. C. Haskell, believed that the campaign could be won by a unanimous white effort combined with conciliatory appeals to the Negro voters.[40] Hence General Gary was omitted from the State Executive Committee

[39]*News and Courier*, May 8, 1876. This entire editorial is quoted by Allen, *op. cit.*, pp. 274ff.

[40]D. D. Wallace, "The Question of the Withdrawal of the Democratic Presidential Electors in S. C. in 1876," The Journal of Southern History, VIII (August, 1942), 375. "Hampton and Gary were agreed in their determination for a 'straight-out' fight, but in little else, either in temperament or in policy, were they in harmony.... Hampton pursued the plan of appealing to the Negroes to desert the Radicals ... and to support their tried, traditional white friends...." Maxwell, *op. cit.*, (March, 1878), p. 418, said, "It was clear that the campaign fought on the straight-out issue required the selection of a man of varied and peculiar qualities. It was essential that the greatest moderation should be united to the highest prudence, the most skillful tactical knowledge to the greatest firmness and perseverance. The provocations to excess and violence would be most exasperating. At this early day it began to be evident that the capital upon which the Radicals were to operate would be the cry of outrages on the part of their opponents to cover the state with troops. It must be made a part of the Democratic creed; it must be the policy of the Democratic leaders to avoid the slightest appearance of force or violence. This was the ruling idea among the wise heads who were guiding the action of the party."

because, though he was the most active of the Straightouts, he was also the leader of those uncompromising extremists who planned to prevent Negroes from voting by violence rather than to appeal for their cooperation.[41] Contrary to Gary's plan, from the time of the August convention the state leaders planned a campaign of appeal to, not attack on, the Negroes. As Haskell testified before a Senate investigating committee, "We did not nominate him [Hampton] as an extreme man, but as a reform man, who was eminently conservative, and who would be able to unite the two races better than anyone else we could select in the state."[42] In other words, Hampton did not accept Gary's theory of race war, though he knew, of course, that the campaign might easily lead to race war. One of his major problems during the campaign was to prevent violence, for the kind of violent action planned by Gary would have given every advantage to the Radicals in the state and in the nation.[43]

A thoughtful reader is likely to ask, "Was Hampton, then, justified in accepting leadership in a movement certain to arouse bitter interracial animosity, likely to precipitate violence and bloodshed?" One answer to this question is to be found in an article written twenty-five years later for the *Atlantic Monthly* by ex-Governor Chamberlain himself, the man who best knew the situation and was least likely to be prejudiced in favor of Hampton's cause:

[41]The detailed plan drawn up by Gary for a bellicose campaign is quoted in full by Simkins and Woody, *op. cit.*, pp. 564ff. and Sheppard, *op. cit.*, pp. 46ff. The original copy is in the Gary manuscript. This plan, however, it should be emphasized, was rejected, not accepted, by Hampton and the State Executive Committee. It is evidence, therefore, of what the official plan of campaign was not, an important point in later developments between Gary and Hampton. See also comments on Gary and Hampton by A. C. Haskell before the Senate Committee investigating the election, *South Carolina in 1876* (Washington, 1877), I, 833. Also see below, pp. 115ff., for the Gary faction accusation that Hampton had been guilty of a "repudiation of the plan of campaign adopted" by Gary and the Straightouts and that instead he had followed a "milk and cider, 'peace and prosperity,' conciliation of Radicals and flattery of negroes policy...." See also Ball, *op. cit.*, p. 178. "General Gary's service after the nomination was, like that of many another, indispensable, but the general method of it was not his."

[42]*South Carolina in 1876*, I, 837. Maxwell, *op. cit.*, p. 426, quoted Colonel J. H. Rion, a violent man by nature, as saying in a speech at the convention, "Let us bear and forbear even to that extent when forbearance ceases to be a virtue."

[43]Leland, *op. cit.*, p. 165. See also Williams, *op. cit.*, pp. 187f. and *passim*; Thompson, *op. cit.*, p. 115; and Ball, *op. cit.*, pp. 157f. John W. De Forest, a well-informed observer, stated in a letter to *The Nation*, XXIII (September 28, 1876), 196, that the violence of extremists in Edgefield was jeopardizing the accomplishment of white supremacy.

If the canvass of 1876 had resulted in the success of the Republican party, that party could not, for want of material, even when aided by the Democratic minority, have given pure or competent administration. The vast preponderance of ignorance and incapacity in that party, aside from downright dishonesty, made it impossible . . . the flood gates of misrule would have been reopened. . . . The real truth is, hard as it may be to accept it, that the elements put in combination by the reconstruction scheme of Stevens and Morton were irretrievably bad, and could never have resulted . . . in government fit to be endured.[44]

While federal troops were still holding the State House in Columbia, *The Nation* informed its readers, "Evidently there is nothing to be done but to let the sham give way to the reality . . . to see without regret . . . the blacks deprived of a supremacy as corrupting to themselves as it was dangerous to society at large."[45]   The overwhelming evidence convinced at the time all but the unconvincible doctrinaires that what Hampton had done was right and necessary.   As Congressman S. S. Cox of New York and Ohio remarked:

Since the world began, no parallel can be found to the unblushing knavery which a complete history of carpet-bag government in these states would exhibit.   If the entire body of penitentiary convicts could be invested with supreme power in a state, they could not present a more revolting mocking of all that is honorable and respectable in the conduct of human affairs.   The knaves and their sympathizers, North and South, complain that the taxpayers, the men of character and intelligence in South Carolina and other states, finally overthrew, by unfair and violent means, the reign of scoundrelism, enthroned by ignorance.   If ever revolutionary methods were justifiable for the overthrow of tyranny

[44]Chamberlain, "Reconstruction in South Carolina," *Atlantic Monthly,* LXXXVII, 482. As early as May, 1877, Chamberlain had admitted in an interview in the *New York Herald,* "Bad leadership and ignorant followers could not work out the problem of good government."   Quoted in *The Nation,* XXIV (May 24, 1877), 302.   In "The Political Issues of 1892," a speech delivered by Chamberlain at The Academy of Music, Philadelphia, on October 28, 1892, and printed as a pamphlet, he said (p. 37f.), "The evils which had arisen at the South under Republican rule had become too grave and intolerable to be borne by the people of the South or to be upheld by the people of the North."   In a letter to the *Boston Herald,* August 29, 1904, he said of his administration in South Carolina, it was "never within the bounds of possibility to keep up a bearable government. . . . [I could] merely retard a little the course of corruption and misrule ever gathering force behind me and sure shortly to overwhelm me." See also Chamberlain, "Present Phases of Our So-Called Negro Problem," *loc. cit., passim.*
[45]*The Nation,* XXIV (March 1, 1877), 127.

and robbery, assuredly the carpet-bag domination in South Carolina called for it. Only scoundrels and hypocrites will pretend to
deplore the result.[46]

Since the Negro constitutes a minority in the nation, much misunderstanding of South Carolina's approach to the Negro problem
has been based on the general moral principles involved in treatment
of minorities. The dominating political fact in South Carolina, however, was the existence of a large Negro majority, a majority that
sought to maintain political supremacy and that resolutely resisted
every effort at minority representation. Moreover, this majority had
demonstrated for almost a decade its utter inability even to maintain
the social, intellectual, economic, or moral heritage of the state, much
less to move forward. Evidence of Hampton's moral justification lies
in the rapid improvement in the welfare of both races after he assumed control.

Speaking in this connection before the Massachusetts Reform Club
at Boston in 1890, ex-Governor Chamberlain cited his own experience:

> I come from the South to-night. . . . I have mingled again dur-
> ing the last four months with the people whom I then knew so
> well. . . . I find that since 1876, both races in South Carolina have
> prospered. . . . I find the Negro more self-respecting, better pro-
> vided with schools, far better, acquiring property more rapidly,
> more industrious, more ambitious for education and property,
> than he ever was before 1876. . . . I proclaim it because it is true.
>
> I do not exonerate the white race at the south from all past or
> present blame. There are wrongs done there to the Negro now,
> but I do say that the Negro has never known such an era of ad-
> vancement and prosperity in all that benefits a citizen and free-
> man as the period since 1876, and if it be treason to say it, I reply,
> in historic words, "Make the most of it!"[47]

4

Within the ranks of South Carolina Democracy there were both
unity and conflict. As had happened in 1868, the absolute need for an
unbroken front against the black vote placed in uneasy conjunction
certain diverging forces. There were so many cross currents that the
two main streams cannot be marked off with exact accuracy, but the
division was unmistakably there. As for personalities, the leaders of

[46]Samuel S. Cox, *Three Decades of Federal Legislation* (Providence, 1888),
pp. 506f.
[47]Speech of February 8, 1890, reported in Boston *Daily Post* and reprinted in
pamphlet. Quoted by Simkins and Woody, *op. cit.*, pp. 544f. See also Chamberlain, "The Political Issues of 1892," *op. cit.*, pp. 38f.

the two factions, of course, were Wade Hampton and Martin W. Gary.[48] Both men had followers throughout the state, but Gary's greatest strength lay in his home county of Edgefield and the surrounding counties. Hampton was loyally followed in all sections, but his longest and strongest support was in the Low-country. Hence, although Hampton himself belonged to the Up-country, the division was to some slight extent a continuation of the old feud between the two sections. As for social classes, members of all classes could be found in both factions, but the pre-war "aristocracy" rallied to Hampton sufficiently to give some grounds to the later derisive epithet of "Bourbons."[49] However, he was also at that time the idol of the masses.

The preponderant cause for division, aside from divergent attitudes towards the Negro, lay in the personal qualities of the two men. Hampton was cool, moderate, conciliatory, self-controlled. Instinctively he sought a legal, orderly, peaceful course to follow. His invariable gentleness and courtesy held his friends and disarmed his foes.[50] Throughout the campaign he never lost sight of his ultimate goal, the liberation of the state. His will was as inflexibly set on the accomplishment of that purpose as was Gary's but he would not resort to violence until every other possible means had been tried. The majority of whites, including most of the leaders, sensed the wisdom of Hampton's course and followed him loyally, though sometimes against every instinct and inclination.

Gary, on the other hand, was rigid and inflexible. His was the narrow intensity of the true revolutionary. He carried into politics the same unyielding logic that his ancestor, John Knox, had applied to theology. From the first he had seen the political problem of the state as one, not of parties, but of races. He had viewed with utmost scorn all preceding efforts at conciliation or fusion, and he did not shrink from any degree of violence necessary to eliminate the Negro majority from the political life of the state.[51] The more extreme white

---

[48]Bowers, *op. cit.*, p. 514.

[49]Wallace, *op. cit.*, pp. 375f. Northern observers, however, soon began calling Gary's faction "Bourbons."

[50]Perry, *op. cit.*, p. 566. See also Maxwell, *op. cit.*, p. 418.

[51]Bowers, *op. cit.*, pp. 502ff. and Sheppard, *op. cit.*, *passim.*, also Williams, *op. cit.*, p. 83. See Gary's speech to the Taxpayers' Convention of S. C., February 19, 1874. Gary asserted that the Negroes were united against the whites and the whites not yet united.... "... it is a question of race, and not of politics." p. 4.

men of the state who preferred direct action to conciliation tended more and more to side with the Gary faction. This tendency culminated in the Tillman movement a decade and a half later.

In this crisis of her history South Carolina needed both men. Without Gary, there might not have been a Straightout movement at all in 1876.[52] Certainly the crisis would not have found the state organized, disciplined, and armed sufficiently to meet the needs of the hour. Without Hampton almost surely the campaign would have ended in race war and military government. The state can honor both of her sons.[53]

5

Both Hampton and Gary recognized the need for tightly organized forces of white men, not only to cope with Negro mobs, but more particularly to counter the numerous companies of Negro militia armed at state and federal expense. These militia companies were as unruly and irresponsible as any mob, but far more dangerous since they could be assembled at any time by their leaders, some of whom were the worst rascals in the community.

The policies of the two men differed in the use that was to be made of these organizations, which were called "rifle clubs" (dismounted), and "sabre clubs" (mounted), though many had no weapons except pistols and shot guns. Gary planned a campaign of aggressive intimidation of Negroes, to culminate in seizure of the polls on election day.[54] Such a course would inevitably have led to clashes with United States troops, who were distributed throughout the state to guard the polls.

Hampton's formula for the campaign was *force without violence.* He understood the Negroes well enough to know that they were unlikely to "start trouble" unless they had an overwhelming preponderance of force, and that they would be very much impressed by large, organized bands of mounted men. His instructions were to have large bodies of armed white men ready at every crucial time and place, but to hold them under the firm discipline of responsible officers so that there would be no outbreak of violence except in absolute protection

---

[52]Leland, *op. cit.*, p. 183, and Ball, *op. cit.*, p. 176.
[53]See Williams, *op. cit.*, pp. 82f. See also Wallace, *op. cit.*, pp 375f.
[54]Sheppard, *op. cit.*, pp. 46ff.

of life and property.[55] This constant show of power was an important cause for the surprising lack of bloodshed during the campaign as well as for Hampton's victory.

Shortly after the election the effectiveness of this plan was revealed before the Senate investigating committee by Henry E. Hayne, Negro secretary of state. He was asserting intimidation by the whites, but repeatedly had to admit that no one was shot or struck or hurt. Finally he complained, "...there is an organized plan throughout the state of South Carolina not to have any violence committed on anybody; but the plan of intimidation was so thorough that there was no need to have any violence."[56] He, like many other Radical leaders, felt aggrieved because, although there was constant pressure, there were few, if any, actionable demonstrations. There is considerable evidence that some Radical leaders actually tried to precipitate outbreaks of violence so as to produce their chief stock in trade, loudly proclaimed "outrages."[57]

As soon as Hampton was nominated, the whites of the state from Hilton Head to the mountains rose in a spontaneous combustion of hope and determination. Never did Hampton have to arouse enthusiasm. His was the infinitely more difficult job of controlling it.[58] His speeches were calm, largely addressed to the Negroes in the audience. Throughout the struggle his constant warning was "keep the peace."

---

[55]Williams, *op. cit.*, pp. 84f. See also Haskell's testimony before the Senate committee, December, 1876: The instructions from the State Executive Committee to the county chairmen were "That they should not resort to any violence—to any illegal means whatsoever—no threats, no intimidation . . . that they should develop the strength of the state, that they should exhibit it that it might have its moral and legitimate influence on our adversaries; that we must show our strength, but that no force should be used." *South Carolina in 1876*, I, 837. Haskell also stated that the Democrats "wished to avoid violence and we wished to make it a reform and reconciliation battle." *Ibid.*, p. 834. See also Haskell, *Recent Election in S. C.* (Washington, 1877), pp. 337f, and pp. 340f. Also p. 342—the force of an order "absolutely no intimidation at the election." See Hampton's testimony, *South Carolina in 1876*, I, 984, and *Recent Election in S. C.*, p. 306. See also Reynolds, *op. cit.*, p. 359.

[56]*South Carolina in 1876*, I, 587.

[57]Reynolds, *op. cit.*, p. 356. Patterson was supposed to have said, "We've got to raise hell with these niggers and get troops down there, or the damned Rebels will carry it in spite of us." Williams, *op. cit.*, p. 154 and p. 224. See also Thompson, *op. cit.*, p. 120. See also below, p. 79, for Judge Cooke's testimony. In September of 1877 the Washington correspondent of the New York *Sun*, commenting on the revelation of how many rifles had been sent to South Carolina, stated, "Everything was done that could be done here to precipitate a color-line fight." *Register*, September 13, 1877.

[58]See note 43 above. See also Maxwell, *op. cit.* (April, 1878), p. 472.

Just as the revolution which had placed the Negro in power was synthetic, so was there something unreal about the counter-revolution. In its essence it was revolutionary, but revolution with rules and a referee. Success to the Democrats depended on their not outraging public sentiment in the watchful North sufficiently to permit a hostile federal administration to interfere. It was Hampton who found the indispensable formula, force without violence. But this was a procedure so alien to Gary's nature that, as the weeks passed, he grew more and more resentful.

W. W. Ball in *The State that Forgot* said of Gary, "He was a gallant, impetuous, fiery and brilliant leader, but the conditions for the conduct of the campaign itself demanded moderation and restraint foreign to his nature. General Gary's patience with the Radicals had been exhausted before the campaign began, and General Hampton's patience was inexhaustible."[59]

Gary's intransigence probably had little effect on the election itself except in his own county of Edgefield.[60] During the trying months that followed, however, when in both the state and nation there were two sets of claimants to victory and when only the coolness of wise and moderate men prevented the outbreak of bloody civil strife, Gary's incitements to violence might well have been a spark in the national powder keg had it not been for Hampton's contol over the men of South Carolina.[61] As it was, Gary during these months made Hampton's difficult task more troublous.

Although Gary died in 1881, his name was a potent one during the Tillman campaign a decade later, and those who were associated with him soon began to boast of the violence with which they had conducted the campaign. Since they strongly opposed Hampton's conciliatory policy towards the black man, they tended more and more to minimize the effects of Hampton's pleas to the Negro voters. Simi-

---

[59]Ball, *op. cit.*, pp. 178f. Haskell told the Senate committee that Gary had made a few speeches from the platform with Hampton at the start of the canvass. He had heard of these "violent speeches ... but it was always heard with great regret, and was directly contrary to the spirit of our party and to our whole campaign. I do not like to make such personal allusions, but it is a fact. His speeches were not approved in that respect. It is a great peculiarity of the man that he uses violent language very often, and he was asked to modify it." *South Carolina in 1876*, I, 833.

[60]*Ibid.* In reply to the question "How extensively did Gary stump the state?" Haskell replied, "He went to very few places."

[61]See below pp. 111f.

larly they greatly exaggerated the degree and effect of intimidation.[62] To them the election was race war, and they denied any white debt to the Negroes of the state, even to those who voted the Democratic ticket. They also greatly exaggerated Gary's part in winning the victory.

Hampton, on the other hand, asserted during the campaign that he was seeking the Negro vote and insisted afterwards that the Democratic Negro vote had enabled him to achieve his majority. In this connection he asserted, "I regarded myself as having been elected by the colored people; that I had received not less than 17,000 votes from them. I felt that I was the governor of the colored people as much as the white people, and that their rights would be protected as fully as the others."[63]

Some accounts of the campaign give the impression of continuous violence and intimidation. These derive either from Radical or from Gary-faction sources; for in this respect, as in many others, extremes meet. Thus in an address delivered at Anderson, South Carolina, in 1909, "Pitchfork" Ben Tillman, who had belonged to a sabre club in Gary's county, said of Hampton:

> He blundered egregiously in urging the policy of persuasion; and of convincing the Negroes by argument to vote with us. He always maintained that sixteen thousand negroes voted for him in 1876; but every active worker in the cause knew that in this he was woefully mistaken. . . . Gary preached the only effective doctrine for the times: that "one ounce of fear was worth a pound of persuasion," and was prepared and did ride rough-shod over the negroes and their carpet-bag leaders. . . .[64]

As will be seen, the great weight of testimony before both the Senate and House investigating committees, particularly that by federal officers, even those stationed in the most troublesome districts, shows very clearly that the campaign and election were amazingly peaceful. In *Hampton and His Red Shirts*, A. B. Williams says, "Let it be remembered that in this campaign there was not an assassination by the whites, that the most bitterly and justly hated robbers and authors of vile insult and wrong went about the state openly and unscathed."[65] In all the much-publicized riots—Hamburg, Ellenton, Cainhoy, and Charleston — with all the causes for fear and hatred

[62]See below, p. 146.
[63]*Recent Election in S. C.*, p. 333.
[64]Tillman, *op. cit.*, pp. 27f.
[65]Williams, *op. cit.*, p. 150.

during several excited months, the total death toll was twenty-one Negroes and nine whites.[66]   As a significant comparison, in one riot in Detroit in 1943, a riot with far less pressing cause for racial antagonism, the cost in lives was greater, twenty-five Negroes and nine whites, with more than a thousand wounded.[67]   It was Hampton's wisdom, moderation and power over the minds and hearts of men that enabled the state to throw off Radical rule with a minimum of violence.

---

[66]Simkins and Woody, *op. cit.,* pp. 487, 505f.

[67]Alfred M. Lee, *Race Riot* (New York, 1943), pp. 2, 84.

Chapter Four

FORCE WITHOUT VIOLENCE

A FIRST-HAND picture of General Hampton during the campaign of seventy-six is found in *Hampton and His Red Shirts* by Alfred B. Williams, who was with Hampton as a reporter for the Charleston *Journal of Commerce.*

General Hampton was not brilliant nor spectacular. He wrote and spoke strong, clear English, but did not attempt the lofty flights of oratory or literature. His speeches in the campaign of '76 were just plain, straight talks. When he addressed the negroes, as he invariably did, whether many or few of them were at his meetings, he talked as if he had been on the steps of his plantation house reasoning with the people on his place seeking information and advice, kindly, friendly and frankly, without offensive condescension, with no wheedling, no sentimental appeals, except in reference to the past glories of the state and hopes for her future. When he introduced a bit of humor it was natural, incidental, on the suggestion of the moment, such as everybody could catch. He never became excited or shouted or gesticulated and never made an impious, coarse or indelicate reference.

He was a big, powerful, athletic man, with rather small dark blue eyes, the face of a good humored, self confident, fearless fighter, carrying just enough extra flesh to become his fifty-eight years. Probably he weighed 240 pounds. When in the saddle he looked as if he and the horse were one. His vanities were manly. He was proud of his horsemanship and never felt so much at home as when on a strong, spirited horse and was frankly vain of his skill as fisherman and hunter.... He liked to discuss with other veterans incidents and events of the Civil War, but never so much as hinted at a boast of his own distinguished part in it. An aristocrat to his finger tips, so far as blood descent and standard of conduct and deportment, in great matters and small went, he never talked of his pedigree and in his contacts with people was essentially and instinctively democratic, ready always, for in-

63

stance, to join in familiar chat on the war with the humblest private of the Confederacy or on the merits and characters of dogs and horses with the lowliest citizen interested in those creatures as he was. In the midst of the campaign our train stalled somewhere between Columbia and Graniteville and all of us got out and walked about, amusing ourselves firing at targets with revolvers. By the way, Hampton never carried a weapon — possibly the one man in South Carolina who didn't — and on this occasion he borrowed. A farmer living nearby recognized the General and after looking him over, spoke —

'Say, Gin'ral, they tell me you're a kind of dog man. I wisht you'd come over here an' look at somethin' I've got."

The General joined him and they tramped together to where there was a litter of new hound puppies and through the next hour were in deep, confidential debate on the breeds and builds of hounds and the possibilities of rescuing a young dog wanted for 'possum purposes from the soul destroying vice of going off after rabbit trails.

That was characteristic of Hampton. He never posed, never tried to look or do like somebody else — always and everywhere just plain Wade Hampton, simple unaffected gentleman, dauntless warrior of South Carolina, loving and reverencing his God, his cause and his commonwealth to the last recess of his clean soul.[1]

1

Hampton was nominated on August 16 and opened his formal speaking campaign at Anderson on the second of September. Between those two dates an almost unbelievable change had occurred in the political atmosphere of the state. On August 15 the white leaders were divided, and the mass of the people was sunk in a political lethargy that had lasted for eight years. Republicans in the state, however, seemed to face only one difficulty, the split between Chamberlain and the corruptionists led by the disreputable Negro, R. B. Elliott, and by Senator "Honest" John Patterson, "whose career and mental processes," remarked The Nation, "are more fitting subjects for examination by the police than by the political critic."[2]

With Hampton's nomination the man and the moment came together. Immediately enthusiasm swept through the state. "From that day," says Williams, "all other work and interest were little matters compared with electing Hampton."[3] Many Democrats, says Henry T. Thompson in Ousting the Carpetbagger from South Carolina, had

[1] Williams, op. cit., pp. 89ff.
[2] The Nation, XXIV (April 12, 1877), 216.
[3] Williams, op. cit., p. 79.

regarded the Democratic nomination as an empty honor, "but they began to look at the matter very differently a few days after the convention had adjourned. They had not counted upon the tremendous enthusiasm which Hampton's name evoked."[4] The state knew that it had found a leader.

By early in September the Republicans were for the first time very much on the defensive. On September 6 former Provisional Governor B. F. Perry quoted President Grant as having said to a South Carolina Republican who boasted that the state was safely Republican, "It was safe until the Democrats nominated Hampton. Now they'll carry it."[5] Many prominent white Republicans, Northerners and Southerners, were already pledging their support to Hampton, a process soon to be known as "crossing Jordan." Radical Republican correspondent H. V. Redfield of the *Cincinnati Commercial* watched Hampton's first meetings and wrote to his paper that the state was going Democratic.[6] Indeed, about the middle of September certain Republicans offered to give up the struggle in the state if Hampton would withdraw the Democratic Presidential electors, an offer that Hampton rejected.[7]

From the first, too, Hampton held the reins; and if Gary had expected him to be a "front man," he very soon realized his mistake. Williams gives an enthusiastic appraisal of Hampton's leadership:

> That was the one campaign I ever have known or read of in which there was not a blunder by the leaders of a people struggling for opportunity to live and hope. . . . That was where Hampton was great. . . . He took supreme command and directed and led with eyes that never misread a sign, hands that never slackened or wavered and a heart that knew nothing of doubt or fear or faltering. . . . A. C. Haskell . . . was ruler of South Carolina more absolutely than any czar. . . . He was obeyed on the instant because he was known to be speaking for Wade Hampton. . . . Men, women, and children obeyed. No army ever was under better or more rigid or beautiful discipline than the white people of the state were during those eight crowded and dangerous months. . . .[8]

This state of discipline, discipline absolutely essential if Hampton's formula of force without violence was to work, received many severe

---

[4]Thompson, *op. cit.*, p. 110.

[5]Williams, *op. cit.*, p. 151.

[6]*Ibid.* By September 14 *The Nation* remarked that Chamberlain's letter to Grant had cost him the state. XXIII, 165.

[7]For more detail on this offer and the accusation against Hampton growing out of it, see below, p. 115ff.

[8]Williams, *op. cit.*, p. 84.

tests during the campaign itself and particularly during the five
months after the election, when two governments existed side by side
in Columbia, Chamberlain's supported by federal troops and Hampton's by nearly every white man in the state. The first important test
came during the Charleston riot of September 6.

Before the end of August many Negroes in Charleston were joining
Negro Democratic clubs, and Republican leaders feared a general
swing. Before September 6 there had been rowdy bands of blacks at
such club meetings, and several white men had been delegated to
protect the two Negro speakers. It seems, however, that because of
overconfidence at the way things were going, Hampton's advice about
overwhelming force was neglected. While the Negro Democratic
club of Ward 4 was meeting, the "Hunkidories" and "Live Oaks,"
Negro Radical organizations, had massed in King Street, armed with
pistols, clubs, and slings consisting of a pound of lead on the end of a
twelve-inch leather strap. When the colored speakers left the hall
preceded by their white guards, the waiting Negroes attacked. Word
was carried to the police, and both white and colored police tried to
disperse the rioters, but were resisted fiercely by the enraged blacks.

Soon many white men and police were knocked out of the fight.
The fifteen white men left on their feet managed to get the Negro
speakers uninjured into the Citadel ground, as a new mob of Negroes
rushed out of John Street, screaming, "Blood!" The Negroes divided
into gangs of fifty to a hundred and rioted through the section, beating
every white man they could find, smashing windows, and shouting
that they would exterminate the entire white population. More than
fifty white men were sufficiently hurt to require medical attention, and
one was killed. Five Negroes were wounded, three of them members
of the police force. Panic spread through the city.

Meanwhile the Carolina Rifle Battalion happened to be at its armory
and heard of the riot. It was marched to a point near the fighting
and held in line until about midnight, when the worst rioting stopped
of itself. The men stood within sound of the shots and screams, and
"every few minutes men would be whispering and talking excitedly
to each other with occasional dry sobs of distress, anger and anxiety
as they spoke of friends and relatives up town perhaps in deadly peril,
and we standing idle with rifles in our hands."[9]

---

[9]*Ibid.*, pp. 119ff. For Allen's brief account of this riot, with Chamberlain's
confession of Republican responsibility, see Allen, *op. cit.*, p. 351. *The Nation*
called attention to the fact that "intimidation" was not all on one side. XXIII
(September 14, 1876), 158.

If these men had been brought to the fighting, there would have been many dead Negroes on the street. Again (as so often before and since) the brutal Southerner would have been held up to the scorn of the nation. Again the "bloody shirt" would have waved throughout the North, and the Radical press would have had the "outrages" it sought. But Hampton had ordered, "Keep the peace." As Williams said, there was rigid discipline in South Carolina, and Hampton's word was law. From the time of this riot until after the election, volunteer squads from the rifle clubs patrolled the streets of Charleston every night, and there were no more serious disorders until after the election, though Governor Chamberlain was insisting that such clubs constituted armed insurrection. Radical leaders strongly resented the "organized plan ... not to have any violence committed on anybody." Hampton had found the way to checkmate their influence in the North as well as in South Carolina.

2

During August and September, the Democrats developed various effective campaign devices, the most dramatic of which was "dividing time" at Republican meetings. This device was initiated by Generals Gary and M. C. Butler just before the August convention for the purpose of intimidating the Negroes and discrediting their leaders. On August 13 Governor Chamberlain, Judge T. J. Mackey (later to "cross Jordan") and Negro Congressman Robert Smalls were scheduled to address a Republican rally at Edgefield. Six hundred mounted white men in cavalry formation rode up to the assembly of fifteen hundred Negroes and demanded division of time. Then Butler and Gary, particularly the latter, gave Chamberlain the worst tongue lashing of his life. The only violence was verbal, but brutal. Repeat performances were soon staged at Newberry and Abbeville.[10]

This Edgefield meeting has been described as typical of Hampton's campaign. On the contrary, it preceded Hampton's nomination and

---

[10]For an intensely pro-Gary account of these meetings, see Sheppard *op. cit.*, pp. 94ff. and pp. 123ff. For Chamberlain's side, see Allen, *op. cit.*, pp 348ff. See also Williams, *op. cit.*, pp. 65ff. Maxwell, *op. cit.*, I (April, 1878), 489, states about these affairs, "The public utterances and the general bearing of a few men of that party [Democratic], particularly at the outset of the campaign, had been provocative, in some cases, of trouble. These men were afterwards made to understand that intimidation was no part of the plans of their leaders." John W. De Forest, too, asserted in September, 1876, that the violence of extremists in Edgefield was jeopardizing the accomplishment of white supremacy. See above Chapter III, note 43.

was engineered by Mart Gary. It was typical, rather, of the kind of campaign that Gary planned, but that Hampton and the State Executive Committee rejected. As soon as the danger inherent in this procedure became clear, Chairman A. C. Haskell sent to all county chairmen instructions that brought the "division of time" into conformity with Hampton's general campaign method of appealing to the Negro for his vote rather than merely intimidating him. As explained by Colonel Haskell, these instructions were ". . . to go to the meetings and to remain perfectly quiet, but ask for a division of time, and if it was rejected to remain perfectly quiet, to keep order, listen to the speakers, and use any means at their command, by the ordinary rules of mass meetings, to indicate their pleasure or displeasure – to hiss or applaud, as they pleased – but by no means to make any demonstration or threaten force or use it."[11]

Such a procedure proved useful for three reasons: It impressed the Negro with the force behind the Democratic movement whether it intimidated him or not;[12] it discredited the Radical leaders in the eyes of the Negroes; and it enabled Democrats to reach with their arguments many Negroes who otherwise could not have been touched. Since very few blacks could read, newspapers were practically useless for this purpose.

Throughout the Reconstruction period the Radical leaders feared that the genuine trust in their old masters that was characteristic of a great many Negroes would be carried over into politics. For this reason the Union League had exacted from each Negro a solemn oath always to vote Republican. For this reason, too, the colored people were constantly told that the Republican Party had freed them and that the Democratic Party, if it were returned to power, would re-enslave them. These deceptions could be maintained only so long as Negroes were kept away from Democratic political discussions. Hence, throughout the period every possible form of pressure was used to keep them away from all but simon-pure Radical meetings. "Division of time" served to counter-balance this influence and caused many

---

[11]*South Carolina in 1876,* I, 837. See also Ball, *op. cit.,* p. 157, and Williams, *op. cit.,* pp. 187f.

[12]Redfield reported to the *Cincinnati Commercial,* "A display of force unnerves them [the Negroes]. The whites understand this, and an immense marching about at night, and appearance at any Republican meeting to 'divide time,' is with a view to impress the blacks with the danger of any longer holding out against white rule." Quoted by Allen, *op. cit.,* p. 350.

cries of outrage from the Radicals, who claimed that their right to freedom of speech was thus violated.

Certainly they were able to speak much less freely than before. Files of grim, red-shirted riders, for example, did not facilitate the holding of "shouts," "a weird mixture of Voodoo rite, Christianity, and politics." During these emotional jags, cynically remarked Carpet-bagger W. N. Taft afterwards, "they're nice and crazy. You can play on 'em like a fiddle and they'll believe anything you tell 'em and do anything you want 'em to do."[13] Certainly, too, the "ordinary rules of mass meetings" were very liberally interpreted, and any Radical speaker who was not careful was interrupted by shouts of "Liar!" Moreover, embarrassing questions were asked various speakers about their own political records, questions in many cases very difficult indeed to answer in public. When "division of time" was granted, the record of Radical government was reviewed for the Negroes, and they were asked what they had gained for their vote. Since most of them were in miserable circumstances, that, too, was an embarrassing question for the Radical leaders, black and white.

These meetings led to violence in only one or two instances like Cainhoy (where several white men were killed) because the whites, who attended in force, were under orders not to start trouble and the blacks were not at all anxious to do so under the circumstances. The whites, too, passed around the word that in case of fighting, white leaders of the Negroes would be killed first. The Reconstruction movement in South Carolina did not develop martyrs, and no one urged the Negroes to violence.

Oddly enough, the mass of blacks were unlikely to show much resentment unless a Negro Democratic speaker was introduced. Many observers noted this fact. George R. Walker, son of the English Consul at Charleston, stated that the blacks at Cainhoy absolutely refused to hear Delany, a Negro Democrat who had been a major in the United States army. Walker noted that "the negroes not only at that meeting, but at several other preceding meetings which I had attended, seemed to be very hostile to any negro democrat speaking; the cry was that any white man had a right to be a democrat, 'but no damned black man had.' "[14] In the Up-country, too, Negro Democratic speakers had a difficult time. Henry Daniels, leader of a band of armed Negroes, said, as Colonel Haskell was about to introduce a Negro

---

[13]Williams, *op. cit.*, pp. 238f.
[14]*Recent Election in S. C.*, pp. 182ff.

speaker, "Colonel, I don't want to hurt you or make any mischief, but the body of men that I command are pledged that no man of our race shall speak on the democratic side of our meetings."[15]

One feature of these, as of all other gatherings of Democrats, was the use of the red shirt as a sort of campaign uniform, worn by white and black Democrats alike. For decades after 1876 an old red-flannel shirt was a precious memento in thousands of South Carolina homes. The touch of romance dear to the Southern heart was added by the long lines of red-clad marching men, mounted and afoot. These impressive parades, too, added to the effect on the Negroes. The origin of the red shirt is disputed, but certainly it started as a gesture of defiance at the traditional "bloody shirt." It apparently had no connection whatever with the red shirt used by Garibaldi as a symbol of liberation in South America and Italy a generation before. Whatever its origin, it was a symbol of the Campaign of Seventy-six.

Less dramatic than "dividing time" and less colorful than the red shirts was a third device developed during the first month of the campaign, a device sometimes known as "preference, not proscription." Since to deny a black man employment because of his politics was contrary to federal law, many communities made a practice of giving certificates to qualified Negro Democrats. The idea was that Negroes holding such certificates would be given preference over Republicans in all employment and trade.[16] Undoubtedly some good Negroes honestly voting their convictions were thus penalized, and the practice was an ugly one. Hampton and the State Committee at no time recommended "preference" or proscription either; and after the election Hampton urged the Democrats of the state not to continue any political proscriptions.[17] Since contracts on farms usually did not expire until January, it seems likely that there was little suffering from the device except in the cities. Most such complaints before the investigating committees were urban.[18]

Finally, in many counties each white voter was urged to pick one Negro and get him by bribery, threat, or persuasion either to vote for

---

[15]*Ibid.*, pp. 344ff. See also *South Carolina in 1876*, I, 797.

[16]Williams, *op. cit.*, pp. 172f. See also [Townsend], "The Political Condition of South Carolina," *Atlantic Monthly*, XXXIX (February, 1877), 186.

[17]*Recent Election in S. C.*, p. 333.

[18]Ball, *op. cit.*, p. 164, stated that the policy had little effect since few Negroes worried about the future. See also Haskell, in *Recent Election in S. C.*, p. 340.

Hampton or not to vote at all.[19] This practice, too, was without the sanction of the State Committee; but Hampton probably would not have condemned it so long as no violence was used. Hampton and his Red Shirts were playing for high stakes, as he had said, and most of the cards were stacked against them. Moreover, their opponents were using every type of fraud and intimidation possible. Small wonder if few Democrats had any scruples about how the victory was won. The point was that it had to be won. It should be added that intimidation and fraud were rare in South Carolina elections before Reconstruction.

3

Some of the side shows of the campaign have been mentioned. The main event was Hampton's swing through the state beginning at Anderson on September 2. Never before or since has South Carolina seen anything like it. It seemed particularly fitting to the whites that their struggle for liberation should come on the hundredth anniversary of the signing of the Declaration of Independence; but nothing during the Revolution equaled the Red Shirt campaign in enthusiasm or unanimity. A force was thus generated that feared no check except from the national government, which at that time, with reason enough, was more feared than loved in South Carolina.

Even a hostile observer, Belton O'Neall Townsend, who anonymously described the campaign for the *Atlantic Monthly* of February, 1877, was profoundly impressed by the fervor of Hampton's followers:

> Such delirium as they aroused can be paralleled only by itself even in this delirious State. Their whole tour was a vast triumphal procession; at every depot they were received by a tremendous concourse of citizens and escorts of cavalry. Their meetings drew the whole white population, male and female (for the ladies turned out by tens of thousands to greet and listen to the heroic Hampton), for scores of miles around, and had to be held invariably in the open air. They were preceded by processions of the rifle clubs, mounted and on foot, miles in length, marching amidst the strains of music and the booming of cannon; at night there were torchlight processions equally imposing. The speakers aroused in thousands the memories of old, and called on their hearers to redeem the grand old State and restore it to its ancient place of honor in the Republic. The wildest cheering followed.

[19]Thompson, *op. cit.*, p. 117. See also [Townsend], "The Political Condition of South Carolina," *op. cit.*, p. 186, "one-man-apiece policy."

The enthusiasm, as Confederate veterans pressed forward to wring their old General's hand, was indescribable.[20]

From one end of the state to the other rang the old-time "rebel yell" and the new war-cry, "Hurrah for Hampton!" The lone horseman shouted, "Hurrah for Hampton!" as he passed a cluster of Negro cabins in the dark. Thousands of Red Shirts yelled it as they marched in "Hampton Day" parades. Since that time, remarked W. W. Ball in *The State that Forgot*, "the cry of 'Hurrah' has ever seemed unnatural and jarring to my ears when used with any other name than 'Hampton.'"[21]

And beneath this hot and frothy shouting was a determination that was cold, hard, and absolute. Negro domination would end, peacefully if possible, violently if necessary, or as a last resort, by federal intervention and military government.[22] This feeling was expressed for Williams by "a belated horseman galloping homeward alone and shouting just once, as if summing up the thought of the day, 'Hampton or Hell!'" Chamberlain himself was aware of this determination on the part of Hampton and his followers. He told the Senate committee, "I know that those who voted for the Hampton government say that they will never recognize any one as governor except Hampton; that no earthly power can make them do it."[23]

Hampton's speaking tour lasted for the two months between September 2 and November 4. During this time, by his own account, he "spoke at fifty-seven large meetings, at each of which there were present from three to ten thousand people."[24] He spoke in all but one of the thirty-two counties in the state. Thus he was seen and heard by nearly all the white men in the state as well as by thousands of Negroes, and the result was the kind of absolute confidence in him that led to implicit obedience to his instructions when the situation became critical.

---

[20] [Townsend], "The Political Condition of South Carolina," *op. cit.,* pp. 183f.

[21] Ball, *op. cit.,* p. 162.

[22] Ball, *op. cit.,* p. 167. See also Williams, *op. cit.,* p. 83.

[23] *South Carolina in 1876,* II, 44. See also Williams, *op. cit.,* p. 244.

[24] *Recent Elections in S. C.,* p. 305. Maxwell, *op. cit.* (April, 1878), *passim,* gives considerable detail about many of these meetings, quoting from many of Hampton's speeches. Many excerpts, too, are given in *Recent Election in S. C.,* pp. 306ff. For more complete texts, see such contemporary newspapers as the *News and Courier* and the Columbia *Register.* As Williams remarked, the speech-makers had a tough time because the printed versions were widely read and variety was difficult to achieve.

Travel in South Carolina in 1876 was difficult, whether by road or by train; and at times Hampton and his staff had to go by horse since the railroad did not reach all communities. Only the hardened endurance of an old campaigner enabled Hampton to remain vigorous in spite of the strain. In a speech in Columbia towards the end of September he was already claiming that he had "broken down all the gentlemen who started with him." He was a bit vain of his strength and, like General Lee, liked to tease his staff.[25]

Throughout the campaign Hampton varied the words of his speeches, but repeated over and over a few fundamental principles. Much that he said was addressed to the Negroes, whom he always sought to attract to his meetings. Extracts from many of these speeches were combined into a pamphlet entitled *Free Men, Free Ballots, Free Schools—The Pledges of General Wade Hampton, Democratic Candidate for Governor to the Colored People of South Carolina,* and this pamphlet was widely circulated by the State Executive Committee. These pledges were designed to assure the Negroes that "not one single right enjoyed by the colored people to-day shall be taken from them. They shall be equals, under the law, of any man in South Carolina. And we further pledge that we will give better facilities for education than they have ever had before."

> The only way to bring about prosperity in this state is to bring the two races in friendly relation together. The democratic party in South Carolina, of whom I am the exponent, has promised that every citizen of this state is to be the equal of all; he is to have every right given him by the Constitution of the United States and of this state.... And I pledge my faith, and I pledge it for those gentlemen who are on the ticket with me, that if we are elected, as far as in us lies, we will observe, protect, and defend the rights of the colored man as quickly as [of] any man in South Carolina.... If there is a white man in this assembly, [who] because he is a democrat, or because he is a white man, believes that when I am elected governor, if I should be, that I will stand between him and the law, or grant him any privilege or immunity that shall not be granted to the colored man, he is mistaken....[26]

Hampton's first speech at Anderson struck the keynote of his campaign. He pointed to the record of Radical government in the state and asked the Radical leaders to explain how they proposed to accomplish the reforms that they promised. He reminded the Negroes that the whites of the state had tried to get good government by backing

---

[25]Williams, *op. cit.,* pp. 217f.
[26]This entire pamphlet is reproduced in *Recent Election in S. C.,* pp. 306ff.

the reform element within the Republican party at every election, and he particularly urged them to trust in politics the men whom they trusted in every other relation of life. "He cited the record to show that he was the first white man in the South, after the Civil War, to advocate giving the negroes the franchise as they proved themselves capable of using it.... He promised peace and protection for all classes and always repeated his slogan 'Reconciliation, Retrenchment and Reform'."[27]

The order of Hampton's speaking appointments illustrates the careful planning that characterized the entire canvass. He began in the northwestern tier of counties, where the large white majorities insured an enthusiastic start. He saved the lower counties, with their large black majorities, until last so that the momentum gained at the first would carry over. The Low-country, however, did not wait for Hampton, but "was ready from the first to do its full part, and more."[28]

Hampton by no means carried the burden of his canvass alone. Not only did he have an able and energetic State Executive Committee, but also the party had selected top-quality men for all offices, men tested in responsible positions through four years of war, most of them with scars to show for it. Throughout the canvass he was supported by a succession of the best speakers in a state noted for good oratory. These men provided for Hampton's sober remarks a background of the eloquence, humor, and fiery denunciation dear to political audiences everywhere.[29] Reputable Republicans in the state, too, like Judges T. J. Mackey and T. H. Cooke "crossed Jordan" so far as the state ticket was concerned and joined Hampton's coterie of speakers.

In every town where the General spoke, "Hampton Day" was decreed, and all business stopped. He was greeted by cheering crowds, booming cannon, blaring bands and long lines of yelling paraders; by banners, "illuminations," and dramatic tableaux. Masses of flowers banked the platforms and decorated the streets. Indeed, the flowers that everywhere filled the General's train made him plaintively wish for old army days, when he "marched with a baggage train." At Greenville on the fifth of September, for example, though the canvass had just begun, Hampton was honored with an escort of fifteen hundred mounted men and, though Greenville at that time was only a small

---

[27]*Williams, op. cit.*, p. 164.

[28]*Ibid.*, pp. 218f.

[29]*Ibid.*, p. 165.

town, the crowd at the meeting exceeded five thousand. Another meeting was held in the evening. "It was a brilliant, noisy, memorable night. The large number of Negro men at the meeting was noticeable, although few were in the processions and these were targets for storms of insult and threat from men and women of their own race."[30]

4

Until the latter half of September everything seemed to point to a Democratic victory. After interviewing Hampton on the eighth, Redfield, Radical correspondent of a Northern paper, advised that Republicans abandon the state offices and concentrate on the Presidential ticket. He saw clearly that the burning issue in South Carolina was not national but state government. He asserted that South Carolina white men were going into this fight "with more determination and desperation of purpose than they went into the Civil War, to which they gave more soldiers than the state had voters." He concluded that "attempts to hold the white people of South Carolina, after the provocations and wrongs that had been put upon them and with such leaders as they had, under any negro majority, however huge, would be like trying to make a pyramid stand on its apex."[31]

The effect of Democratic activities in the state was demonstrated, too, in various town elections on September 11. In Abbeville, for example, out of 143 colored voters, seventy-five voted the straight Democratic ticket. Kingstree, in the Low-country, showed the result of the new spirit by electing its first Democratic municipal government since Reconstruction began. Other town elections showed that the Radicals were losing the support of many Negroes.[32]

The Republican state convention met September 15-17, however, and soon came the Radical counter-attack. Orders passed down from party headquarters that Chamberlain would have to be the candidate

---

[30]*Ibid.*, p. 167.

[31]*Ibid.*, p. 180.

[32]*Ibid.* Maxwell, *op. cit.* (April, 1878), pp. 478ff, tells in considerable detail about this Negro swing to the Democrats. As one Negro put it, they were "utterly disgusted with the faithlessness and Radical rascality." Tom Hamilton, prominent Negro planter, urged his fellows to realize that their welfare depended on the prosperity of the whites (*ibid.*, p. 479). There were about five hundred Negroes in the procession at Abbeville, Maxwell, *op. cit.*, II (May, 1878), 44, and on September 23 at Cheraw Hampton announced, "There are already colored men enough in the Democratic party to carry this election" (*ibid.*, p. 49). On October 8 nearly a thousand Negroes were in the procession at Sumter (*ibid.*, June, p. 168).

for governor; no other available Radical would save the party's face
in the North. After considerable name-calling all around, Chamberlain
was nominated, the nominating speech, amusingly enough, being
made by Senator "Honest" John Patterson himself.[33]

On the ticket with Chamberlain were placed three of the anti-
reform element, among them one of the most disreputable Negroes in
the state, R. B. Elliott.   Seven months after the election, Chamberlain
wrote to William Lloyd Garrison that because of Elliott's being on the
ticket he "took the resolution ... to walk into the Convention and
throw up my nomination ... because I would not run on a ticket with
Elliott." Chamberlain explained his remaining in the race by saying
that he was over-persuaded by his "most devoted colored supporters."[34]   At any rate, he justified, at that time, Elliott's being placed
on the ticket.   It is worth noting, too, that testifying under oath before
the Senate committee soon after the election, Chamberlain, in answer
to a question about his nomination, asserted, "I should not have been
a candidate for the nomination if there had been any doubt in my own
mind as to whether I ought to accept it or not. . . . I was talked to by
some republicans about it who thought that perhaps it was a question
whether I should remain on the ticket; but it never was a question
with me."[35]

Whatever Chamberlain really thought about his ticket, it caused
many reputable Republicans to "cross Jordan," notably Judge Cooke.
By election time, according to one observer, fewer than five hundred
white men in the state, not counting office-holders, supported the Republican state ticket.[36]   Even ex-Governor Scott, of odorous memory,
had "crossed Jordan," though in timid and hesitant fashion.[37]   Chamberlain admitted to the Senate committee that almost all white men
voted for Hampton.   Besides, any slight hope that Chamberlain might
have held for support from those Democrats who opposed the Straightouts was entirely lost.   In other words, Chamberlain had to depend
entirely on his Negro majority — and that seemed to be slipping.

---

[33]Allen, op. cit., pp. 352ff. Allen does not mention that Chamberlain was
nominated by his old crony and, later, opponent, "Honest" John Patterson. For
a description of this convention in the words of Judge T. H. Cooke, a participant,
as he "crossed Jordan," see Sheppard, op. cit., pp. 137ff., quoting the Abbeville
Press and Banner for September 20, 1876.   See also Reynolds op. cit., pp. 366ff.
[34]Allen, op. cit., pp. 504f.
[35]South Carolina in 1876, II, 44.
[36]Williams, op. cit., p. 238.   See also, for example, General Hagood's testimony, South Carolina in 1876, I, 550.
[37]Williams, op. cit., p. 248.

Such a situation demanded only one remedy — more federal troops. A change in the political atmosphere in the North and the impending national election, however, made such use of troops politically unwise for the Republicans unless there was obviously adequate cause. Even Grant and Morton knew that. The day after Chamberlain's nomination, some riots near Ellenton, in the same county as Hamburg, gave the Governor his excuse. Like the Hamburg riot, the Ellenton riots were in no way political, wherever the major blame lay, except in the use made of them by the Governor.

They started with the clubbing of a white woman and her nine-year-old son by two Negroes in an attempted robbery. A posse of white men secured a warrant from a Negro trial justice and went seeking the criminals.[38] From there on, accounts differ widely, but certainly a large body of armed Negroes protecting the criminals met this posse, and a sort of Indian type of bushwhacking ensued for several days until federal troops arrived. A careful reading of many pages of testimony from both sides does not reveal any preconcerted plan by either race, (though each charged the other with conspiracy, and conspiracy to prevent freedmen from voting was the federal charge on which subsequent arrests of whites were made), only the very ugly general situation denounced many months before by Judge Mackey. The whites requested troops at the outset to check Negro destruction of property, but they were denied. In this, as in other instances, federal troops apparently were not sent into any area so long as Negroes seemed to have the upper hand,[39] as they did at first in this affair, when they ambushed several bodies of white men, tore up the railroad tracks, wrecked a train, and burned several buildings. Reynolds states that the casualties were probably as follows: whites, two killed and eight wounded; blacks, fifteen killed and two wounded. The officer commanding the federal troops, which were rushed in when the whites had assembled in large numbers, stated that there was about to be "a slaughter of nearly all the negroes in the place" when he arrived.[40] Certainly the Negroes were about to be disarmed and dispersed, and very likely a few leaders would have been shot, as at

---

[38]Voluminous testimony on this affair was recorded by investigating committees of both the Senate and the House. See all three volumes of *South Carolina in 1876* and also *Recent Election in S. C.*, *passim*. See also Simkins and Woody, *op. cit.*, pp. 505f.

[39]Williams, *op. cit.*, p. 208.

[40]Report of commanding officer of federal troops at Aiken, dated September 21, 1876, quoted by Allen, *op. cit.*, p. 417. Reynolds, *op. cit.*, p. 378.

Hamburg. A large-scale killing, however, was at least unlikely. According to this same officer the whites dispersed readily as soon as the arrival of troops insured protection of their homes.[41] At no time did they resist the law, as Chamberlain and Corbin both admitted during cross-examination. Radicals claimed, however, that more than a hundred innocent Negroes had been murdered. It should be noted that the blacks greatly outnumbered the whites at the outset, but as fighting progressed the number of whites rapidly increased while many Negroes faded away. Hundreds of Negroes who remained quietly in their homes throughout the area were in no way molested. Undoubtedly, however, brutal deeds were done by both sides during the fighting.

As he had done immediately after the Hamburg affair, Chamberlain (in spite of a plea to him to remain in the state by Judge Mackey, at that time a Republican) hurried North during the Ellenton riots and probably talked the situation over with his political bosses. On his return he sent D. T. Corbin, United States district attorney, into the area to make an "investigation." As Corbin himself testified, "all the authorities there at that time were Republicans," but there was "some doubt" about the party loyalty of one sheriff, who had stated publicly that there was no obstruction to legal processes. William Stone, the state attorney general, had gone to the area first; Corbin was called in two days later. Stone, who was a fairly honest man, made no public report; Corbin's report, two weeks after the riot, was the first from the scene of action to assert political causes.[42]

Corbin's report, which was published, was based solely on the accounts of Negro participants. As Corbin testified before the Senate committee, "I did not send for the white men" to give their side of the affair "because the white men in that neighborhood [three entire counties] were reported to me to be all guilty, and I thought from the examination that they were — all that were old enough and young enough."[43] Corbin also admitted that he arrested none but Democrats. He told the committee that he had issued about five hundred warrants on this purely *ex parte* testimony, and he admitted, further, that he had no difficulty making arrests. By his own account, the only three Negroes for whom warrants were issued were Democrats.

[41]Allen, *op. cit.*, p. 417.
[42]This entire report quoted in Allen, *op. cit.*, pp. 391ff.
[43]*South Carolina in 1876*, II, 52ff.

These Negroes had issued a statement that "perfect order prevailed in the county."[44]

Judge Cooke testified before the same committee that Corbin had remarked about a month before that "if two or three riots or rows could be gotten up in South Carolina, and about thirty, fifty, or one hundred negroes killed, it would be the means of saving the State to the republican party, and perhaps the nation to the republican party." Corbin, however, denied having made such remarks.[45]

The verbal sparring between the Governor and Chairman A. C. Haskell which followed Corbin's report was too lengthy to relate here.[46] The upshot was that although nearly every judge in the state and the sheriffs of the counties most involved (Republicans all) denied any insurrection or obstructions to normal legal processes, Chamberlain decreed a state of insurrection and asked President Grant to send more troops. At the time Grant was in California, but on his return the following telegrams were exchanged.[47]

HEADQUARTERS OF THE ARMY
WASHINGTON, OCTOBER 14, 1876

TO GENERAL RUGER, COLUMBIA, S. C.:

WE ARE ALL BACK FROM CALIFORNIA. IF YOU WANT ANYTHING SAY SO. I WANT ALL MEASURES TO ORIGINATE WITH YOU. GET ALONG WITH THE MINIMUM FORCE NECESSARY, BUT YOU SHALL HAVE ALL WE CAN GIVE IF YOU NEED THEM.

W. T. SHERMAN
GENERAL

COLUMBIA, S. C., OCTOBER 16, 1876

TO GEN. W. T. SHERMAN, WASHINGTON, D. C.:

THINK I HAVE TROOPS SUFFICIENT UNLESS CIRCUMSTANCES CHANGE. HAVE NINETEEN COMPANIES IN STATE NOW IN STATIONS OF ONE TO FOUR COMPANIES. HAVE SOME COMPANIES STILL IN RESERVE. NO SPECIAL DISORDER HAS OCCURRED SINCE ELLENTON RIOT LAST MONTH. IF I NEED MORE TROOPS I WILL ASK FOR THEM. I SHALL BE HERE TO-DAY.

RUGER.

---

[44]*Recent Election in S. C.*, pp. 269f., and Williams, *op. cit.*, p. 254.
[45]*South Carolina in 1876*, I, 893; *ibid.*, II, 61.
[46]See Allen, *op. cit.*, pp. 365ff. and pp. 406ff. See also Simkins and Woody, *op. cit.*, pp. 506ff. and Reynolds, *op. cit.*, pp. 380ff.
[47]These telegrams quoted by Thompson, *op. cit.*, p. 126.

In spite of this statement from General Ruger, on the following day, October 17, Grant ordered all Democratic "rifle clubs" in South Carolina to disband and ordered that all available troops in the military district of the Atlantic be transferred to the state —[48] decisions that were obviously political rather than military.

The white people of the state were indignant with both the Governor and the President. The State Executive Committee issued an address, in which it warned the people of the nation that the "domination of our election by the bayonet and by soldiers as the irresistible instrument of a revolutionary local despotism, if successful, will become the precedent before which the whole fabric of American liberty will fall, and will be applied to other States just as soon as party exigencies require it." The committee, however, instructed the people of South Carolina "to yield full and entire obedience to the President's proclamation."[49] Hampton telegraphed various prominent citizens, "Urge our people to submit peaceably to martial law."[50] There was no violent resistance to this martial law, but a deeper bitterness was added to the campaign. Also the movement of Negroes towards the Democratic camp was checked.

Governor Chamberlain had acted shrewdly, but not honestly and certainly not in the best interests of the state that he had sworn to serve. General James Conner, Democratic candidate for attorney general, testified before the House committee in regard to the influence of Hampton's campaign on the Negroes and to the later effect of the introduction of troops:

> I have told you the line that we worked through the whole campaign, and the nature of the appeals we made to the colored people, and wherever General Hampton went he excited a great deal of interest among them. They are a curious race, and judge more by the eye than by the ear. It is not what you say that affects them, but they look at you and note what manner of man you are and how you say it. . . . His [Hampton's] presence was very fine and he had a wonderful effect and influence upon them. Before he came down to the low-country, when I went up to the Combahee, negroes were anxious for him to come down. Every gentleman who came down from that section to Charleston would come to me and appeal to me to get General Hampton to come

[48]Allen, op. cit., pp. 406f. See Williams, op. cit., p. 252, for denial of need for troops.

[49]Reynolds, op. cit., pp. 388ff.

[50]Ibid., p. 387. At Aiken on October 20 Hampton urged his listeners not to resist the troops, Maxwell, op. cit., (June, 1878), p. 171.

down to the low-country, the negroes were so anxious to see and hear him; and after he did go down, we heard from negroes down there pledges of support; that they would vote the Hayes and Wheeler presidential ticket, but they would vote the Hampton state ticket. That was the line that they all ran on . . . and I suppose in Charleston alone we must have had from 2,000 to 2,500 negroes who pledged their support to the Hampton local ticket. Everything was as smooth and prosperous as it could be in the low-country and in the upper part of the State, and it was changed on the introduction of the troops. . . . The impression was that the troops had come there to see that they voted the republican ticket; that was their idea.[51]

The testimony of many colored men indicates that General Conner's conclusion as to the effect of the influx of federal troops on the blacks was correct. Said one, Chamberlain "was going to send down the Yankees to shoot down every democratic nigger that 'sists after the election." Another Negro testified that he was told that the troops "were brought here to see that every man that wanted to vote the republican ticket could do it, but any man that wanted to vote the democratic ticket, as soon as he done voted it, the troops would take the names down, and soon as Chamberlain would give them the power they would go down and shoot them all. . . ." Another asserted, ". . . they said Chamberlain was going to have troops coming in here, and 'every one of you niggers that vote the democratic ticket will be killed, sure.' That day [the election], sure enough, the troops did come down, and that made me believe they was going to do it, sure enough. It did make me feel kind of skeerish, and I was going to run down in Wooster Hollow until Mr. Childs told me better." Another Negro told about taking a group of blacks to vote the Democratic ticket: "I carried eight; there was more than eight, but they drew off because they had heard that Chamberlain was going to send the Yankees down to shoot them down, and some niggers when they hear about Yankees they willing to go and eat the ground alive; but I won't be scared about Yankees."[52]

This sending of troops to South Carolina was violently objected to by the Democratic press in the North, of course, and viewed with deep suspicion by independent periodicals. *The Nation* for October 19 said of this use of force, "The negroes think that it has been sent down by their Republican friends in Washington to help them to win; the

---

[51]*Recent Election in S. C.*, p. 372. See also Haskell's testimony, *South Carolina in 1876*, I, 818.
[52]*Recent Election in S. C.*, pp. 400ff.

whites, that it has come to assist in their defeat."[53]   Prophetically, *The Nation* could find only one possible "good" in the action:

> When a government undertakes to use all its powers to secure a free election to an inferior race, and for this purpose, 1st, gives them the ballot; 2d, passes laws to prevent all interference . . . 3d, stations judges and marshals with full power . . . 4th, requires all the local laws to be made to conform with these changes; and 5th, not satisfied with all this, sends down cavalry, infantry, and artillery . . . for it to compain afterward that the election was not fair is an absurdity.[54]

Yet, in less than a month, that is exactly what the Radicals were going to do.

Undoubtedly Chamberlain and Grant decided to garrison the state of South Carolina, not to preserve the peace, but to preserve the Republican Party. In spite of their efforts Hampton won a clear majority, including thousands of Negro votes. Very probably his majority would have been made much larger by freely given Negro votes if federal troops had not intervened. Certainly there would have been less bitterness as the campaign progressed.

5

Throughout late September and October, party and race lines were drawn more closely. There was less and less good-natured badinage, and resentment from indignities that had to be meekly borne bit deep into the hearts of the white men of South Carolina. Spurred by the indefatigable Corbin, federal courts were used even more blatantly for party purposes than were federal troops.[55] Arrests of prominent men concerned in the Ellenton riots so multiplied that the jail in Aiken had become a social center for the entire section.[56] Elsewhere white men were being arrested for disturbing Republican meetings and for "intimidation."[57] Division of time became pretty much a thing of the past. "Honest" John is said to have boasted that seven hundred Democrats were arrested in all during the campaign.[58] Negroes, so

---

[53]*The Nation*, XXIII (October, 1876), 237. *The Nation* wrote a solemn article on this use of troops, who "are really an armed force in the service, and acting under the orders of one of the parties to the political contest. The force . . . is not looked on by either side as a mere minister of law."

[54]*Ibid.*, p. 233.

[55]Williams, *op. cit.*, pp. 254, 292.

[56]*Ibid.*, pp. 254, 267f., 289, 315. See also Thompson, *op. cit.*, p. 122.

[57]Williams, *op. cit.*, p. 291.

[58]Wells, *op. cit.*, p. 137.

the report went, were selling affidavits against white men for "a dollar and a half apiece, eighteen dollars a dozen;"[59] and Chamberlain was writing to the Northern papers about his "legal evidence" of "outrages" and "intimidations."[60] As *The Nation* was moved to comment, if a white man "speaks to a negro about politics," it is called "intimidation."[61]

Hampton's orders were still, "Keep the peace," and he was obeyed; but hate increased on both sides. Williams describes this condition:

> No favors or toleration of any kind by Democrats for Republicans was the accepted and unanimously approved policy and the Republicans were fighting on the same line as they found opportunity. Birnie was prevented from becoming postmaster at Charleston by withdrawal from his bond of all Democrats. Every Democratic workman — which meant every white workman — on the custom house was discharged and replaced by a negro. No Republican could get credit for a pound of meat in any store kept by a Democrat. That was the situation until election day, with the Red Shirts everywhere in the country districts riding almost every hour of every day, more troops arriving continually, swarms of United States deputy marshals being appointed, Charleston city held peaceful by the rifle clubs, supposed to have been disbanded, every white man in half a dozen counties living in daily expectation of arrest.[62]

Still, the order was, "Keep the peace." There was no violence.

Meanwhile, Hampton's canvass was a continued and increasing triumph. Each town sought to outdo anything that had gone before, and many succeeded. But the struggle had a deeper tone than a mere political campaign. Most meetings opened with prayer. October 26 was declared a day of fasting and prayer in the state, "not for Hampton, nor for the Democratic party, but for South Carolina, stricken, troubled, her civilization and life at stake."[63] Protestant churches throughout the state held services; Catholic churches were forbidden by their rules, but remained open for prayer. The mood of bitter determination strengthened.

Only once did Hampton face a hostile audience, at Beaufort, center of an overwhelming Negro majority and of the most rabid Radical sentiment. Williams gives an eye-witness account:

[59]Williams, *op. cit.*, p. 254.
[60]Allen, *op. cit.*, pp. 415, 423.
[61]*The Nation*, XXIII (October, 1876), 237.
[62]Williams, *op. cit.*, pp. 318f.
[63]*Ibid.*, p. 309.

Hampton could have had an escort of from five hundred to a thousand armed men, but he preferred to go with nobody but the speakers and reporters. Possibly the spice of danger appealed to his spirit of adventure. Possibly he thought best to avoid possibility of serious collision between his followers and the intensely antagonistic Beaufort population. He went unguarded and unattended, except by his regular party, and stepped directly from a warm atmosphere of love and adulation to chilling surroundings of hostility. When he arrived ... nobody met him but a few friendly, faithful white men, silent, dubious of what the next day would bring. A stand had been built at the club house and the white women had decorated it handsomely and tastefully, but the night of the twenty-fifth negro roughs showered the stand and decorations with brickbats. ... The Rev. Mr. Johns offered prayer and Hampton began his first speech before an unfriendly audience. What kind of devil, or angel, or giant the Beaufort negroes expected to see is beyond white imagination. As the General arose one old fellow in the crowd shouted, in tones of amazement and relief, "Why he ain' nuttin' buttah man, attah all!"

It is something in negro psychology beyond Caucasian comprehension, perhaps, or maybe it was the power of personality. Whatever the cause, the crowd picked and sent, as appeared from later developments, to disturb and interrupt and start a riot, listened to Hampton silently and as attentively as it was allowed to do. The intendant of the town and the police, on pretence of keeping the road clear, did all they could to prevent the speaker from being heard and to make trouble by pushing back everybody, of either color, who tried to approach the stand. Hampton spoke along steadily, taking no heed of the noisy efforts of the officials. He challenged Lieutenant Governor Gleaves, colored, who was circulating busily about the town almost within ear shot, to come on the stand and speak and defend his party and chief, if he could. He ... flatly accused the Governor of cowardice in failing to come out and face the people. Even this was heard without show of resentment ...

.   .   .   .

When Hampton concluded his speech ... the meeting took a new turn. LeRoy F. Youmans, of Columbia, spoke next. He, too, was heard in silence until he began attacks on the Republican governments and officials. Then shrieks and howls arose from front and rear and center and both flanks, from men, women and boys. The crowd was permitted to approach and from it came a tangle and mixture of epithet and insulting and derisive cries. ... He yielded at last and Judge Cooke tried it. The storm became wilder and louder and more furious and epithet began to change to definite threat. ... He lost his temper, became so hoarse with shouting defiance that he could not hear himself and at the end of his strength had the mortification of retiring amid a roar of

FORCE WITHOUT VIOLENCE

85

African laughter. . . .Then came another marvel. Hampton advanced again, and again there was silence. He spoke quietly and without show of resentment, like a man rebuking a crowd of disorderly children. . . . This concluded the one failure of the campaign, if it really was a failure in the long run. Three or four United States deputy marshals were in the crowd and did nothing towards suppressing disorder. Five days later in Pickens, at the other end of the state and in the white belt, twelve white men were arrested for appearing at a Republican meeting, one of them accused of giving a speaker the lie and the others with aiding and abetting. . . .[64]

Hampton's final meeting was at Columbia on November 4. For days the women of the city had worked on plans and decorations. Mrs. Thomas Taylor in *South Carolina Women in the Confederacy* gives a lively account. One feature was thirty-two little girls on a fire truck to represent the counties of the state, and "as the truck with the thirty-two little silver-winged girls was entering the gates the Negroes, women and men, threatened and insulted them, and a soldier (from Edgefield) cried: 'Have we got to take this?' 'Keep the peace,' was the General's order, and he obeyed. . . . And win we did, by the masterful reticence, the glorious power held by the spirit of one man over the spirits of our other men."[65]

Pathos was added to this last meeting by the fact that the General had just buried in Columbia his young grandson, Wade Hampton Haskell. But the meeting was a triumph and a fitting climax to the most remarkable speaking tour that the state has ever witnessed. Tension seemed unbearable until the election. No one imagined that the voting would only begin, not end, the real stress and danger.

---

[64]*Ibid.*, pp. 325ff. For Hampton's account see *Recent Election in S. C.*, pp. 329f.
[65]*South Carolina Women in the Confederacy* (Columbia, 1903-7), I, 383ff.

Chapter Five

VICTORY

AFTER the polls closed on November 7, 1876, the entire country was tense, awaiting the result. For months no one knew which of the two candidates would be President of the United States. "The Nation," says Bowers in *The Tragic Era*, "faced the most serious crisis in its history."[1] A month before the election Hayes had written in his diary that a contested election might "lead to a conflict of arms."[2] Republican Senator Pool had asserted that should the Democratic candidate, Tilden, be elected, the North would not permit his inauguration.[3] Remarked *The Nation* in January, "The Republican extremists would prefer war (i.e., 'a new rebellion') to the chance of losing their power by the forms of law, while the Democratic extremists would sooner try to get Tilden elected by the house, and then have him overthrown by Republican violence...."[4]

The stage was set for even more Senecan tragedy than the Civil War of fifteen years before. South Carolina again, though for very different reasons, would play a leading role. Hampton was among those wise, moderate, self-controlled statesmen, many of them Southern "Bourbons," who prevented another tragedy of blood. Just as, to quote Bowers, the Republicans had "learned in the twelve-year revolution the power of audacity and effrontery," Southern leaders had learned in a bitter school to value peace with a hard, realistic appraisal. They knew, too, that in case of armed conflict all of the onus and most of the fighting would fall on the South. "In all the debates in the House over the Presidential dispute, ever since the election," wrote *The Nation* in late February, "the Southern members have been

---

[1] Bowers, *op. cit.*, p. 531.
[2] *Ibid.*
[3] *Ibid.*, p. 498.
[4] *The Nation*, XXIV (January 25, 1877), 49.

foremost in supporting a policy of peace and moderation; they held the violent Northern Democrats in check in the earlier days of the controversy; they threw their influence in favor of arbitration.... We now call attention to it once more for the sake of the light it throws on the conduct of the Republican leaders last summer in wickedly converting the canvass into a 'bloody shirt' crusade against the South...."[5]

1

In South Carolina the state returns came in slowly, and the final results were awaited in an agony of hope and fear. Through November 8 and 9 returns dribbled in, with Hampton leading but with Chamberlain piling up large majorities in the "black belt." By the night of the tenth the returns showed a victory for the Democratic state ticket. Hampton was serenaded in Columbia, and he made a brief, moderate speech. "He was taken on the shoulders of colored Democrats and given a triumphant progress ... while flags were flown from all windows and house tops, and cannon boomed more loudly and faster than ever before."[6] Hampton issued the following address:

To the People of the State:

In offering to our people my heartfelt congratulations and gratitude for the grand victory they have won, I venture to beg them to prove themselves worthy of it by a continued observance of good order and a rigid preservation of the peace. Let us show that we seek only the restoration of good government, the return of prosperity and the establishment of harmony to the whole people of our State.

In the hour of victory we should be magnanimous, and we should strive to forget the animosities of the contest by recalling the grand results of our success. Proscribing none for difference of opinion, regarding none as enemies, save such as are inimical to law and order, let us all unite in the patriotic work of redeeming the State. By such conduct we can not only bring about good conduct among all classes, but can most surely reap the best fruits of victory[7]

The returns were sent from precinct managers to county election commissions, all Republican controlled, though, for the first time during Reconstruction, with Democratic representation. From these

---

[5]*Ibid.* (February 22, 1877), p. 110.
[6]Williams, *op. cit.,* pp. 373f.
[7]Reynolds, *op. cit.,* pp. 396f.

county commissions the returns went to the State Board of Canvassers, which consisted entirely of Republican state officials. The tabulation of this group, watched by selected Democrats, gave Hampton 92,261 votes; Chamberlain, 91,127. The "face of the returns," as this tabulation was called, also gave the Democrats 64 members of the lower house of the legislature to the Republicans' 60; in the senate, Democrats 15, Republicans 18, including hold-overs. Thus, on the "face of the returns" the Democrats had all major state offices, control of the house, and a majority of one on joint ballot, this on an official count by a Republican board. As for the national election, this same count showed all Republican electors ahead in South Carolina by majorities of from six hundred to a thousand.[8]

Democratic leaders in the state were willing to abide by this tabulation, though they protested the count in Richland and in several of the "black" counties; but Chamberlain had just begun to fight. His struggle kept the state in dangerous suspense for five full months, until federal troops were withdrawn April 10, 1877.

The election law framed by the Radicals had provided, among other things, for just such a contingency as a Democratic victory at the polls. In an open letter to Colonel W. L. Trenholm written May 8, 1871, Chamberlain himself had described it as "that most unjust and scandalous election law."[9] Republican Judge Carpenter had stated to the 1871 Congressional committee, "I cannot suppose that a law of that sort was made for any other purpose than to keep the party in power, to prolong their power, whether the people voted for them or not."[10] United States District Attorney Corbin, whose zeal for his party we have noted, had told the same committee how this law was designed to make fraud easy for the party in power. "It is a matter I regret exceedingly," he had concluded piously, "but the truth must be told and ought to be told."[11] All had agreed on the iniquity of the law, but the Radicals in control had refused to change it.

Perhaps the most glaring injustice in this election law lay in the broad, undefined powers vested in the State Board of Canvassers, which had the duty of making the final tabulation and which had long assumed the right of deciding just which votes should be counted and which should not. This board consisted of the Comptroller General,

[8]*Ibid.*, pp. 393ff., Simkins and Woody, *op. cit.*, p. 514.
[9]Charleston *Daily Republican*, May 8, 1871.
[10]*Ku Klux Conspiracy*, S. C., p. 228.
[11]*Ibid.*, pp. 82f.

the Secretary of State, the Treasurer, the Attorney General, and the Adjutant General. All of them were intensely partisan Radicals, three of them were Negroes, and three of the five were candidates for re-election, passing on the merits of their own cases.[12] Through this board Chamberlain planned to remain in power.

His strategy was simple. Since the election of governor and lieutenant governor was confirmed, not by the board, but by the legislature, the board would declare the election void in enough Democratic counties to give the Radicals control in the legislature. That body would then declare enough Democratic votes void to give the election to Chamberlain. Meanwhile the board would declare Republicans elected in such other state offices as it pleased. The election was clearly a victory for the state Democratic ticket, and Chamberlain's plot was just as clearly a bare-faced theft, though with the color of legality.[13] It was particularly criminal in view of the dangerously inflamed condition of both the state and the nation.

Chamberlain's plan was anticipated by the Democrats, and an effort was made to checkmate it. The legal contest was long and involved, but it may be briefly summarized. Democratic lawyers applied to the State Supreme Court, which, of course, was Republican, for the necessary orders to require the State Board of Canvassers to do the following: to supply the court with an official tabulation of the face of the returns; to certify all candidates thus elected; and to abstain from judicial inquiry into the validity of the vote, such inquiry being, according to the constitution, the function of each body of the legislature in regard to itself. The court so ordered.

The board complied with the Supreme Court's order to supply its tabulation to the court; but, delaying until the last hour of its legal time limit, it completely invalidated the elections in Edgefield and Laurens Counties on the grounds of "intimidation and fraud"; it certified according to the returns the members-elect, Democrats and Republicans, of all other counties; and then it adjourned, declaring itself out of existence and therefore no longer subject to any order of the Supreme Court. The court promptly fined and imprisoned the members of the board for contempt, but they were just as promptly

[12]Reynolds, op. cit., pp. 397ff.

[13]For accounts of the legal maneuvering that followed the election, see ibid.; see also Simkins and Woody, op. cit., pp. 516ff. See also Recent Election in S. C., Appendix, pp. 78ff. For a pro-Chamberlain account, see Taylor, op. cit., pp. 250ff.

released by federal Judge Bond, who was "sure that my brother judges of the state courts will not think me wanting in courtesy."

Moreover, the elections in Laurens and Edgefield were invalidated solely on affidavits from Republicans there, without any investigation or questioning and without the Democrats' having any opportunity to hear or answer the charges. Indeed, Hayne, the Negro secretary of state, voted against excluding these counties from the tabulation on the grounds that the evidence was entirely *ex parte*.[14]

Fifty-nine certified Republican members-elect of the house, all but three of whom were Negroes, met and organized. Their legal quorum was sixty-three, but they declared that the failure of an election in Laurens and Edgefield automatically reduced the quorum. This body then declared Chamberlain elected by again invalidating the votes of the two counties in dispute. Chamberlain was thereupon "inaugurated."

Meanwhile, as we shall see later, a great many other things were happening in the state. The well-oiled plot of the Republicans was not to run quite so smoothly as they had hoped.

2

The Republicans justified their actions on the grounds that throughout the state many Republican Negro voters had been kept from voting by intimidation and that, particularly in Edgefield and Laurens, there had been an excessive degree of intimidation and fraud. Chamberlain stated to the Senate committee, "I consider it was an election that was characterized, on the part of the democratic party, by two great facts: first, violence; and second, fraud...."[15] Hampton and the other Democratic leaders, on the other hand, insisted that the election had been notably peaceful.

An accurate judgment on the subject is further complicated by the fact that, stimulated by Gary and Tillman, a legend has developed in South Carolina of outrageous extremes of violence and fraud. As the legend grew, many reputable South Carolinians boasted of utterly impossible feats of "repeat voting" and of intimidation. Such tall tales should be checked against the cold facts of two Republican managers at every poll, with marshals, deputy marshals, state constables, and United States troops within easy calling distance, particularly at the very places where Democratic frauds were alleged. Assertions that

---

[14]*Recent Election in S. C.*, p. 77.
[15]*South Carolina in 1876*, II, 25.

the election was won by violence and fraud were from the first the answer of the Gary faction to Hampton's recognition of a debt to the colored Democrats of the state,[16] though the legend did not fully develop until about a decade later.

Leading Republicans testifying before the Congressional committees and, indeed, most writers investigating this election have used the state census of 1875 as the basis for their most telling evidence of intimidation and fraud.[17] According to this census there were 110,744 Negro voters in the state. R. B. Elliott, Republican candidate for attorney general, asserted that thousands of Negroes were afraid to vote and cited figures to "prove" it, complaining to the Senate committee that "the deficiency of the colored vote of 1876, as compared with the census of 1875, amounts to 7,180 for the whole state."[18] Such a deficiency in such an election, it was claimed, strongly indicated successful widespread intimidation. Likewise the white vote in excess of that predicated by the state census has been accepted as fairly conclusive proof of successful and excessive fraud by the Democrats.

The Democrats could answer these charges only by questioning the accuracy of the state census. As Hampton told the House investigating committee, "Our idea was — we may have been wrong — that they had endeavored to show a much larger majority than actually existed in the colored vote in this state, so as to discourage any effort to overcome it."[19] This reply, of course, was very unconvincing at the time, but a comparison of the state census of 1875 with the federal figures of 1870 *and* 1880 gives a strong indication that Hampton's suspicion was justified. Such a comparison indicates that if, as the state census showed, the Negro voting population increased 25,269 during the five years from 1870 to 1875, then from 1875 to 1880 the increase in Negroes of voting age was only 8,145, less than one-third as much.[20] If we grant, however, a uniform rate of increase in the number of Negro voters during the decade, the much-complained-of deficiency of Negro votes disappears. In spite of the seeming discrepancy between the Negro vote and the state census, Hampton insisted to the

---

[16]See below, pp. 144ff.

[17]See, for example, Simkins and Woody, *op. cit.*, p. 514. See also Taylor, *op. cit.*, p. 250.

[18]*South Carolina in 1876*, II, 473ff.

[19]*South Carolina in 1876*, I, 986f.

[20]See below, pp. 99ff. The accuracy of the federal census of 1870 has been questioned.

committee that there had been a "full Negro vote," that few if any blacks had been frightened from the polls.[21]

Another approach to this subject of intimidation is through the testimony of those on the spot. With obviously partisan observers making exactly opposite assertions, one looks for the non-partisan third person. Such persons were hard to find in South Carolina in 1876; but if any could qualify, they were the officers in command of federal troops at the various polling places. These Northern officers, be it noted, were under orders to watch for violence or intimidation, and they were subject to the requisition of intensely partisan marshals and deputy marshals, who, in turn, were backed by rigid federal laws designed to prevent such practices. Such troops, too, were placed at all polls where Democratic violence was anticipated (or later claimed), though Democratic requests for troops at danger points in the "black belt" were uniformly denied.

The testimony of these officers before both committees strongly supports the contention that the election was a quiet one. Brevet Lieutenant Colonel H. G. Litchfield, who was at Winnsboro, testified, "I had excellent opportunities for observing. The polls were held directly across the street from my hotel; I never witnessed a more quiet election in any country... a more quiet election than I would expect to see at any place."[22] Lieutenant F. H. Barnhart, in Abbeville County, saw no "intimidation of any class of voters, or... disposition to prevent them from voting," though during the day he saw one man hit on the head with a rock.[23] Lieutenant R. F. Bater, in Newberry, who was "on the streets nearly the whole day," said of the election, "It was very quiet and orderly." His subordinates throughout the county reported to him "that everything passed off very quietly."[24] Captain T. J. Lloyd, also in Abbeville, "There was no violence whatever. It was very quiet there."[25] Second Lieutenant G. L. Turner, in Chester County, "It seemed to me an exceptionally quiet election."[26] First Lieutenant Edward Davis at Union, "I never saw a more quiet election in my life."[27]

Since alleged violence, intimidation, and fraud in Laurens and Edgefield Counties were used by the State Board of Canvassers to

---

[21]*Recent Election in S. C.*, pp. 31f. and *South Carolina in 1876*, I, 990f.
[22]*Recent Election in S. C.*, pp. 381f.
[23]*Ibid.*, pp. 382ff.
[24]*Ibid.*, pp. 387ff.
[25]*Ibid.*, pp. 390ff.
[26]*Ibid.*, pp. 392ff.
[27]*Ibid.*, pp. 394ff.

justify invalidating the vote in those counties, testimony from officers stationed there deserves a more full treatment. It should be remembered that all this testimony was under oath and was accompanied by sharp cross-examination by Republican members of the committees. Captain James Stewart commanded all troops in Laurens. He had told the United States Commissioner that he would hold himself "in readiness to respond to any requisition that either he or the United States marshal might make." He was within two hundred yards of the polls throughout the day. No requisition was made on him and "the general character of the election in the town" was "very quiet." There was no "disturbance during the day" nor was any reported by troops elsewhere in the county. On being asked, "If there had been any trouble to amount to anything, you, as the commanding officer for the county, would have heard of it?" he replied, "Yes, sir." To the question, "Was there any word of any account sent to you that men were intimidated or prevented from voting, or that there was trouble at the polls?" he replied, "There was not."[28]

As for Edgefield, lurid tales were told by the Radicals and, later, by Gary and Tillman in political speeches, as to intimidation there. The sworn testimony of responsible officers taken shortly after the event and agreeing with that of General M. C. Butler, who was also on the spot, however, is surely more trustworthy. There were seven companies distributed throughout the county. Brevet Colonel A. W. Randall testified in part as follows:

> I was sent to the polls, the first precinct, at seven o'clock in the morning by direction of General Brannan, on account of a report made to him by the deputy marshal that the polls were obstructed. On my arrival there, I found that there was no obstruction, and that there was perfect peace and good order. I conversed with several of the colored men there, and also with several whites. . . . Voting was progressing in an orderly manner, and on communicating with the managers (two to one Republican) as to whether there was any obstruction, they sent me word that there was not . . . and I saw that there was no obstruction and no evidence of any obstruction on the part of either party, but the utmost good feeling prevailing.
> Q. Did you see any riotous conduct, any violent demonstration of any kind there? — A. Not at all, sir; not the slightest unless you call cheering by both parties. There were cheers for Hampton and cheers for Chamberlain by the respective parties. . . .

[28]*Ibid.*, pp. 385ff.

I visited this same precinct several times during the afternoon and towards evening, and I saw nothing in the way of disturbance or intimidation, or anything else. Towards nightfall there were quite a number of mounted men listening to harangues or speeches made to them by General Butler and General Gary — congratulatory speeches; and they were rather near the polling-place, and an officer was sent by General Brannan to this polling-place, and at his approach they moved back and left the place clear. When it was reported to General Brannan that the polls were obstructed he sent for the deputy marshal, Beatty, and I saw that marshal take in parties of six and ten men to vote. They passed right through this crowd and the crowd gave way for them. . . .[29]

This account of the obstruction at the first precinct should be compared with Tillman's dramatic narrative of the same incident — of how Gary defied General Ruger and dared him to try to bring Negroes to the polls.[30]

Randall further testified that the town of Edgefield "was remarkably quiet. . . . I have seen elections in the North ten times more noisy." In answer to the question, "Did you see anything in the town of Edgefield during that day that indicated a disposition on one side or the other to intimidate voters or prevent a fair expression of their opinion?" he replied, "In my opinion, no, sir; I did not." Randall was acting "as a sort of assistant or aid to General Brannan" and consequently heard reports sent to headquarters. In answer to the question, "How many colored men were hurt that day within your knowledge?" he replied, "Within my personal knowledge there were none. There was not a blow struck nor an injury received or given during the day." He had heard, however, of one Negro's being hit on the head. He did not visit Precinct Number Two, where there was the nearest approach to a riot. The only event in Edgefield that gave the slightest color to Republican accusations was this near-riot at Precinct Number Two. Two officers who were concerned testified before the Senate committee as to this affair. Theirs was the only testimony given by federal officers that could be called at all damaging to the Democrats.

Captain Kellogg testified that about nine-thirty in the morning obstruction at Box Number Two was reported, and he was sent with his company to "receive instructions from the deputy United States marshal, a Mr. Beatty."

I located my company about fifty yards from the voting place, and the deputy marshal came to me then and reported that there

[29]*Ibid.*, pp. 378ff.
[30]See below, pp. 96f.

was a large crowd of white men, mounted men, in front of the
house in which the box was, and that they were preventing the
admission of anyone to the box except democrats. . . .
All these white men in front of the building and near it were
shouting and cursing, and a great many of them shouting out,
"Shoot! Shoot! God damn it, shoot!" I really apprehended that
there would be some trouble, and I knew that if there should be
that there would be bloodshed. I spoke to General Gary then,
and asked him if he would not endeavor to quiet the crowd. . . .

In the meantime, Lieutenant Hoyt, with four men, had opened a
way through this crowd so that the Negroes could vote.

When I worked myself through I found that Lieutenant Hoyt
had made a passage of from four to six feet in width to the boxes.
These men who had their pistols drawn were the men right next
to the soldiers. I saw a number of them with their revolvers in
their hands and with their thumbs on the locks and their fingers
on the triggers. I stayed there a few minutes until there was less
disorder than there had been, and then returned to my company,
where I remained during the day. . . .

Captain Kellogg admitted, however, "There was no obstruction,
though, to any man's going in there after Lieutenant Hoyt opened
that passage. They usually went in then in squads; one of the managers would open the door and call for voters, and from six to ten
would go in at a time." He believed that there were a good many
Negroes who did not get to vote, but did not know.[31]

He complained, too, of noise before and after the election. "Well,
sir, I never saw more disorder or boisterousness in my life than I saw
there, both the day before and during election day, and the day
after. . . . I know my own family complained to me that they were not
able to sleep any. . . . It was disgraceful, the way that many of them
behaved. . . ."[32]

Lieutenant Hoyt saw the only violence outside the imagination of
habitually outraged Radicals and the later elaboration of the veterans.

I went inside the building through a window, used as an exit
for the voters, and then out the door and opened the way from
the door through these horsemen so as to give the people a chance
to come through. I had four men with me, and as we marched
out I ordered the horsemen to give back, and they crowded their
horses back so as to give way for the men to come out. I then

[31]A near-contemporary account of this incident may be found in Appendix B.
[32]*South Carolina in 1876*, II, 395ff. See also *Recent Election in S. C.*, pp.
266ff.

posted sentinels to keep the way open. . . . At the time I went down to the house there were some men, who had voted, coming out. . . . They opened the door to admit some more, and the negroes in front tried to get up to the door through the white men, but they would not allow the negroes to do so; two or three did, however, get through between their horses in some way, and came up on the platform. One of them was struck over the head by a club in the hands of a democrat, and knocked off the platform.[33]

Major Jacob Kline's testimony agreed with that of Brevet Colonel Randall, except that Kline did visit Precinct Two at six-fifty in the morning. He saw the barrier of mounted men referred to by Captain Kellogg. He entered the building and inquired about the matter of the managers, one white man and two Negroes. He learned that the managers had agreed to allow only ten Negroes at once to approach the booth so as to prevent undue crowding. At the time he inquired, a Negro was inside being questioned preparatory to voting.[34]

So much for the violence for which Chamberlain sought to invalidate the total vote of two counties and by virtue of which, with the aid of federal troops in the State House, he held on to the government of South Carolina for five full months after the election. As *The Nation* had prophetically remarked, for Republicans "to complain afterward that the election was not fair is an absurdity." But it was a grim and bitter absurdity to South Carolina; and but for Hampton's wisdom, moderation, and power over the people of the state, it might well have been tragedy instead of farce.

Tillman's dramatic account, in a speech at the state constitutional convention in 1895, of this election in Edgefield is pure legend — typical of the Gary-Tillman exaggerations of an election won by fraud and violence:

"You must make your men give way and let these negroes to the ballot box," said Ruger.

Gary's gray eyes flashed, and his voice vibrated with a desperate resolve:

"By God, sir, I will not do it. I will keep the compact I made with you this morning, that whites and blacks shall vote at different boxes, and if you think your bluecoats can make way for these negroes to vote again, try it."

---

[33] *South Carolina in 1876*, II, 425ff.
[34] *Ibid.*, pp. 106ff.

The whites yelled lustily, the negro politicians quailed, retired — and the crisis passed.[35]

This is typical and stirring legend, head man against head man. Perhaps such tales gained Tillman, whose thesis seems to have been that Gary won the election in spite of Hampton's interference, many votes against supporters of the too-cautious Hampton when the Tillmanites set out to "right the wrong done Mart Gary." But sober fact will not support this version. General Ruger, commander of all federal troops in South Carolina, was not even in Edgefield on election day.[36]

General M. C. Butler gave the real explanation of the incident. For years it had been the custom of the Negroes to arrive at the polls before daylight and to stand around all day, particularly massing around the box itself so that no Democrats could detect "repeat voting." White men could not vote until all negroes had voted without shoving through the dense crowd of blacks. "But on this occasion," said Butler, "the white people had resolved to vote, and had got possession of the polls and resolved to keep them until they got through voting." Butler assisted Lieutenant Hoyt in managing the crowd and suggested that he get more soldiers since the four he had

[35]Tillman's speech, in the constitutional convention, 1895, as quoted by Bowers, *op. cit.*, p. 521. See also Sheppard, *op. cit.*, pp. 154ff., for an even more dramatic account of this incident. See above, p. 94 for Colonel Randall's account—"and an officer was sent by General Brannan [commanding officer in Edgefield], and at his approach they moved back and left the place clear." Tillman asserted in 1909, *op. cit.*, p. 28, that Gary's "daring refusal on the day of the election to obey General Ruger's order to have the whites vacate the court house at Edgefield really gave us the victory." By all accounts the event took place shortly before the polls closed; so even if it had happened as Tillman told the story, not enough Negro votes could have been cast to have had a decisive effect. General M. C. Butler told of this incident before the House investigating committee without mentioning Gary or Ruger. *Recent Election in S. C.*, pp. 295f. J. C. Sheppard's testimony agrees with that of Colonel Randall and General Butler. *Ibid.*, pp. 406f. Sheppard, *op. cit.*, p. 156n., cites for authority Mrs. Kellogg in Edgefield *Advertiser*, November 20, 1876. Mrs. Kellogg was the wife of the Captain Kellogg who gave testimony unfavorable to the Democrats before the Senate investigating committee. She wrote a highly colored account of the election in Edgfield to a friend in the North; and her letter was printed in a Northern paper. The *Advertiser* copied the account from Mrs. Kellogg's copy of the paper, illegally as her husband complained to the committee. Under cross-examination Captain Kellogg admitted that his wife's account was unfriendly and inaccurate. See *Recent Election in S. C.*, pp. 266ff.

[36]General Ruger was probably at his headquarters in Columbia where he belonged on such an election day. General Brannan is frequently mentioned by

were having to use their bayonets to keep back the crowd of Negroes.[37] There was no riot.

As for fraud, there simply is no non-partisan testimony. Even sober
tradition in South Carolina, however, indicates that some whites
bought Negro votes outright. Probably, too, some white men crossed
the river from Georgia and voted, particularly in Edgefield County.[38]
"Repeat voting" was probably in favor of the Republicans since they
controlled the election machinery. They could have prevented it by
meeting the constitutional requirement of a registration of voters;
presumably they refused to do so, in spite of Democratic protests, because the *status quo* worked to their advantage. Certainly there was
evidence of both intimidation and fraud by Republicans in the "black
belt," where at one precinct Negroes actually drove the Democratic
manager away from the polls.[39]

Every evidence points to more Democratic fraud in Edgefield
County than anywhere else in the state. In fact, election returns elsewhere do not indicate fraud at all. In Laurens, for example, the
county next to Edgefield most suspect, Hampton received only 657
more votes than the white votes in the county by the state census of
1875.[40] Even granting that this census was correct, 657 votes can be
explained by the number of white men normally coming of age in a
year plus a perfectly reasonable Negro vote for Hampton, who averaged about 500 Negro votes per county. The figures in Edgefield,
however, cannot be thus explained. There Hampton received a majority of 3,160 votes. But the customary comparisons with the election
of 1874 are misleading (Chamberlain, 3,398; Green, 2,900); for both
candidates were Republicans, and Gary despised all efforts at "fusion."
Green's vote cannot, therefore, be considered the normal Democratic
vote of the county. Census comparisons are uninformative in Edgefield, too, because after the 1870 census the county was divided in

---

the officers and others who testified about the election in Edgefield; General
Ruger, not at all. Colonel Randall's "an officer was sent by General Brannan..."
is overwhelmingly more probable than that the commanding officer of all the
troops in the state would personally investigate alleged obstruction to voting at a
ballot box in a small town distant from the capital. Finally, when Tillman told
this stirring tale in 1895, General M. C. Butler remarked that Ruger wasn't even
there. See D. D. Wallace, *The History of South Carolina* (New York, 1934), III,
312n.

[37]*Recent Election in S. C.*, pp. 294ff. See also the account of the school house
poll in Appendix B.

[38]Simkins and Woody, *op. cit.*, pp. 514f.

[39]*Ibid.*

[40]*South Carolina in 1876*, III, 578.

the formation of Aiken County. There was fraud, no doubt, in Edge-field, but probably not to the extent alleged. Most later stories of fraud and intimidation stem from Edgefield, the home of both Gary and Tillman; but this county was the exception, not the rule, as to the campaign in the state at large.

That there was some intimidation and fraud on both sides no one will deny. The extent of such practices, however, and their effect on the outcome of the election have been grossly exaggerated. The Rad-ical pretext and the South Carolina legend of extreme violence and fraud are not based on the facts. Hampton, as usual, was telling the simple truth when he stated that the election was a peaceful one, largely won by appeals to the Negro. Louis F. Post, who had served as secretary to the ubiquitous Corbin, writes in "A 'Carpetbagger' in South Carolina":

> William Stone (Mr. Corbin's brother-in-law and law partner), who was Attorney General of South Carolina in 1876 and ex-officio one of the State canvassing board, assured me after he came to New York that at this election Wade Hampton honestly carried the State for Governor while Rutherford B. Hayes as hon-estly carried it for President. It required Stone's assurance to make me believe this, but upon his assurance I do believe it.[41]

As to the number of Negro votes cast for Hampton, no one will ever be certain. Chamberlain estimated to the Senate committee that the total was about three thousand.[42] S. L. Hutchens, an intelligent Negro lawyer who had canvassed the state, estimated that "at least twelve thousand black men enrolled their names to vote the Demo-cratic ticket" and that about ten thousand did vote it.[43] Colonel A. C. Haskell estimated fifteen thousand,[44] and Hampton, seventeen thou-sand.[45] Casual references in newspapers of the state during 1877 and 1878 were usually to sixteen thousand Negro votes for Hampton. Certainly enough Negroes did vote for Hampton to give him a major-ity even on a Republican count.

For an analysis of the vote, the state census of 1875 is valueless for two reasons: the previously mentioned padding of the Negro total,

<hr />

[41]Post, op. cit., p. 72.
[42]South Carolina in 1876, II, 40.
[43]Ibid., I, 605.
[44]Ibid., I, 823.
[45]Recent Election in S. C., p. 333. But Tillman, op. cit., p. 28, said that Hamp-ton "always maintained that sixteen thousand negroes voted for him; but every active worker in the cause knew that in this he was woefully mistaken."

which justified a suspicion that any figure in the census might have been distorted for party advantage;[46] and the fact that several thousand voters of both races must have come to voting age during the full year between the taking of the census and election day, November 7, 1876. A theoretical estimate of the voting population, however, may be calculated from the federal censuses of 1870 and 1880, figures presumably without political bias. Such an estimate indicates a voting population very close in number to the actual "face of the returns."

TABLE I[47]

1. Negro males over 21, 1870...................... 85,475
2. Negro males over 21, 1880...................... 118,889
3. Ten-year increase (2—1)...................... 33,414
4. Average yearly increase 3,341
5. Theoretical six-year increase, 1870-1876.......... 20,046
6. Theoretical Negro voting population, 1876 (1+5)
   (5,223 fewer than Negroes in state census of 1875) 105,521
7. White males over 21, 1870...................... 62,547
8. White males over 21, 1880...................... 86,900
9. Ten-year increase (8—7) 24,353
10. Average yearly increase 2,435
11. Theoretical six-year increase, 1870-1876.......... 14,610
12. Theoretical white voting population, 1876 (7+11)
    (2,859 more than whites in state census of 1875).. 77,157
13. Theoretical total voting population, 1876 (6+12).. 182,678
14. "Face of the returns" for Hampton.............. 92,261
15. "Face of the returns" for Chamberlain........... 91,127
16. Total vote counted (14+15) 183,388
17. Excess of total vote counted over total theoretical
    voting population (16—13) 710

Within the obvious margin of error in such a calculation, the "total vote counted" is sufficiently close to the "theoretical voting population" to eliminate the necessity for explaining the size of the vote by excessive additions through fraud or by subtractions through intimidation, unless, of course, the two counteracted each other. This analysis may be carried further to indicate the division of the vote on the basis of race. It was generally admitted, even by Chamberlain,

---

[46]See, for example, Williams, op. cit., pp. 372f., and testimony of men like Haskell, Connor and Hagood before the investigating committees. Also see note 19 above.

[47]Figures for 1870 and 1880 taken from South Carolina Handbook, 1883 (Charleston, 1883), p. 397.

that nearly every white man in the state voted for Hampton, though, of course, such an assumption adds to the margin of error.

TABLE II

1. "Face of the returns" for Hampton (14 above)   92,261
2. Theoretical white voting population, 1876 (12 above)   77,157
3. Theoretical Negro vote for Hampton (1–2)   15,104
4. Theoretical Negro voting population, 1876 (6 above)   105,521
5. Negro votes theoretically remaining for Chamberlain (4–3)   90,417
6. "Face of the returns" for Chamberlain (15 above) . .   91,127
7. Excess of Chamberlain's actual vote over Negro votes theoretically remaining for Chamberlain if 15,104 Negroes voted for Hampton (6–5)   710

This analysis, inconclusive though it must be, indicates that accusations of successful wholesale intimidation and fraud on the part of the Democrats (which were based largely on the excessive white vote and deficient Negro vote as compared with the questionable state census of 1875) are not necessarily true. In other words, the "face of the returns" is perfectly consistent with this probable estimate of the voting population in both total number and racial division.

There is further evidence substantiating this conclusion. In his testimony before the Senate committee Colonel Haskell gave his own analysis of the election returns. Entirely disregarding the state census of 1875, he reached some interesting conclusions about the Negro vote through an analysis of the returns in the counties. Out of thirty-two counties, according to Colonel Haskell, only twenty-four furnished complete poll lists of voters separating blacks and whites, as the law required. Of the eight that failed to do so (Republican tables, etc., vary from two to four counties that so failed), all but three, Aiken, Edgefield, and Laurens, polled large Republican majorities.[48]

In the table below are given Colonel Haskell's figures without change or interpretation. These agree substantially with both the "theoretical voting population" and the "face of the returns."

[48]The counties failing to differentiate races were, according to Haskell, Aiken, Beaufort, Charleston, Edgefield, Kershaw, Laurens, Williamsburg, and Colleton. Simkins and Woody, op. cit., p. 514, list only four counties, Charleston, Edgefield, Laurens, and Williamsburg.

TABLE III[49]

1. Number of Negro votes cast in 24 counties where races were distinguished...................... 60,607
2. Chamberlain's vote these 24 counties............. 52,416
3. Negro votes to Hampton these 24 counties (1–2).. 8,191
4. Ratio of Negro votes between Chamberlain and Hampton these 24 counties.................... 74:10
5. Chamberlain's vote in 8 counties that did not distinguish races (assumed all Negro).............. 38,711
6. By ratio 74:10, number of Negro votes cast in these 8 counties................................... 44,759
7. Total Negro vote (1+6)...................... 105,366
   (Theoretical Negro voting population, Table I, 105,521)
8. By ratio 74:10, Negro vote for Hampton, these 8 counties 6,046
9. Total Negro vote for Hampton (3+8)............ 14,237
10. Total Negro vote remaining for Chamberlain (7–9) 91,129

"I confess," said Haskell, "that I was surprised by the result of my own figures, because the vote returned for him is 91,127."

It should be noted that the analysis of Tables I and II, disregarding all election returns and using only the federal censuses, arrives at a total Negro vote of 105,521. Haskell, on the other hand, disregarding all census figures and using only the election returns, arrives at a total Negro vote of 105,366. These figures are about five thousand less than the Negro voting population as given in the state census of 1875. The fact that the two entirely independent calculations on the Negro vote differ by only 155 out of more than a hundred thousand gives a certain validity to the lower estimate. The matter is significant because the divergent policies of Hampton and Gary (and, later, Tillman) towards the Negro were largely justified by their contradictory claims as to how the election had been won. Hampton was to assert that the election of 1876 had proved that many Negro voters could be won by the appeals of white men whom they trusted. Gary was to insist that the election was won only by intimidation and fraud and that any other course with the Negro was treason to Straightout Democracy.[50]

Perhaps, then, in appealing to the Negroes for their vote, Hampton had not blundered so egregiously as Tillman later asserted. Certainly one of the very few unanimous reports of Congressional committees during the period was that of the House committee to the effect that

---

[49]*South Carolina in 1876*, II, 568ff.
[50]See below, pp. 141ff.

a majority went to Hampton in the state but to Hayes on the national ticket.[51] After taking testimony on the election in South Carolina to the extent of nearly a thousand pages of very fine print, members of this committee, Democratic and Republican, agreed that the election was sufficiently fair for the "face of the returns" to stand as tabulated.

3

If Hampton had no other claim to greatness, his wise leadership during the five months following the election of 1876 would entitle him to both state and national honor; for during this crisis he maintained peace in an area where but for him violence would have erupted. Even Tillman gave Hampton full credit for this part of his campaign: "Hampton's calm determination, his poise, his moderation, his good judgment in dealing with the perplexing conditions produced by the dual government . . . were absolutely necessary to the success we achieved."[52]

Chamberlain, too, when the dust of battle had long settled, could see Hampton as something more than the leader of a gang of cutthroats.

> It has been remarked that South Carolina has no great leader or leaders after Mr. Calhoun. This was true until 1876, but not later. Great new occasions usually bring leaders. At the head of the Democratic forces in South Carolina, in June, 1876, appeared General Wade Hampton, known only, one might say, till then, except locally, as a distinguished cavalry officer. He had led the life of a planter on a large scale, and possessed well-developed powers and habits of command. Totally unlike Calhoun, Hampton's strength of leadership lay, not in intellectual or oratorical superiority, but in high and forceful character, perfect courage and devotion to what he conceived to be the welfare of South Carolina. Not even Calhoun's leadership was at any time more absolute, unquestioned, and enthusiastic than Hampton's in 1876; and it was justly so from the Democratic point of view, for he was unselfish, resolute, level-headed, and determined. He was for the hour a true natural leader; and he led with consummate, mingled prudence and aggressiveness.[53]

---

[51]The Senate committee (majority Republican) gave the usual majority and minority reports on party lines. The House committee (majority Democratic) presented a unanimous report approving the face of the returns. *The Nation*, XXIV (January 4, 1877), 1, commented in ironic vein, asking the Democrats of the House committee if they were unaware that well-established custom made it the duty of such a committee to strengthen the party, not to get the truth.

[52]Tillman, *op. cit.*, p. 27.

[53]Chamberlain, "Reconstruction in S. C.," *op. cit.*, p. 480.

One very important result of the policy followed by Hampton from November to April, a result of extreme significance at the time, was the effect of events in South Carolina on public opinion in the North. Gary might fume at indignities meekly borne, but meanwhile Hampton's moderation and the obvious rightness of his actions disarmed the supporters of what even Republicans were calling "Grantism." Moreover, as the facts in the case emerged, the country as a whole began to penetrate the thick smoke-screen of Radical propaganda and to recognize to some extent the arrogant high-handedness of carpetbagger-Negro government in the South. As *The Nation* put it, the question "was not so much whether black men should be free, but *whether white men should be slaves.*"[54]

Hampton's position in the state was not unlike that of Tilden in the nation. He had won his majority at the polls by a small margin, but it was subject to legal theft by the machinations of state and national administrations with no perceptible scruples where the perpetuation of their power was concerned. If, unlike Tilden, he should show undue caution or the slightest uncertainty, again like Tilden he would lose in the conference room what he had won at the polls. If, on the other hand, he were unduly aggressive or if for even one hour he lost control of his already over-tried Red Shirts, riot and military government were the inevitable sequel.

Unlike Tilden, Hampton was probably determined to fight as a last resort. After the state was safely in the hands of the Democrats, Williams asked Hampton if he would have fought the United States government. "His reply was solemn and deliberate," wrote Williams, "and I believe he meant every word of it — 'The people of South Carolina gave me their banner to carry. I intended to carry it as far as they would follow me.' "[55] Unlike Tilden, too, Hampton had a following sufficiently desperate to accept even war and certain defeat as an alternative to the intolerable *status quo*. Much later Chamberlain himself admitted that under such government as then existed in South Carolina (he cited as an example the fact that at the beginning of his administration two hundred trial justices in the state could not read or write), armed rebellion would be the inevitable result for any Caucasian community if other recourses failed.[56]

---

[54]*The Nation*, XXIV (March 22, 1877), 174.
[55]Williams, *op. cit.*, p. 447.
[56]Reynolds, *op. cit.*, p. 294.

As early as 1871 Hampton had been asked by the Joint Congressional committee then in Columbia if he believed that current conditions would "culminate in resistance to the state government." He had replied, "If it were merely the negro majority to continue, I do not think it would produce a conflict.... But if they go on as they have been going on ... I am afraid it may end in a collision."[57] In 1876 he believed that the issues involved justified fighting in the state, but not in the nation.

Unlike General Gary and many another impatient Carolinian, he did not give up hope of a peaceful solution during the post-election imbroglio, though again and again he had a "good right" to be fighting mad. His formula of force without violence was still the key to the situation. The certainty that thousands of Red Shirts would converge on Columbia if Hampton gave the word was a potent factor in all negotiations; but the complete lack of violence and the moderation of everything Hampton said and did left Chamberlain with few supporters in the country except Radical leaders.

As early as November *The Nation* was observing, "The people of South Carolina are displaying great moderation and self control under circumstances which put these qualities to as severe a test as any community accustomed to free government was ever tried by."[58] By the end of December the same periodical remarked, "The Democrats in South Carolina have taken an unassailable position, and they must either succeed or the State must be changed into a military despotism — a change which they may rest assured will not be permitted by the rest of the country to last long."[59]

In December, too, the *Philadelphia Times* observed, "Every utterance of the legally elected Governor of South Carolina brings his character out in striking and pleasing contrast to that of the man who has stolen the office, and whose crime is upheld by the administration at Washington. General Hampton's inaugural address is characterized by the spirit which might be expected of a popular leader, who, under great provocation has kept his own temper and restrained the just indignation of an outraged people."

Yet, as Senator Randolph of New Jersey told the Senate, when he had taken a message to President Grant from Hampton, saying that Hampton had been confirmed in office by the State Supreme Court,

---

[57]*Ku Klux Conspiracy*, S. C., p. 1236.
[58]*The Nation*, XXIII (November 30, 1876), 320.
[59]*Ibid.* (December 28, 1876), p. 376.

Grant's reply "in angry tone and uncivil manner was, 'I won't withdraw the troops; I don't regard the decision of the Supreme Court; and if I had any message to send to General Hampton, it would be that his message to me is an impertinence.' "[60]

By the last of February, however, Grant, the "Old Man" himself, commented wryly, "In South Carolina the contest has assumed such a phase that the whole army of the United States would be inadequate to enforce the authority of Governor Chamberlain." "The people of that state," continued Grant, echoing the complaint made to the Senate committee two months before by Secretary of State Hayne, "have resolved not to resort to violence, but have adopted a mode of resistance much more formidable and effective than armed demonstration. . . ."[61] "Evidently there is nothing to be done," commented *The Nation* on Grant's pronouncement, "but to let the sham give way to the reality . . . to see without regret, if we can, the blacks deprived of a supremacy as corrupting to themselves as it was dangerous to society at large."[62]

By late March *The Nation* could observe with relief the "change of tone" throughout the country. "The telegraph brings no news of 'outrages'. . . . Every Republican has become disgusted with military control of states, and thoroughly convinced that a state government which cannot support itself should not be propped up by national soldiers. . . . We can discuss state governments without being accused of treason against humanity if we fail to approve of bayonet support."[63] Hampton had won his victory, not by political adroitness, but through the fundamental rightness of his character.

On April 10, 1877, federal troops left the State House; and, almost exactly twelve years after the surrender, the Civil War was over in South Carolina, though troops remained in Columbia. In a bloodless victory Hampton had won not only independent statehood for South Carolina, but also much understanding and respect in the North.

4

On November 22, three weeks after the election, the South Carolina State Board of Canvassers held the meeting in which it threw out the vote of Edgefield and Laurens Counties; and as an awareness of their purpose spread through the state, a flood of anger began to rise, a

---

[60]This incident is related in *The Nation*, XXVIII (April 24, 1879), 275.
[61]Quoted in *The Nation*, XXIV (March 1, 1877), 127.
[62]*Ibid.*
[63]*Ibid.* (March 29, 1877), 188.

flood that Hampton alone could control. He immediately issued an address to the people of the state: ". . . your cause, and it is the cause of constitutional government in this country, has been carried to the highest court of the State, and we are willing to abide by its decision, feeling assured that this tribunal will see that the laws shall be enforced and justice succeed."[64]

November 28 was the day fixed by the state constitution for the organization of the new legislature. At midnight of the twenty-seventh, under the orders of Grant and the "advice" of Chamberlain, a company of United States infantry occupied the State House. All legislators certified by the Board of Canvassers were permitted to enter; members-elect from Laurens and Edgefield with certificates of election from the State Supreme Court, however, were stopped at the door by sentinels with loaded rifles and fixed bayonets. Hampton and Haskell were also denied entrance.

The Nation (by no means a special pleader for Southern white men but a friend of honest and constitutional government) commented on this use of federal troops:

> They were in possession not only of the State House, but of the hall of the Legislature, and the members could only reach their seats on satisfying the corporal of the guard, who in his turn appears to have been under the orders of one Dennis . . . a carpetbagger, an old member of the Scott ring . . . and in other respects like most of his kind. . . .
>
> Has the spectacle ever been witnessed out of the United States of an armed corporal of the guard passing on the validity of election certificates at the door of a legislature? Troops are used under military monarchies for all sorts of purposes which we consider reprehensible, but we do not think they have ever been used with such gross indecency as in this case. . . .[65]

As news of soldiers in the State House spread through the community, a large crowd of angry men assembled about the building. Many of them believed, undoubtedly with relief, that the time of waiting had ended and that the time for fighting had come. They were ready, about five thousand of them.

In considerable agitation the officer in command of the troops requested Hampton to have the crowd disperse. Hampton spoke to them briefly and simply from the State House steps: "My friends, I am truly doing what I have done earnestly during the whole exciting contest,

---

[64]Reynolds, *op. cit.*, pp. 402f.
[65]*The Nation*, XXIII (December 7, 1876), 337.

pouring oil on the troubled waters. It is of great importance to us all, as citizens of South Carolina, that peace should be preserved. . . . Keep perfectly quiet, leave the streets, and do nothing to provoke a riot. We trust to the law and the Constitution, and we have perfect faith in the justice of our cause."[66]

The crowd dispersed quietly and promptly, not because his words inspired them, but because they trusted his judgment and his courage and because they knew that his purpose was as inflexible as their own. Two years later in an interview for the Boston *Globe*, Hampton said simply, "I told them we wanted no disturbance, and asked them to go away. Every one of them had left within three minutes."[67]   General B. T. Johnson, who was standing near Hampton, wrote years later, "I know of no more remarkable illustration of moral force. . . ."[68]

The correspondent of the *New York Herald* gave his eyewitness account:

> The bearing of South Carolina citizens in the great trial to which they were subjected yesterday was admirable. There has never been a more critical and dangerous conjunction in the history of American politics. The whole country had its attention focused on the proceedings at Columbia and there was a great strain of anxiety and apprehension lest scenes of violence and bloodshed should set the whole country on fire and inaugurate a new civil war. Public passion was in so inflamed a state that a mere spark might have kindled a conflagration of which the consequences might have been appalling. As no spark fell into the dry tinder there we felicitate the country that the period of danger is past.
>
> The credit of preserving the peace at Columbia yesterday is due to General Wade Hampton, Democratic candidate for Governor. He had only to lift his finger, he had only to signify the slightest assent and the State House would have been rescued from the Federal soldiers and his supporters could have controlled the organization of the Legislature. . . . It is fortunate that they have a leader so strong, so sagacious, so self-possessed and so thoroughly trusted as Wade Hampton. He perfectly understands the situation, and as we may judge by his conduct yesterday, he will make no mistake. . . . His supporters have so much confidence in him that they will do nothing against his wishes and he understands the situation too well to permit any resort to violence.[69]

---

[66]Reynolds, *op. cit.*, pp. 41f. See also Williams, *op. cit.*, pp. 394f. For Hampton's quieting influence on the excited Democrats in Columbia during the preceding days, see *ibid.*, p. 389.
[67]Boston *Globe*, November 29, 1879, quoted by Thompson, *op. cit.*, p. 143.
[68]*Ibid.*
[69]*New York Herald*, November 29, 1876, quoted by Thompson, *op. cit.*, p. 144.

Meanwhile the Republican house had organized, though, as has been explained, without a legal quorum, and had elected E. W. M. Mackey speaker; thereafter it was known as the "Mackey House." The Democratic house organized in a nearby hall and elected General W. H. Wallace speaker; it, of course, was called the "Wallace House." Counting the members from Edgefield and Laurens, from the first the Wallace House had a legal quorum of sixty-four members, and soon it received five deserters from the Mackey House (four Negroes and one White Republican), giving it a majority of members actually certified by the Board of Canvassers. Not to be outdone, however, the Mackey House by resolution unseated the Democratic members elected from Abbeville, Aiken and Barnwell Counties and seated their Republican opponents.

On Thanksgiving Day, November 30, all members of the Wallace House, in a surprise move occupied the regular legislative hall before the Republicans could organize resistance. For five days and four nights the rival bodies remained in the same hall, neither willing to give place to the other. There were tense moments during this co-occupation, but no violence. At one point General Ruger sent notice that he would oust the Laurens and Edgefield delegations, but he was sent a very strong written protest signed by Hampton, Haskell, and Senator Gordon of Georgia and never took the threatened action.[70]

On Sunday, December 3, Hampton received an anonymous letter, sender still unknown, which indicated a new crisis. Chamberlain, it informed him, had imported a hundred or more Negro "Hunkidories" from Charleston and planned to deputize them and use them to expel members of the Wallace House. The resulting violence would justify the interference of troops, who would be waiting nearby. Those in the hall learned of the plan, and all Sunday afternoon and night they waited for a bloody fight to begin. Meanwhile, messages in pre-arranged code were sent to nearby towns to assemble the Red Shirts. That to Greenville, for example, read, "Ship first train 200 game chickens state fair, with sufficient gaffs."

Williams, who was there as a reporter, describes the scene:

> Sunday night, December 3, and the day following made the last hours of real danger in the revolution and the last occasion for a general rally of the Red Shirts. Late Saturday evening a new and valuable ally was gained by the Democrats when Tom Hamilton [well-to-do Negro farmer of Beaufort and Chamberlain's

---

[70]For a play-by-play account of this transaction, see Williams, *op. cit.*, pp. 399ff.

strongest supporter at the Republican convention in September],
after a scathing speech, before which his party associates cowered,
walked to Speaker Wallace, took the oath as member of the Wallace House and returned defiantly to his place on the Republican
side in the front row, a position of special advantage if it came to
shooting and of special danger. . . .

Probably each man had his own plan of battle. We reporters
decided that we would push our table over on its side, jam chairs
against it and stuff our overcoats into the space between. . . . Mr.
Austin, the *London Times* man, was not disturbed. His program
was to find a place on the floor where he would be safe from all
but stray bullets. . . .

Why Mackey delayed his signal to the Hunkidories never has
been known. . . . It is certain that Captain Kellogg, one of the few
army officers in sympathy with Chamberlain, was all night near
the entrance to the hall, ready to call up his company, kept under
arms downstairs, when the negro deputy sergeants-at-arms made
their rush from the committee rooms. All entrances to the State
House were guarded by soldiers and nobody was admitted without a pass from Mackey or unless vouched for by the Republican
officials.

So we waited. . . . Just as daylight came, negroes began to cluster at a window looking down the hill of Gervais Street. . . . Just
to be moving and to satisfy an idle curiosity, I went to another
window to see what was attracting attention. By the living pal-
metto tree! There they were! Red Shirts![71]

By noon Monday there were about three thousand Red Shirts in
Columbia, all organized under their local officers and assigned to previously prepared quarters. Now Hampton could lead from strength,
not from weakness. Force without violence. To the consternation of
most Democrats and the bewilderment of the Republicans, Speaker
Wallace at noon read a dry, legalistic submission under protest to the
federal government and suggested that the Democrats withdraw to another hall.

What was a shrewd strategic withdrawal seemed like abject surrender to many men in the hall. "All agree now that the course taken
was wise," says Williams, "but it was a bitter pill then, apparently a
retreat before an ignominious and insolent foe with victory in sight."
Several members, notably John C. Sheppard of Edgefield, pled for a
fight to the finish. A large majority, however, voted for withdrawal,
and the weary men gathered up their blankets and filed out. "The
Republicans showed no exultation. They knew they were in the

---

[71]*Ibid.*, pp. 411ff.

power of formidable and exasperated men, hardly held in leash, and had learned from experience that every move the Democrats made was likely to work against Chamberlain, whatever its outward or immediate aspects."[72]

The crisis was not yet over. On the following day, the fifth, the Mackey House met with Republicans in the Senate and declared Chamberlain elected. This sequence of "defeats" was more than Gary, who lacked the general confidence in Hampton, could patiently bear. His apologist, W. A. Sheppard (in *Red Shirts Remembered*), who accuses Hampton of a discreditable "bargain" with Hayes, describes what Williams calls "an excited and exciting speech, demanding action."

> In the meantime, Mart Gary was thrust into the role of oriflamme for the men to whom compromise was abhorrent. Letters of congratulations and commissions poured in on the Bald Eagle [Gary]. Red Shirts gathered in the streets and shouted his name. . . .
>
> Demanding more immediate attention were the Red Shirts who leaped to the defense of the Wallace House. Released from close supervision of their officers, mocked by Hampton for their heroic response to a desperate summons, they surged through the capitol, crying for vengeance upon the political usurpers. Climbing upon a box, Gary called down maledictions upon Chamberlain and his crew. He advocated purging the state of the men who dragged its Government through the slime. This was music to the ears of those who recognized the battle-cry of a warrior, cogent logic to yeomen who had forsaken every private interest for the redemption of South Carolina. Skilled only with weapons for the field of honor, they were ignorant of covert trades and bargains.[73]

After General Gary had thus poured oil on the troubled fires, excitement reached a dangerous intensity. Let Williams take up the narrative:

> In the evening five thousand men assembled around Choral Hall . . . and cheered and screamed against further delay or yielding and for a fight to the finish then and there. As Hampton mounted a box on the sidewalk, he was met by many cries, mingled with the cheering.
>
> "We'll leave everything we've got with you and tear down the State House with our hands, if you'll just give us the word, General!" shouted one man with a powerful voice, and a wild yell of approval responded.

---

[72]*Ibid.*, pp. 416f. For an anti-Hampton account see Sheppard, *op. cit.*, pp. 176ff.

[73]Sheppard, *op. cit.*, pp. 180f.

"When the time comes to take the State House I'll lead you there," was Hampton's quiet answer, evoking a new and more general cheer. His manner, his intense earnestness but avoidance of excitement and gesture, his fatherly, friendly tone, carried conviction that he was master of the situation and to be trusted and followed, even when leading in apparent retreat men eager to advance. . . . That evening of December 5 the last serious danger to the peace of the republic and the state of that perilous period vanished . . . as the crowd, tuned for war, dispersed quietly, obedient to the advice and plea of the chosen leader.[74]

Like Thad Stevens, Gary had a one-track mind, saw one truth intensely, but only one. To such men any compromise of conflicting human claims and needs is far worse than defeat after a stand-up fight. If South Carolina had elected to follow Gary in the counter-revolution of 1876 as the North had followed Stevens in the revolution of 1867, Gary's leadership would have been as disastrous for the state as Stevens' had been for the nation. Lincoln, like Hampton, might have controlled the doctrinaires of '67, but President Johnson could not. Credit is due to the Red Shirts in Columbia that they subdued their impulses to Hampton's moderation, but General Gary was a bitter man.

Only once again did pressure even approach the danger point. Chamberlain was "inaugurated" on the seventh and made a gloomy address to his scanty audience. "Neither the public peace nor the life of any man who now opposes the consummation of this policy of fraud and violence," he said, "is safe from the assaults of those who have enforced that policy."[75] That night a crowd again called for Hampton. He spoke briefly, again counseling self-control, patience, and the strictest preservation of the peace. It was this speech that he concluded with his only stirring phrase of the campaign: "The people have elected me Governor, and, by the Eternal God, I will be Governor or we shall have a military governor."[76]

On December 6 the state Supreme Court had formally recognized Hampton's Wallace House as the lawful legislative body. On the fourteenth this house with the Democrats in the senate declared Hampton elected, and he was inaugurated on the same day. In his address he reviewed the events leading to the occasion and then reiterated the pledges that he had made during the campaign:

A great task is before the conservative party of this state. They entered on this contest on a platform so broad, so strong, so liberal,

---

[74]Williams, op. cit., p. 418.
[75]Allen, op. cit., pp. 445ff.
[76]Reynolds, op. cit., p. 425; Thompson, op. cit., p. 153.

that every honest citizen could stand upon it. They recognized
and accepted the amendments of the Constitution in good faith;
they pledged themselves to work reform and to establish good
government; they promised to keep up an efficient system of public
education; and they declared solemnly that all citizens of South
Carolina, of both races and of both parties, should be regarded as
equals in the eye of the law; all to be protected in the enjoyment
of every political right now possessed by them.

To the faithful observance of these pledges we stand committed, and I, as the representative of the conservative party, hold
myself bound by every dictate of honor and good faith to use
every effort to have these pledges redeemed fully and honestly.
It is due not only to ourselves but to the colored people of the
State that wise, just and liberal measures should prevail in our legislation. We owe much of our late success to these colored voters
who were brave enough to rise above the prejudice of race and
honest enough to throw off the shackles of party in their determination to save the State. To those who, misled by their fears,
their ignorance, or by evil counseling, turned a deaf ear to our appeals, we should not be vindictive but magnanimous. Let us show
to all of them that the true interests of both races can best be secured by cultivating peace and promoting prosperity among all
classes of our fellow citizens. . . .[77]

After Hampton's inauguration his power increased steadily as that
of Chamberlain declined. The state treasury was empty, and the
state's credit was nil; moreover, not even Republicans in the state
would pay their taxes to the Chamberlain government. Hampton, on
the other hand, had levied a small voluntary tax which had been
promptly paid by members of both parties — for example, by 938
Negroes in Barnwell County alone.[78] Consequently, all state institutions had to go to Hampton for money and thus, like the Supreme
Court, recognize him as the lawful governor. By the time that troops
were withdrawn, the Hampton government was already functioning,
if not normally, at least effectively, unresisted except in the State
House.

On March 12 Senator Stanley Matthews, an adviser of President
Hayes, wrote Chamberlain, advising him to withdraw; but Chamberlain refused, saying, among other things, "To permit Hampton to reap
the fruits of a campaign of murder and fraud, so long as there remained power to prevent it, is to sanction such methods."[79] Hayes,

---

[77]*Ibid.*, pp. 427ff.

[78]Williams, *op. cit.*, pp. 436f.

[79]For copies of these communications see Allen, *op. cit.*, pp. 469ff. See also
Reynolds, *op. cit.*, pp. 451ff.

as Williams relays the rather doubtful story, "hinted at a new election to determine the South Carolina governorship. Hampton rejected this defiantly, saying that if General Hayes would consent to a new election for the presidency he would consent to a new election for the governorship, not otherwise."[80]

On March 23 President Hayes requested both Chamberlain and Hampton to confer with him in Washington so that he could "put an end as speedily as possible to all appearance of intervention of the military authority of the United States in the political derangements which affect the government and afflict the people of South Carolina."[81] Speaking to those assembled at the railway station to see him off, Hampton explained his purpose:

> I go to Washington simply to state before the President the fact that the people of South Carolina have elected me Governor of that state. I go there to say to him that we ask no recognition from any President. We claim the recognition from the votes of the people of the State. I go there to assure him that we are not fighting for party, but that we are fighting for the good of the whole country. I am going there to demand our rights — nothing more — and, so help me God, to take nothing less.[82]

President Hayes consulted with both Hampton and Chamberlain, and on April 3 he and his cabinet decided that troops would be withdrawn on April 10. Hampton wired the Lieutenant Governor, "Everything satisfactorily and honorably settled. I expect our people to preserve absolute peace and quiet. My word is pledged for this. I rely on them."[83] The transfer of office was quietly accomplished. Twelve years after the end of the war Reconstruction was over in South Carolina, and reconstruction could begin.

5

There had been, however, one distinctly sour note in the general Democratic harmony in the state during the five months following the election, an indication of conflict to follow. The "face of the returns" showed a Democratic majority for the state ticket but a Republican majority for the Presidential electors. This unusual division is easily explained by the small margin of both majorities combined with the fact that many Republicans, white and black, supported

---

[80]Williams, *op. cit.*, p. 441, and the *Register*, February 28, 1877.
[81]Reynolds, *op. cit.*, pp. 452f.
[82]*Ibid.*, pp. 453f.
[83]Williams, *op. cit.*, p. 444.

Hampton for honest government in South Carolina, but remained true to their party on the national ticket.[84] Nevertheless, this discrepancy made plausible the suspicion either that inadequate effort for the national Democratic ticket had been made in the state or that Hampton had bargained with the national Republican Party.[85]

On January 10, while both state and national elections were in dispute, this suspicion found its sharpest expression in an anonymous letter to the Augusta, Georgia, *Chronicle and Sentinel*.[86] This letter, signed "A Tilden Democrat," undoubtedly expressed the views of General Gary. That he himself wrote it, however, though he has been suspected, is very doubtful; for his nature demanded frontal attack, and his worst enemy would hardly accuse him of cowardice, moral or physical. Gary himself continued this attack on Hampton two years later, but did so openly.[87]

The letter embodied two accusations: It asserted that throughout the canvass Hampton had shown indifference towards the national ticket and that in one specific instance near the beginning of the campaign he was "willing and anxious" to make (not that he did make) a treacherous deal with the national Republican Party. The second accusation was that Hampton had been guilty of a "repudiation of the

---

[84]There was a considerable amount of testimony on this point before the two investigating committees. For example, Republican Judge T. J. Mackey explained that he was for Hampton in the state but for Hayes in the nation. From the Democratic platform he urged other Republicans to vote as he planned to do. He quoted Hampton as saying in his Winnsboro speech that he saw no reason why supporters of Hayes and Wheeler should not support the Democrats in the state, *South Carolina in 1876*, II, 680. See Republican Judge Cooke's declaration to the same effect in his Abbeville speech in September. Sheppard, *op. cit.*, pp. 137ff., quoting from the Abbeville *Press and Banner*, September 20, 1876. Maxwell, *op. cit.*, p. 331, stated that very many Negroes who voted for Hayes in the Presidential contest supported Hampton in the state. Hampton, in *South Carolina in 1876*, I, 990f., explained that he welcomed the votes for the state ticket of Republican Negroes who would vote for Hayes as President.

[85]For general accounts see Wells, *op. cit.*, pp. 179ff.; Reynolds, *op. cit.*, pp. 445ff., and Williams *op. cit.*, p. 433. A detailed accusation against Hampton on this point is made in Sheppard, *op. cit.*, pp. 136ff. and pp. 280ff.; an answer to Sheppard's attack is in Wallace, "The Question of the Withdrawal of Democratic Presidential Electors," *op. cit.*, pp. 374ff. Sheppard answered Wallace in two pamphlets, "Some Reasons Why Red Shirts Remembered" (Spartanburg, S. C., 1940) and "An Open Letter to David Duncan Wallace, *etc.*" (Spartanburg, S. C., 1943).

[86]Augusta *Chronicle and Sentinel*, January 10, 1877, quoted in Sheppard's "Some Reasons Why Red Shirts Remembered."

[87]In an interview with the Columbia, S. C., representative of the *New York Herald*, published December 12, 1879; Hampton's answer, December 13. Cited in Wallace's "South Carolina Presidential Electors," *op. cit.*, p. 381.

plan of campaign adopted" by Gary and the Straightouts and that instead he had followed a "milk and cider, 'peace and prosperity,' conciliation of Radicals and flattery of negroes policy...."[88] There was enough truth in these "charges" to make the false accusation of treacherous purpose towards the national Democratic Party damaging to Hampton, particularly at a time when the electoral votes of one state would have given the Democratic candidate the presidency.

Hampton, it is true, was concerned with the campaign in the state much more than in the nation. He had frankly stated his attitude in a brief speech at the August convention before he was nominated:

> Men whose patriotism is beyond question, and in whose wisdom I have great confidence, think that my nomination would injure the Democratic party of the United States. If it were left with me to decide between that party and the interests of South Carolina, I would not hesitate in my choice. But I believe the success of the Democratic party of the United States will bring success to South Carolina, and that if Tilden is elected we can call South Carolina our own.[89]

Not only at that time but in speeches during the canvass Hampton expressed his major interest in the state, not the national, contest. As he put it in his Abbeville speech, "I am not in that big fight, however. I am in this little fight to save South Carolina...." It was clearly understood, too, that the state Democracy invited the votes of Republicans who would desert their party in the state to support Hampton, however they might vote on the presidency. Judge Mackey and Judge Cooke, both Republicans, spoke from Hampton's platform on that theme.[90] It was thus that the Democrats won their majority in a state with a normal Republican majority of near thirty thousand. Chamberlain's accusations of a monstrous conspiracy, on the other hand, and cries of rage from Republican "stalwarts" in the North were based on the odd assumption, frequently condemned by *The Nation*, that every Negro vote was the rightful and permanent possession of the Republican Party and that any Negro who voted the Democratic ticket could do so only through terror or fraud, an assumption that creeps into some later accounts of the election.

It was true, too, as the letter stated, that there was little cordiality between Hampton and Democratic national headquarters. Hampton's candidacy had been strongly objected to at the national Democratic

---

[88]See above, pp. 53f.

[89]Reynolds, *op. cit.*, pp. 350f.

[90]See note 84 above.

convention, where Tilden's nephew, Colonel Pelton, "urged that some man of less prominence and of more known conservative views" should be the state candidate. At the August state convention this objection to Hampton was again strongly pressed by the national headquarters. Before the August convention, too, Hampton had written to Tilden, asking advice about accepting the candidacy, but had received no answer to his letter.[91]

About the middle of September Judge Cooke and Judge Mackey had suggested the "deal" that gave rise to the accusation. Their offer was rejected. Not only Hampton and A. C. Haskell, but also J. S. Cothran, Samuel McGowan, and Robert Toombs, who were present at the conference where the offer was discussed, denied in writing that Hampton ever favored accepting it.[92] In a letter to the *Chronicle and Sentinel* on January 15, General McGowan said that "the proposition was not entertained for one moment." He added that he believed that Hampton "considered the election of the State ticket as more important than the election of the national ticket, but I know he desired the election of both." According to "A Tilden Democrat" and General Gary (who were not present at the conference), however, Hampton wished to accept the offer and to withdraw the Democratic Presidential electors; but, according to "A Tilden Democrat," did not do so for lack of time, though, it should be noted, this conference was held about seven weeks before the election.

Hampton had been aware of the complaint that his campaign would prove a burden to the party in the North; consequently on September 19 he had written to Manton Marble, chairman of the National Democratic Executive Committee, explaining his position:

> I have made the canvass thoroughly conservative, and it has been a perfect success so far. With aid from abroad the State can be carried for Tilden. There is no doubt of its being carried for our State ticket, for our opponents would gladly agree to let us elect our men if we withdrew from the Presidential contest. Of course we are most anxious to aid in the general election, but you can understand our solicitude to find out how we can best do this. If our alliance is a load, we will unload. If our friends desire us to carry on the contest as begun, we shall do so.[93]

Marble telegraphed to Haskell, "IT IS AGREED HERE THAT YOUR FRIEND'S PERSISTENCY AND HIS PRESENT EFFORTS AND PLANS ARE WISE

---

[91]Wallace, "South Carolina Presidential Electors," *op. cit.*, pp. 378f.
[92]*Ibid.*, pp. 377ff.
[93]*Ibid.*, pp. 378f.

AND ADVANTAGEOUS."[94]   Thereafter no more was done about withdrawing electors. Nevertheless, the National Committee gave no aid to
South Carolina, money or speakers, but rather collected funds for use
in "doubtful" states.[95]

Before the Electoral Commission had been created by Congress to
determine the Presidential contest, Hampton had favored a peaceful
national settlement. Even after the Electoral Commission had shown
its partisan character by its consistent division on party lines, Hampton's conviction, like that of most Southern leaders, was that, "right
or wrong," the decision of the Commission should be accepted. Hampton, of course, did not fight so earnestly for the national ticket as he
did for the state, but he certainly was guilty of no treacherous or
dishonorable practice or purpose towards national Democracy. If
he had made a straight party fight, as "A Tilden Democrat" implied
that he should, he would probably have lost on both the state and
national tickets, unless, of course, he had seized the polls by armed
force as Gary apparently wished. But who can believe that the Radicals would have allowed the counting in of Presidential electors thus
elected? With federal troops guarding the polls to be so seized, the
result much more surely would have been the counting-in of Republican electors and prolonged Republican control of the state under
military supervision. That game was the one Grant knew best how
to play. The result of Hampton's policy demonstrated its wisdom.

The real grievance behind the attack of "A Tilden Democrat," a
continuation of the old feud between South Carolina moderates and
extremists, is to be found in the second charge against Hampton, that
he rejected the belligerent plan of campaign devised by Gary and the
Straightouts before the August convention. This accusation is entirely
true. Just as the letter complained, "Though the straight-outs brought
about his nomination in the face of a tremendous opposition from
within the Democratic Party and though their courage and skill had
much to do with redeeming the State, they claim to have been practically ignored by General Hampton when he selected the State Executive Committee."[96] In other words, the August convention had accepted the "governor to coroner" aspect of the Straightout program but

[94]*Ibid.*
[95]Wells, *op. cit.*, pp. 181f. See also letter by J. S. Cothran, quoted in Sheppard,
"Some Reasons Why Red Shirts Remembered," pp. 13f., and see the *News and
Courier*, August 15, 1878.
[96]*Chronicle and Sentinel,* January 10, 1877. Gary, for example, was left off
the committee, which was composed of moderate men.

had rejected Gary's elaborate blue-print for a violent recapture of the state. The "tremendous opposition" had been more against Gary's proposed campaign of armed force than against Hampton as a candidate.

The difference between Hampton and Gary in their attitudes towards the Negro was of long standing. Just as Hampton since the end of the war had been recognized as a leader of those who sought racial harmony and cooperation, Gary had long been foremost among those who scorned any compromise with the Negro.

Gary's fundamental objection to the conciliatory canvass conducted by Hampton was forecast by Article Fourteen in Gary's detailed plan of campaign:

> In speeches to negroes you must remember that *argument* has no effect upon them: They can only be influenced by their *fears*, superstition and cupidity. Do not attempt to flatter and persuade them. Tell them plainly of our wrongs and grievances, perpetrated upon us, by their rascally leaders. Prove to them that we can carry the election without them and if they cooperate with us, it will benefit them more than it will us. Treat them so as to show them, you are the superior race, and that their natural position is that of subordination to the white man.[97]

Gary's divergence from Hampton's plan of campaign became clear, too, during the canvass. He made a few speeches from the platform with Hampton. In answer to a question about these "violent speeches," Colonel Haskell told the Senate committee that he had heard about them, "but it was always heard with great regret, and was directly contrary to the spirit of our party and to our whole campaign. I do not like to make such personal allusions, but it is a fact. His speeches were not approved in that respect. It is a great peculiarity of the man that he uses violent language very often, and he was asked to modify it."[98]

From Gary's point of view, therefore, Hampton had betrayed the true cause by his "milk and cider, 'peace and prosperity,' conciliation of Radicals and flattery of negroes policy, instead of the bold and aggressive policy inaugurated by the straight-out leaders, and thus a majority of ten or fifteen thousand votes were lost to Tilden in South Carolina, while the State ticket was only elected by a bare majority."[99]

---

[97]Simkins and Woody, *op. cit.*, pp. 566f.

[98]*South Carolina in 1876*, I, 833. See also Wallace, "South Carolina Presidential electors," *op. cit.*, pp. 375f.

[99]*Chronicle and Sentinel*, January 10, 1877.

Gary's point of view, a decade after his death, triumphed over Hampton's in the Tillman movement of 1890. Which of the two men was right depends on the judge's own point of view.

Hampton's chief political struggle during his term as governor of South Carolina was to be with the Gary faction and the Gary point of view towards the Negro. Ironically enough, however, it has been Hampton and his fellow "aristocrats" and "Bourbons" who in the North have unjustly borne much of the onus for the exclusion of Negroes from the political life of the state. The term "Bourbon" is still sometimes used in the North to characterize anti-Negro Southern politicians, though, like Tillman, such leaders usually have drawn their strength from the "wool-hat, one-gallus boys." The race struggle in the South has resolutely refused to conform to the Marxian concept of a class struggle; but, rather, it has consistently reversed that concept.[100] The Tillmans of Southern politics have always attacked "aristocrats" and "nigger-lovers" in the same breath.

---

[100]Stephen Powers, ex-federal soldier, began in January, 1868, a journey afoot that carried him from Raleigh, N. C., through Charleston, S. C., Macon, Ga., on to the Pacific. He observed closely and shrewdly the lives of ordinary men along the way, black and white. In *Afoot and Alone*, p. 28, he observes, "Tolerance towards the negro broadens with the planter's acres. Let a man be in such abject poverty as to own no land whatever, and he finds himself thrown in direct competition with the freedman and hates him; let him own but sixty acres, and work with his hired negro occasionally in the field, and he already acquires towards him a kindlier feeling." Testimony throughout *Ku Klux Conspiracy in S. C.* demonstrated this same tendency.

Chapter Six

HAMPTON'S ADMINISTRATION
1876-1878

B Y April 11, 1877, Governor Hampton had succeeded in leading to peaceful victory a people not slow to resent wrong with violence. Immediately he set himself an even more difficult task. As early as 1865 Hampton had sought a political road that both white and black could follow without strife, believing as he did that the future welfare of the state demanded political harmony between the races. At first he had appealed to the whites; but when the Reconstruction Acts had shifted political power to the Negro majority, he had urged in vain that the blacks trust those local men they knew rather than "go into the camp of strangers." When the political bias of the colored vote had become clear, however, Hampton had joined with the extremist white elements in the state in an unsuccessful effort to prevent Negro supremacy. In 1877, with political control of the state back in the hands of the whites, Hampton again sought a formula that would result in a peaceful political combination of whites and blacks without Negro domination.

In 1877 such a formula was even more difficult to find than it had been ten years before. In the hour of his triumph the Negro, in spite of the warnings of thoughtful and friendly white men like Hampton, had himself drawn a hard and fast political color-line and had maintained it for a decade. Moreover, after the Democratic victory many Negroes continued their political organization under former corrupt leaders like Bowen, Whipper, Smalls, R. B. Elliott and E. W. M. Mackey, some of whom had promptly been given federal jobs in the state.

The political habits and attitudes of the Negroes, however, were by no means the only obstacle to the kind of political amalgamation that

121

Hampton sought, for by 1877 most white men in the state had confirmed their fear and resentment of the colored man in politics. Then, too, the existence of the Reconstruction amendments to the federal Constitution with rigid federal laws for the special protection of Negro voters, the constant agitation of the "Southern problem" in the North, with attendant "waving of the bloody shirt," and the perennial recurrence of various even more stringent "force" bills in Congress, combined with the ever-present fact of a large Negro majority in the state, made most white men regard the Negro vote as a sword of Damocles, an eternal danger. Moreover, as *The Nation* wisely observed in 1878, the Negro's cause in the South was most injured by "indiscriminate Northern denunciation supported by a solid Negro vote" which forced all white factions in the South "to unite in a common pride of race."[1] Undoubtedly elimination of the Negro vote rather than any genuine cooperation with it was the political ideal of most white men in the state.

Hampton's own policy towards the Negro, which dominated most political activity in the state during the two years of his administration, was expressed in the platform of his party in 1876 and in the pledges to Negroes and other Republicans which he reiterated in his speeches throughout the canvass and reasserted in his inaugural address. These pledges were, briefly, to accept in good faith the Thirteenth, Fourteenth and Fifteenth amendments to the Constitution, to recognize the perfect equality of all citizens under the law, to make no discrimination because of race or party in administering the laws, to provide better education for black and white alike, to accept the Reconstruction debt as consolidated by the General Assembly in 1873, and to welcome the help of all citizens, regardless of race or party, in reestablishing good government.[2]

Hampton differed from many members of his party in his sustained determination to carry out these pledges in letter and in spirit. The dominant theme of the two years of his administration, one too slightly noted by most historians of this period, is his struggle to end discord in the state — between parties, between the two races, and between the North and South — and to redeem his pledges in a political atmosphere that made such redemption extremely difficult, if not impossible. The true measure of Hampton's goodness is his persistent effort during

[1] *The Nation*, XXVII (November 28, 1878), 325.

[2] *News and Courier*, August 5, 1878, said that the Democratic platform of 1878 was really Hampton's speeches of 1876.

his administration to effect conciliation where hatred had long been the rule; the true measure of his greatness is the large — almost unbelievably large — degree of success that he achieved.

Hampton's general method was to win the Negroes' trust by unfailing justice and to win their political support by giving them better security, more prosperity, and better schools than they had been able to achieve under their own leadership. By obliterating the political color line drawn by Radical leadership, Hampton expected to hold in the Democratic Party a sufficient number of the better Negroes in the state to insure continued white supremacy.[3]

But in addition to giving very real non-political advantages to the Negro, Hampton differed from most white men in his state — indeed, in the entire nation — in giving to the Negro as large a share in the actual governing of South Carolina as could be done without harm to the commonwealth. His announced policy was to appoint the men best qualified without reference to race.[4] As early as August of 1877 ex-Governor Scott told an interviewer in Ohio, "Hampton is honestly carrying out the promises he made during the campaign. He has already appointed more colored men to office than were appointed during the first two years that I was Governor...."[5] The opposition that Hampton aroused, which was led by General Gary, was based in large part on his "Negroism"; and the Tillman movement that overthrew him in 1890 (and brought to an end Negro political activity in the state) was a last phase of the counter-revolution of 1876, which Hampton and his supporters had refused to carry to its cyclic conclusion.

Thus, of course, Hampton failed in his purpose. The narrower view of Charles Sumner and Thad Stevens had embraced only the Negro's rights; that of Gary and Tillman, only the white man's rights,

---

[3]In a speech in Darlington, September 24, 1878, Hampton said, "I am striving to obliterate the colored line in politics. Be assured, my colored friends, that the colored men or the color line will never get control of this government again." Reported in the *Register*, September 28, 1878. See also the report of Hampton's speech in *Register*, October 16, 1878.
[4]For example, Adjutant General E. W. Moise asserted in his Greenville speech on August 17, 1878, that he was willing to accept for the militia any men up to standard, regardless of color. For strong objection to the appointment of Negro militia officers, see Sheppard, *Red Shirts Remembered*, pp. 216ff., citing Abbeville *Press and Banner*, August 15 and 29, 1877. See also General Hagood's speech at Barnwell, *Register*, May 9, 1878: Accord the Negro "within the ranks of the party ... every right that you accord to the white man, neither more nor less. If he is fit for office give it to him...." A few Negroes were elected on the Democratic ticket at each election until 1890.
[5]Toledo, Ohio, *Sunday Journal*, quoted by *Register*, August 28, 1877.

extreme begetting extreme. The broader vision of Hampton encompassed the rights and needs of both races, but his long effort to translate that vision into reality was defeated by the extremists of both sections: first by the Stevens-Sumner and later by the Gary-Tillman point of view. The decades following the Civil War were a time for demagogues, North and South, not for statesmen; but more earnestly and more nearly successfully than any other leader, Hampton sought a political ground where white and black could stand together in near equal numbers without hatred and strife. Perhaps there is no such ground; perhaps Stevens and Gary were right in their refusal to seek or sanction any middle way. But if Hampton was wrong in his conviction that such a way can be found, if the ultimate solution must be one extreme or the other, then the costly and fruitless struggle between the sections over the status of the Negro in the South is far from its end.

2

The quality of Hampton and the men who supported him insured the rapid return of South Carolina to the ante-bellum standard of honest, efficient, and economical government. But we are concerned not with that process but rather with the continuing division of white men in the state into hostile factions, largely on the issue of the Negro.

Two conditions dominated the politics of South Carolina during the decade following the victory of seventy-six. One was the absolute need for white unity against the Negro vote — about that, right or wrong, there was no dispute. Hampton was credited (or discredited) with saying, "An independent is worse than a Radical." Whoever said it, it was the *sine qua non* of South Carolina politics, the one guarantee against the return of Negro supremacy. The second condition during the decade was the high prestige of Hampton himself with all classes throughout the state. As the luckless Gary was to prove, open opposition to Hampton meant political death. Therefore hostility towards him and his supporters was self-suppressed. When it did break out a decade later, its bitterness and intensity amazed all observers. The ever-present threat of the Negro vote prevented, of course, the normal development of two-party government. Although Gary led the opposition to the Hampton faction, this opposition usually had to conform to the party line and vote for men and measures it did not approve.

Shortly after the departure of federal troops from the State House, Hampton called a special session of the legislature. Immediately the need became apparent for a rigid Democratic caucus to prevent indirect domination by the Negro minority in the legislature. The constricting force of absolute conformity thus became the essential but baneful condition of continued white supremacy, that is, of the prevention of a return to Negro supremacy.

The first violent disagreement arose over filling the vacancy in the Supreme Court caused by the death of Chief Justice Moses, father of the robber governor. Hampton backed the candidacy of Associate Justice Willard, a Northerner and a Republican, but an upright judge and, as senior associate justice, the logical successor to the Chief Justice. Fulfilling his pledge that his victory was not of party or race but of honest government, Hampton insisted on Willard's election. In the resultant Democratic caucus the contest was long and hard, with Gary leading the opposition in favor of General McGowan, a distinguished and popular South Carolinian. During the election itself there was the ironic spectacle of most Democrats sourly voting for Republican Willard, but the Negro Republicans, to complicate the issue, voting for Democrat General McGowan.[6]

Disagreement over the election of Willard as Chief Justice — "conciliation of Radicals" — was by no means the only point of conflict between Hampton and Gary. Hampton called a special session of the legislature for April 24, 1877, shortly after federal troops were withdrawn. In his first message to that body he strongly recommended immediate action to provide for the public debt, as he had pledged that he would do.[7]

In a speech on May 25 Gary met Hampton's request with a frontal attack on the platform and pledges of the campaign of 1876, particularly on the pledge to uphold the Consolidation Act of 1873 and the pledge of a constitutional amendment to provide a two-mill tax for the education of both races. His argument was that the Democratic Executive Committee had had no right to make such pledges and that therefore all such pledges were binding on no Democrats except the members of the committee.[8] Gary wanted to relieve the state of the debt accumulated by the Republican administrations, which he considered to be fraudulent. After extended discussion and investigation, a

---

[6]For a pro-Gary account of this election see Sheppard, *Red Shirts Remembered*, pp. 200ff.

[7]See *News and Courier*, April 27, 1877.

[8]Martin W. Gary, "Finance and Taxation" (Columbia, 1877), pp. 1ff.

compromise was agreed on which met the spirit if not the letter of Hampton's pledge in regard to the debt of the state.

In this controversy Gary bitterly attacked those who were insisting on what he called "Quixotic schemes of public honesty." In a style that Tillman was later to make famous, he lashed out at those "elegant, smooth-mannered, oily-tongued bond holders, bond speculators, bankers and members of the financial boards who have produced a magical influence upon the law makers of this General Assembly."[9]

On May 2 he had already attacked the ruling class of the state: "It was this same spirit of aristocratic exclusiveness which . . . established an aristocratic ring, who ruled the affairs of this State with such a proscriptive spirit as to drive many of her most gifted sons to seek their fortunes in the West, because the accident of birth did not place them within the charmed circle."[10]

Gary also opposed Hampton's recommendations in regard to education, particularly the education of Negroes, which *The Nation* described as "all that could be asked for by the most exacting advocate of free schools and equal rights."[11] He wanted no appropriation for education — only the proceeds of the poll tax for the public schools and no state support for the University.[12] Sheppard summarizes a speech made by Gary shortly after the close of this special session:

> Continuing his plea for economy and retrenchment in government, Gary announced his opposition to ratification of the annual tax of two mills upon all property of the state for educational purposes. Nine-tenths of this tax would be paid by white people, and three-fourths of it would be spent in educating piccaninnies. This was discrimination. He advocated education, but the impoverished condition of the people was a handicap in furnishing schools for white children. He was unalterably opposed to taxing whites to supply the teachers for blacks.[13]

Hampton, however, had his way in this regard, as on most other issues. The constitutional amendment providing a two-mill tax for the education of both races was ratified, and an act was passed

---

[9]*Ibid.*, pp. 5f. See also Sheppard, *Red Shirts Remembered*, p. 215, for Gary on the "bond ring" in his speech at Abbeville.

[10]Martin W. Gary, "Address on Bill to Regulate the Rate of Interest" (Columbia, 1877), p. 4.

[11]*The Nation*, XXIV (May 3, 1877), 258.

[12]Gary, "Finance and Taxation," p. 6. This opposition to the University points to another road that Tillman followed.

[13]Sheppard, *Red Shirts Remembered*, p. 216.

that his Excellency the Governor and the Board . . . shall . . . devise plans for the organization and maintenance of one university or school for the white and one for the colored youths of the State, which said universities or colleges shall be kept separate and apart, but shall forever enjoy precisely the same privileges and advantages with respect to their standards of learning and the amounts of revenue to be appropriated by the State for their maintenance.[14]

Thus Hampton, during the special session of 1877, established his political control of the state, and Gary, whose unsuccessful bid for the United States senatorship won by General M. C. Butler laid him open to the charge of being a disappointed officeseeker,[15] became the recognized leader of a generally unpopular opposition — unpopular more because of Hampton's high personal standing in the state than because of any grass-roots opposition to Gary's views.[16]

Thus had Gary blazed many of the trails that Tillman was to follow a decade later, when Hampton's personal power had so faded as to no longer be the dominant political factor in the state. Gary probably came closer than Hampton to expressing the convictions of a majority of the white voters of the state, and he was defeated because of his opposition to Hampton rather than because of his political views.[17] If he had lived through the next decade, he would probably have received the support that went to Tillman. As it was, he had won the fighting loyalty of those who were close to him, many of whom were to provide leadership for the Tillman revolt. And Tillman inherited

[14]*Acts, etc., of General Assembly,* S. C., Extra Session 1877, p. 315.

[15]See Sheppard, *Red Shirts Remembered,* pp. 182, 184.

[16]For example, on August 2, 1877, the *Register* warned against "Independent Democrats," though on September 14 it cited the Spartanburg *Spartan* and the Anderson *Intelligencer* as siding with Gary on the University issue. By March 3, 1878, the *Register* quotes the Batesburg *Monitor* against "ambitious office seekers" who want to supplant Hampton, men "of some ability and much cunning." On March 14 it quoted a warning from the Kershaw *Gazette* against "the opposition to Governor Hampton by a few members of the Legislature." Hampton, the article continues, "has kept his pledges, done his duty, and knows full well that extreme measures will ruin the state . . . continue to govern in the interests of all races, and our perpetuity of power is assured. But nominate extreme men, and the end no man can predict." On March 27 the *Register* noted that the entire country was praising Hampton's administration. "Only a small coterie of politicians in South Carolina form the exception, and at every opportunity the objection is interspersed that Hampton has not adhered to the 'straightout' policy adopted in 1876." As the campaign of 1878 warmed up, such comments multiplied.

[17]For Gary's able defense of his course in the legislature, see Edgefield *Advertiser,* April 25, 1878, quoted at length in Sheppard, *Red Shirts Remembered,* pp. 247ff.

from Gary not only many political convictions and the foundations for a strong party, but also an accumulation of resentment against the Hampton faction which gave the populist movement in South Carolina its unexpected tone of violent bitterness.

A speech delivered in April of 1878 by Major Tom Woodward, the man who in 1867 had plaintively asked why "Southern nigger-worshipers" like Hampton did not leave the Negroes alone and let them do their work, reveals this odd combination of objection to Hampton's conciliatory policy and of personal loyalty for Hampton himself that was characteristic of many citizens:

> When Governor Hampton . . . brought to bear his great influence against men like McGowan . . . in favor of a Carpetbagger, I thought then, and I think now, that he did violence to the sentiments of Straight-out Democracy and went beyond any pledges I heard him make in his brilliant and unparalleled campaign.
>
> When he appointed Gleaves, the vile Negro mulatto ex-president of the most infernally infamous Chamberlain Senate, to the position of Trial Justice, I said then, and say now, that he temporarily lowered the standard of Democracy. . . .
>
> When the Legislature, through what I now believe to have been the influence of Governor Hampton . . . seated the dirty, thievish blackguards of the Mackey House, I asked, "In God's name, are these the fruits of the Democratic victory. . . ."
>
> When again, Mr. Chairman, the good citizens of this county . . . prayed a Democratic Legislature not to seat the member, Prince Martin, who was known to be the most corrupt and scoundrelly Radical in the state, and found themselves checkmated, as I believe, by Governor Hampton, I cried aloud. . . .
>
> But, sir, despite all this, and more that can be alleged, I honor and love this man. I know, personally, that he possesses those magnetic attributes of head and heart which will endear him to this people, and will keep the honor of the old Palmetto State and the welfare of its citizens uppermost in his mind.[18]

3

In his efforts at achieving conciliation — an end to old animosities — Hampton was faced not only with dissent within his own party and long-standing racial and party hatreds within his state; he had to reckon with honest suspicion in the North as well as with the conventional bloody-shirt waving of the extreme Radical press. His restraint and good judgment had gained him much favorable opinion, and the

---

[18]*Register*, April 5, 1878. Quoted also in Sheppard, *Red Shirts Remembered*, pp. 245f.

justice of his administration won him many more friends and admirers in the North.

Many Northern papers, Republican and Democratic, were praising his work during 1877 and 1878.[19] His address at the Winnebago County Fair, Rockford, Illinois, in September, 1877, was a forthright and manly plea for an end to sectional animosities,[20] and somehow he struck the right note to awaken an enthusiastic response throughout the country.

During the spring of 1878, E. P. Clark, managing editor of the Springfield, Massachusetts, *Republican*, visited South Carolina, travelled over the state, and wrote a shrewd, well-informed estimate of Hampton's accomplishments during the first year of his administration. Dated Columbia, April 10, and copied in the Columbia *Register* for April 19, 1878, his account serves both as a statement of what Hampton had done and as evidence of well-informed liberal Northern Republican reaction to his administration.

Clark first called attention to the changes "nothing less than wonderful" which had resulted from a year of Hampton's administration. A year before, the people of South Carolina had been "divided into two opposing parties — the Democrats flushed with their long-delayed victory, the Republicans embittered by their final defeat and genuinely distrustful of the future." Racial relations, too, were dangerously tense. "The negroes saw at last the success of that party which they had been sedulously taught for years would signalize its accession to power by relegating them back into slavery...." The close of the year, Clark continued, "finds everything absolutely changed. The political excitement which had long kept the state in turmoil has disappeared, and complete peace prevails. Financial distrust has given way to a feeling of growing confidence.... The relations of the two races have steadily improved, till a far better feeling is already reached than was ever before known."

Although he considered himself "somewhat familiar with the course of events," Clark was surprised at the universal Republican admiration for Hampton that he found in the state. He made a careful survey of Republican opinion, Up-country and Low-country, Negro and white,

[19]See, for example, *The Nation*, XXIV (April 26, 1877), 241; *ibid.* (May 3, 1877), 258; *ibid.* (May 24, 1877), 302 and 306; *ibid.* XXVI (January 24, 1878, 49). See also many favorable comments quoted in the *Register* and *News and Courier* from the press of the nation, particularly after his speech at Winnebago, Ill., in September, 1877. See, for example, *Register*, September 19, 1877.

[20]Quoted in *News and Courier*, September 18, 1877.

high and low — judges, postmasters, the Collector of Internal Revenue as well as the Negro "I might chance to have for my driver," so that he had "sounded all phases of Republican feeling."

> The concurrent testimony of all these Republicans, white and black, is the most sweeping commendation of Governor Hampton's course and the most implicit confidence in the man. Said Dr. Boseman, Postmaster of Charleston, "You may quote me as expressing absolute confidence in Governor Hampton and entire satisfaction with his course. . . . He has kept all his pledges." Said Postmaster Wilder of Columbia, "Governor Hampton has done everything we could have asked. . . ." The striking testimony of these colored men is reechoed by their white associates.

Clark continued his political analysis with the observation that Hampton's "victory over the malcontents in his own party has been no less complete." For the benefit of his Northern readers he explained the division of the Democrats in the state into two factions, the Gary Group (whom he calls Bourbons[21]), "which looks regretfully and longingly at the past," and the Hampton group, "which cuts loose from that past and fixes its eye on the future."

> The Democratic Bourbons were willing enough to have Hampton talk fair in the canvass . . . but did not expect the official to live up to the promises of the candidate. The result was that when Hampton commenced trying to enforce the liberal policy he had promised, opposition began to spring up in the Legislature and the press. . . . But, as time went on, the Governor steadily gained strength, and the malcontents lost power, till finally the opposition in the Legislature was completely crushed out, and a Democratic caucus, just before adjournment, gave Hampton a unanimous endorsement — at the same time, by the way, that all the Republicans in the Legislature joined the other party in supporting a resolution introduced by one of the leading Republicans heartily commending the Governor. Meanwhile the opposition to Hampton among the Democratic press has been swamped by the irresistible tide of popular approval, till now it is a unit in his favor. . . .

Clark gave Hampton full personal credit for the greatly improved political climate of South Carolina. "The success that Governor

---

[21]As early as May 24, 1877, *The Nation* liked what it had heard and seen of Hampton and was convinced that "he means to do what he can to keep his pledges." But because of the opposition of "Bourbons" in the Up-country, *The Nation* doubted "whether he will be able to sustain himself," XXIV, 306. This meaningless term, "Bourbon," still heard at times in the Northern press, did yeoman service for Tillman, by him, however, applied to the Hampton, not the Gary faction.

Hampton has thus achieved ... can only be described as one of the greatest personal triumphs of the present generation. Indeed, I do not recall another case in our history where a man has made within the brief space of a year so complete a conquest of the party that opposed him, at the same time that he has retained, and even strengthened, his hold on his own original followers." Moreover, Clark attributed Hampton's success to the rightness of his character and policies rather than to mere political adroitness. Hampton, Clark decided, "is inspired by an overruling desire to serve the state.... The conviction of his sincerity is wide spread, and strongest among those who have watched him most closely. As one eminent Republican ... remarked, 'I don't think it is simply policy. It *is* policy, of course, but I give Hampton the credit of being inspired by patriotism....'"

Prophetically Clark discerned that the essential weakness in Hampton's policy lay in this dependence on Hampton himself.

> Popular enthusiasm for the man has finally suppressed all open opposition to his course, but there is a large element of the party which at heart does not like Hampton's liberal course. I have ... put this question to a good many people: "How ... many Democrats ... would support any other man carrying out the same policy?" ... One very intelligent Republican said, not one in ten; several agreed in saying, not a majority. Fair-minded Democrats took this latter view....
>
> Weighing all the evidence, I think it fair to say that a majority of the Democrats have supported the man rather than the policy for the past year, and that any other person who had attempted to embody similar ideas would have failed to carry the party with him.

In the light of these observations Clark made a long-time prognostication regarding race relations in the state that time and chance — or, perhaps, inescapable necessity — proved to be over-optimistic.

> At the same time a year of Hampton's policy, however and whyever accepted, has had an immense educative effect.... There can be no reasonable doubt that another term of Hampton would carry the good work beyond the possibility of ever being undone....[22] Every Republican whom I questioned on this point expressed grave apprehension whether Hampton's work could as

[22]In a speech in Spartanburg on August 15, 1878, General Hagood made this same point about the Negro: "Two more years of good faith and justice, and we would have the confidence of the colored people in every county of the state. We must obliterate the color line in politics, and invite the colored man into our ranks the same as we invite the white man, and accord him every right we accord the white man."

yet be taken up and carried through by any other man. . . . Intelligent, far-sighted Democrats admitted that there would be greater opposition to Hampton's policy if Hampton were to drop out, but they regard it as too manifestly the policy of the future to be ever overthrown. . . . He [Hampton] recognizes the situation very clearly, and is too true a friend of the state to leave the government if he feels there is any danger of harm thus coming to the cause he represents. . . .

Clark was more fortunate in his prediction of the outcome of the state election scheduled for the following November:

He will be elected Governor in November with as near an approach to unanimity as was ever seen at an election in the United States. It is hard to tell which party will support him with more enthusiasm — for it is already settled that the Republicans as well as the Democrats will support him. . . . a colored Republican club held a meeting the other evening, and the sentiment in favor of supporting Hampton was simply unanimous; there was absolutely not a dissenting voice. And this is the universal feeling among Republicans throughout the state, black and white.

Ironically enough, the fulfillment of Clark's prediction, a vote of 169,550 to 213 in favor of Hampton, has been accepted as evidence of a thoroughly bulldozed Negro electorate.[23] And similarly with Clark's further prediction, not quite so accurate, that "the Negro enthusiasm for Hampton will of course carry a considerable colored vote over to the Democratic legislative ticket as well, and it will need no cheating or returning board to elect a majority. Where the Republicans do elect men, they will be given their seats. . . ."[24]

As Clark's account indicates, then, Hampton's policy had not only established confidence and good will within the state, but also it commanded the respect of well-informed, fair-thinking Republicans as well as Democrats in the North.

4

One further reconciliation was essential if Hampton was to secure for South Carolina the complete peace for which he was striving. Throughout the eight years of Grant's administration there had been virtual war between the President of the United States and the white men of South Carolina; Hampton wanted peace and mutual trust. Fortunately he discovered in President Hayes another moderate and

---

[23]See Simkins and Woody, op. cit., pp. 547f.
[24]This entire letter, dated Columbia, April 10, was published in the Register, April 19, 1878.

patriotic statesman, and very soon the two men trusted one another so well that they could work together for the welfare of the state and nation in spite of outraged extremists in both sections. In South Carolina Gary, of course, urged that the people "unseat the usurper" — that is, President Hayes — thus, oddly enough, taking the same ground as Radical extremists like Conkling. Hampton, he said, was guilty of "consorting with, aiding and abetting one Rutherford B. Hayes in his usurpation upon the Presidency of the United States."[25] Hampton, on the other hand, defended Hayes: "He did not propose the Electoral Commission, and is not responsible for its results. The Democratic party is responsible for the Electoral Commission.... The Commission gave Mr. Hayes the office and the Democrats were a party to it, and in accepting it he did as any American citizen would have done, and it is well for us that he did...."[26]

The cordial relations that Hampton soon established with the President, which benefited both the state and the nation, caused the Gary faction to suspect some venal deal between the two men, and Sheppard in *Red Shirts Remembered* advances every possible argument for such a conspiracy.[27] If one accepts the theory that there was fighting war between Democrats and Republicans, then Hampton *was* guilty of communication with the enemy. If, however, one admits that there was a state of peace, Hampton and Hayes were acting together for the best interests of all concerned. Gary, like extreme Radicals in the North, probably sincerely believed — or felt — the former alternative; Hampton and Hayes accepted the latter.

The story of Hampton's relations with Hayes is an essential part of an account of the Governor's administration. The accusation that early in the election of 1876 Hampton had been "willing and anxious" to betray the Democratic Party in the Presidential race in return for a guaranteed victory in the state has been disputed above.[28] Furthermore, Hampton had no part in the much-misunderstood "bargain" between Southern Congressmen and friends of Hayes. The point of the Southerners' agreement is not that they "sold their Party down

---

[25]Speech at Spartanburg August 15, 1878, quoted in the *Register*, August 17, and *ibid.*, March 2, 1878. See also Gary's comment at Darlington on September 25, quoted in the *Register*, October 1.

[26]Hampton's speech at Anderson, quoted in full in the *Register*, March 29, 1878. In this same speech Hampton denied any "shadow of a bargain with Mr. Hayes or anyone else, looking to the seating of the Governor of South Carolina."

[27]Sheppard, *Red Shirts Remembered*, p. 136, p. 141, p. 186, p. 189, p. 199, p. 240, p. 284, and *passim*.

[28]See above, pp. 116ff.

the river," but that they agreed to abide by the decision of the Electoral Commission, a method of reaching a decision between Tilden and Hayes that the Democrats, North and South, had strongly supported. When the blind partisanship of the commission became clear, however, extreme Northern Democrats in the House wanted a filibuster to prevent a decision by Inauguration Day. The Southern Democrats blocked such a maneuver. The very probable alternative was war, and Southerners of that generation knew too well the cost of civil strife.[29]   Hampton agreed that his party should abide by the commission's decision. Indeed, on December 23, 1876, even before Congress had decided on the Electoral Commission, he had written to both Tilden and Hayes that it was the "firm and deliberate purpose" of the people of South Carolina "to condemn any solution ... that involves the exhibition of armed force or that moves through any other channel than the prescribed forms of the Constitution, or the peaceful agencies of law."[30]

Before Hampton and Hayes met face to face, each distrusted the other; afterwards, there is every evidence of mutual confidence and respect. Hampton's three letters to Hayes which immediately preceded this conference[31] are therefore coldly formal, so much so, in fact, that Hayes' biographer complains of "questionable taste."[32]

There is no record of what transpired in the first meeting between the two men, but they took each other's measure and liked what they

---

[29]See H. J. Eckenrode, *Rutherford B. Hayes, Statesman of Reunion* (New York, 1930), pp. 216ff.   When the inside story came to light in 1878, *The Nation* commented, "Under such circumstances the 'bargain' was simply an engagement on the one side not to interfere further with the settlement by Congress of the Presidential dispute in the manner which had already been virtually agreed to; and on the other, in consideration of this, a promise that the United States troops should not be longer used to bolster up the rotten Republican 'machines' in Louisiana and South Carolina. . . . If any 'bargain' in politics is allowable, certainly this one was. . . ." XXVII (August 1, 1878), 61.

[30]On December 23, 1876, Hampton sent similar letters to Hayes and Tilden, asserting his claim as Governor of South Carolina and his determination to "leave its vindication to the proper legal tribunals"; as for the national problem, he asserted, "it is their [the people of South Carolina] firm and deliberate purpose to condemn any solution of existing political problems that involves the exhibition of armed force. . . ." I quote from a copy of Hampton's letter to Hayes.   His letters to Hayes are preserved at the Hayes Memorial Library, Fremont, Ohio. Mr. Watt P. Marchman, Director of Research, has generously sent me copies of these letters.   All with political significance are printed in Appendix C.

[31]See note 30.

[32]Charles R. Williams, *The Life of Rutherford Birchard Hayes* (Boston, 1914), p. 56n.

saw. At last, moderate and courageous men, North and South, men with the power to implement their convictions, were consulting as to the status of the Negro in the South. As has been true throughout the course of our history, such men could find essential agreement on every important point; tragically, though, the course of our history has rarely given them a chance. The Sumners and Stevenses, the Garys and Tillmans — not the Hamptons and Hayeses — all too often have forced political action on the Negro question by the concentrated intensity of their convictions. For just a little while after 1877, moderate men controlled the destiny of the Negro in South Carolina. The result merits most careful and thoughtful consideration; it has received only the scantiest attention.

In a letter immediately following the conference, Hampton wrote to Hayes what he conceived to be the essence of their agreement:

> ... you sincerely desire to see a peaceful and just settlement of the questions which are distracting our people and injuring so seriously the material interests of our State and I trust that you are equally convinced of my earnest wish to aid in accomplishing this happy end.... if Federal troops are withdrawn from the State House, there shall be on my part, or that of my friends no resort to violence.... With the recognition of the perfect equality of every man before the law, with a just and impartial administration of the laws: with a practical secure exercise of the right of suffrage: with a system of public education which will open the services of knowledge to all classes we may hope to see our State soon take the position to which she is entitled.[33]

This mutual trust and respect between Hampton and Hayes meant much in the settlement of vexing problems between state and federal governments during the next two years. That Hampton and Hayes could work together with confidence and understanding made far easier South Carolina's hard road back to true statehood.

A need for understanding soon arose. About eight hundred South Carolina Democrats were under federal indictment as a result of the activities of United States Attorney Corbin during the campaign of '76.[34] Since an "ironbound" test oath excluded from federal juries "all

[33]See Appendix C for the entire letter and others from Hampton to Hayes. Three weeks later (April 22) Hampton could write, "The papers have shown you what policy I have advocated here, and I am glad to say that it is strongly sustained by the people. You have seen, too, that events have followed since the removal of the troops from the State House, precisely as I indicated to you, would be their course. I therefore hope, that we shall have now enduring peace and good government in the state."
[34]See *Register,* April 4, 1878.

who voluntarily participated in rebellion," such juries were virtually limited to Negroes and carpetbaggers. Trial before these juries under the federal election laws then in operation was no light matter. Moreover, three South Carolinians were still in federal prison as a result of the Ku Klux trials, and many others were prevented from returning to the state for fear of arrest.

On the other hand, many Republicans who had participated in the state Reconstruction government were manifestly guilty of various crimes, and a few had been tried and convicted. Most people in the state quite naturally wished for and expected the prompt punishment of numerous Radicals, particularly those whom the current investigation showed to be worst offenders.

Hampton knew, however, that such trials would arouse old animosities and would set off hysterical demands for retaliation in the Radical press, which was objecting even to the investigation of frauds, conducted by a committee with a Republican chairman, as a violation of Hampton's pledges and as political persecution.[35]   In his Anderson speech in March, 1878, Hampton publicly stated his purpose:

> I think the wisest statesmanship is amnesty. I want the cases in the United States courts against our people dismissed – the Ku Klux, Hamburg and Ellenton and revenue cases. If we give general amnesty, we shall have amnesty for our own people."[36]

Negotiations to that effect had already begun ten months before in a telegram from Hampton to Hayes, dated May 11, 1877, accompanying a concurrent resolution of the General Assembly. Hayes' reply, dated May 12, contained a guarded agreement that "a general amnesty should extend to all political offenses except those which are of the gravest character."

A long letter from Hampton to Hayes, marked "personal" and delivered by South Carolina's Attorney General Youmans (dated March 25, 1878), indicates how far Hampton's policy had progressed during the intervening ten months.

Hampton began his letter with an explanation of what he had done to minimize prosecution of Radical offenders in the state. He had sponsored in the General Assembly "a resolution authorizing me to 'nol pros' any of the cases which are regarded as political" since it "is very desirable that all agitation should cease in the state" and he desired "as full amnesty as can be granted." There had been "but three

---

[35]See extract from *New York Times* quoted in *Register* September 1, 1877.
[36]*Ibid.*, March 29, 1878.

trials of cases of this sort, though there is evidence sufficient for two hundred," and Hampton had arranged for the pardon of the three men convicted.

In return, Hampton urged Hayes,

> You can strengthen my hands in carrying out the policy of amnesty greatly by the exercise of executive clemency in behalf of those who are charged with violation of the U. S. laws and I appeal to you to do so. . . . I feel sure that you could do nothing which would be more grateful to our people, than to end at once all this irritating source of anxiety.   Public opinion would then sustain me in the course I wish to pursue here and all political causes of dissension would be removed.

Hampton explained to Hayes the difficulties that had faced him during the first year of his administration: "My position has been a very difficult one, for besides the opposition to me from political opponents, I have had to meet and control that of the extreme men of my own party. That this latter has been bitter, the enclosed article published here will show you, but I can crush out all opposition, if you can grant amnesty to our citizens."

As an indication of what his policy could accomplish in the state, Hampton reviewed his accomplishments towards securing peace and good will:

> It is very gratifying to me to learn that I have gained the confidence of the Republicans here, by my administration of the government, for this proves that justice has been done.   A Republican Senator offered resolutions endorsing the course I have pursued, saying that I had redeemed every pledge made, and every Republican in the legislature voted for them.   The colored people urge me to be a candidate for the next term, and assure me that there shall be no opposition if I will run.   We have peace throughout the state, and goodwill between the races is growing up.   As you have seen, the people and the volunteer troops respond readily to my orders to assist the Revenue officers, and the laws are enforced everywhere.   You have been largely instrumental in bringing about these happy results, by your policy to the South, and I feel therefore that I can approach you in full confidence that you will sympathize with my objects.   We have in this, a common end in view, and if you will trust my judgement in the matter, you can accomplish a great work, one that will do much towards pacification.

Not until 1884 were all legal knots formally and publicly untied, but by the middle of June, 1878, Hampton could write to a friend that "your brother and all others concerned with the Ku Klux troubles, can return to the State, with perfect safety. Mr. Hayes promises that no action shall be taken against any of these parties. . . . It is not desirable to make any public announcement as to the action of the President just at this time. . . ."

The state *quid* for this federal *quo* made a distasteful pill for South Carolinians to swallow. The idea of refraining from prosecuting the bribe givers and bribe takers, the forgers and embezzlers who had bankrupted the state, was a hard one to take, and many and loud were the complaints.[37] But Hampton had his way — surely, all things considered, the best way. The letters from Hampton to Hayes reveal how difficult politically for both men this "exchange of prisoners" really was, and how impossible it would have been without the mutual trust that they had achieved.[38]

A potentially troublesome conflict between state and federal governments over the collection of internal revenue — "revenuers" in the mountains — and acts of illegal violence by both moonshiners and revenue officers, also yielded with a minimum of excitement to the personal communications between the two men, thus removing another dangerous source of hatred and strife.[39]

Early in the fall of 1877 President Hayes toured several Southern states to promote reconciliation, the first such gesture since the war, the federal government having been more prone to send troops than Presidents into the South. Hampton accompanied the President, who introduced him to a Kentucky audience as "a noble and patriotic man." As Hampton said of Hayes, ". . . he serves his party best who serves his country best. . . ."[40] Hampton and Hayes worked faithfully together, one in Washington and the other in South Carolina, to end the animosities of war and Reconstruction. Both men jeopardized

---

[37]Though the *Register* (March 25, 1878) asserted, "The State can afford to be magnanimous . . ." most other papers wanted the leaders, at least, prosecuted. See, for example, Winnsboro *News and Herald*, "too much amnesty," quoted in the *Register*, May 26, 1878. Even the *Register* had to swallow hard to take the whole program, see May 30, 1878.

[38]See Appendix C, communications dated May 11, 1877; from Hayes, May 12, 1877; June 24, 1877; September 25, 1877; March 25, 1878; June 14, 1878; June 14, 1878 to Colonel Bratton; August 5, 1878; August 7, 1878; letter from D. T. Corbin to Hampton, August 13, 1878; August 13, 1878, "The clemency which you have exercised has produced the most favorable results . . ." and July 2, 1880.

[39]See letters dated January 9, 1878; March 25, 1878; June 14, 1878; July 15, 1878; July 31, 1878; August 13, 1878; and Resolutions from Spartanburg, July 26, 1878.

[40]C. R. Williams, *op. cit.*, II, 249ff.

their political fortunes in the service of their country, and the result was good.

5

During the spring of 1878 political interest began to stir in anticipation of the state elections in November. Two questions dominated political speculation: What would be the attitude of the Negro majority towards the now dominant whites? What would be the theory and practice of the whites towards the Negro?

There was soon fairly general agreement as to what the Negro Republicans would do. Early in March the Augusta, Georgia, *Chronicle and Constitutionalist*, a new name for the old *Chronicle and Sentinel*, was saying, "It is an open secret that the most influential members both black and white, of the Radical party in South Carolina, recognizing the beneficent influence of Governor Hampton's wise, moderate, and just administration, have determined to make no factious opposition to his reelection."[41]

In August, J. J. Wright, a Radical Negro who had resigned under pressure as associate justice of the State Supreme Court shortly after Hampton's election, told a reporter of the *Philadelphia Times* that Hampton "has kept every pledge he has made, and on the seventh of next November he will be re-elected Governor almost unanimously. He will get nine-tenths of the colored vote. I speak advisedly on that point. There is not a decent Negro in the state who will vote against him."[42] Soon the consensus of the state was that the state ticket would have no difficulty.[43]

---

[41]Quoted in *Register*, March 15, 1878.

[42]Quoted from Philadelphia *Times* in *Register*, August 21, 1878.

[43]Such action was implied, of course, in the resolution approving his administration referred to by E. P. Clark (*ibid.*, April 19, quoted above) and by Hampton in his letter to Hayes dated March 25, 1878 (see Appendix C). See also Yorkville *Enquirer* quoted in *Register*, March 22, 1878; Hampton has won the "confidence of a vast majority of the colored Republican voters.... We doubt whether the Republican party will attempt to place a candidate in the field, preferring to support one ... serving them regardless of party, race...." See also E. P. Clark, *loc. cit.* "It is hard to tell which party will support him with the more enthusiasm—for it is already settled that the Republicans as well as the Democrats will support him...." See also Orangeburg *Times*, quoted *ibid.*, June 16, 1878, "The colored people in Orangeburg, as well as elsewhere in our State, have been very favorably impressed with the liberal and consistent course Governor Hampton has pursued, and ... he will receive the entire colored vote of Orangeburg...."

There was considerable fear, however, that, nominating no state ticket, the Republicans would seek to dominate the legislature by concentrating on the county tickets. Warnings were issued in various editorials for the whites to keep busy and to countenance no bolters or "independents."[44] Late in March in his speech at Anderson Hampton said, "... we cannot afford to be divided on State matters. Your county is the first to adopt the system of primary elections — be governed by its results, and allow no independents to run. . . ."[45]

The Union Republican Party Convention met at Columbia early in August. The old corruptionist wing of the party was in control of the convention, and C. C. Bowen, a not too delectable specimen of white Radical politician, was elected president.[46] Early in the meeting, however, a strong pro-Hampton resolution was offered: ". . . we recognize in the course of Governor Hampton the fulfillment of all the liberal pledges made by him in the last canvass, the discharge of all the duties of his high office without favor or distinction because of race or condition, the repression of crime, the cessation of violence and the impartial administration of law." This resolution was strongly supported, and then it was violently attacked by Bowen in a bitterly denunciatory speech. It was rejected, but nevertheless the convention refused to nominate a state ticket, thus virtually ceding the election to the Democratic state nominees. This convention, dominated by irreconcilable Radical extremists, also included in the Republican platform a condemnation of Hampton's administration and the assertion that he had not kept his pledges, one of the very few contemporary assertions to that effect. Opposition to Hampton in the state was thus confined to the two opposite poles: Bowen and Gary — extreme again meeting extreme.

Various Republican clubs in the state, however, repudiated the convention,[47] and throughout the state Republican county conventions

---

[44]As early as August 2, 1877, the *Register* gave a strong warning of the need for unity against the Radical vote in the counties. See also *ibid*, March 16; the *Register* urges county primaries, which were then being initiated in place of the old-style county conventions, and were being discussed throughout the state. The *Register* advised that these primaries be "virtually elections as far as we can make them so." "Division in our ranks," it continues, "are most to be feared and would prove fatal."

[45]Quoted in the *Register*, March 29, 1878.

[46]This convention reported in the *Register*, August 8 and 9. For brief sketch of Bowen's record, see Chapter II, note 65.

[47]For example, in Barnwell, reported in the *Register* September 7, 1878, and Richland, *ibid.*, October 16. The Richland Republican County Convention passed resolutions disapproving the platform of the state convention on the

were very scantily attended, many placing previously nominated Democratic county candidates on their tickets, five out of nine, for example, in Marion.[48] A month before the election E. P. Clark's prognostication was clearly justified, "The Negro enthusiasm for Hampton will of course carry a considerable colored vote over to the Democratic legislative ticket as well, and it will need no cheating or returning board to elect a majority."[49]

The second question — what would be the theory and practice of the whites towards the Negroes — found no such simple or complete answer. The very success of Hampton's program proved an embarrassment, for Negroes came over to the Democrats in such numbers as to threaten Negro domination within the party.

As the St. Louis *Republican* put it, "The South Carolina whites . . . are evidently puzzled over the new question how to allow the blacks to join their party without permitting them to rule it." Gary's county, Edgefield, characteristically solved this problem by not allowing Negroes to vote in the county primary at all, a practice that under Tillman became general; but in 1878 it was condemned by the Hampton faction, and in that year no other county followed suit.[50]

In his Blackville speech on July 4, Hampton condemned this practice:

> You went to the colored people and told them that their rights
> would be protected . . . You appealed to them to come out and
> help you work out the redemption of the State. They came by
> hundreds and did help you. . . . And now would you turn your
> backs on them, and, after trying for ten years to convince the

ground that Hampton had "performed his pledges to the people, and, as far as possible, protected all classes of citizens. . . ." Fred Nix, Jr., a prominent Negro politician, said at the Barnwell Republican County Convention, ". . . if the Democrats of Barnwell County will put such men in nomination as will cause the colored people to feel safe in their rights, the Republicans will put out no ticket. I speak for the party, and I know what I say." Quoted by *News and Courier*, August 7, 1878.

[48]*Ibid.*, October 2 and 3, 1878.

[49]E. P. Clark, *loc. cit.*

[50]The *Register*, July 11, 1878, thought that Edgefield "made a mistake in restricting primary elections to the whites . . . they are making the race issue squarely and definitely, which is in conflict with the platform . . . two years ago. . . . Edgefield stands alone so far in this respect, and all the indications are that the state will again make the fight upon the line of success achieved in the last campaign." See also Newberry *News*, quoted in the *Register* May 26, 1878. The Negroes "have already learned that they are just as safe under Democratic rule as Republican, that is, Democratic rule as expressed and exemplified in the policy of such a man as Hampton, though we doubt if they would feel safe if the spirit of the Edgefield resolutions should become dominant."

colored man that his true interests lay with the Democratic party, would you say, "Now we have no use for you. You shall not vote even at the primary election."? If this be the policy of South Carolina, then am I sadly mistaken in the people of South Carolina and the people are mistaken in me, because *I can carry out no such policy as that.*[51]

It soon became clear, of course, that the state was divided into irreconcilable factions on the basis of the political status of the Negro, just as it had been at the constitutional convention of 1865. Now, however, the matter could not be "ignored *in toto.*"

Major Theodore Barker, who had been prominent in the campaign of 1876, explained this division in the New York *Herald*:

> There exists some divergence of opinion among the Democrats as to the best line of policy to be pursued in these exceptional counties [those with strong Negro majorities]. Hampton, Hagood, and others recommend a liberal policy, reiterating the platform of 1876 and endeavoring by argument and persuasion to induce the negroes to abandon their carpetbaggers and go in with the Democrats. . . . This agreement plan is impatiently rejected by the extreme straightout Democrats, who advocate a bolder and more self-reliant line of policy . . . and some of them go so far as to avow that they prefer the defeat of the entire Democratic ticket rather than make any concessions to the Republican enemy.[52]

At his March speech in Anderson before the campaign got under way, Hampton had firmly enunciated his principles:

> If the State Convention, when it meets, stands squarely on the platform of two years ago, and nominates a conservative ticket, I say that the Republicans will not put a ticket in the field. . . . By doing justice to all men, our colored people will stand by us. . . . One of the pledges of that platform was that all men were equal before the law. I can say that I have favored no race, party or people in the administration of the laws of the State. I defy any man to place his finger upon a single pledge of that platform, and say that I have not carried it out.

In his July speech at Blackville he expressed the same point of view even more strongly, warning his listeners not to "harken to extreme men who tell you that the glorious platform of 1876 was very well as a promise to be kept only to the ear and broken to the heart. . . ." "You can carry the election," he continued, *"by standing squarely on*

[51]Quoted in the *Register,* July 7, 1878.
[52]Quoted *ibid.,* August 4, 1878.
[53]*Ibid.,* March 29, 1878.

the platform of 1876.... You can succeed by carrying out the principles you have solemnly initiated, and *in no other way.* Do that and if I can aid you again I'll do it.... If you are to inject into it any new and abhorrent principles ... I should have to decline. I would give my life for South Carolina, but I cannot sacrifice my honor, not even for her."[54] This position Hampton maintained without qualification throughout the canvass.[55]

Hampton also repeatedly warned that no fraud or violence would be supported by his administration. In his Blackville speech he told the people of the state that if they made a practice of countenancing fraud, before many years "they would not be worth saving." The administration was pledged to a "fair count" "... and I tell you the men you have placed in power would *cut off their right arms before they would violate their pledges....*" That Hampton meant what he said is evidenced by the fact that in the special elections of 1877 Republicans of Sumter were seated by the house when four ballot boxes were stolen by the Democrats.[56]

Other political leaders carried Hampton's message. Speaking at Barnwell in May, General Hagood said, "Invite every citizen to aid you in the combat for equal rights to all and good government for the whole.... Obliterate the color line in politics. Invite the negro to the ranks of the Democracy as you invite the white man...."[57] Most newspapers in the state reasserted these Hampton principles,[58] though there was a certain amount of sharp dissent."[59] Democratic county

[54]*Ibid.*, July 7, 1878.

[55]See *ibid.*, August 13 for speech at Edgefield; August 17, speech at Spartanburg; September 20, speech at Greenville.

[56]*House Journal, S. C., 1877-78*, pp. 166ff., 180.

[57]*Ibid.*, May 9. See also *ibid.*, August 17. See also Democratic speeches reported in the *Register* and the *News and Courier* throughout the summer and fall, for example, James A. Hoyt in the *Register*, March 6, 1878, and General John D. Kennedy, *ibid.*, October 5, 1878.

[58]The *Register* and the *News and Courier* were particularly faithful and reasserted Hampton's thesis throughout the canvass. Their quotations from the smaller county papers of the state show the same conviction. See, for example, Kershaw *Gazette*, in the *Register*, March 12 and April 6; Barnwell *Sentinel* in *ibid.*, March 16; Yorkville *Enquirer* in *ibid.*; Newberry *News* in *ibid.*, May 26; Orangeburg *Times* in *ibid.*, June 16.

[59]The Augusta *Chronicle and Constitutionalist* frequently expressed the Gary-faction point of view. See quotations in *Register*, March 15, 1878; April 18; September 3. The Winnsboro *News and Herald* at times sounded pro-Gary; see quotations in the *Register*, January 4 and May 26, 1878. In Sheppard, *Red Shirts Remembered, passim.*, see numerous pro-Gary sentiments quoted from Abbeville *Press and Banner.*

conventions throughout the state, too, adopted resolutions endorsing Hampton's policy, with, however, strong objections here and there.[60]

Early in April, 1878, the Augusta *Chronicle and Constitutionalist*, which frequently expressed the Gary-faction point of view, warned that a policy of conciliation of Negroes was a return of "fusion," which had so signally failed to effect any good results during Reconstruction.[61] A few days later the same paper gave much stronger expression to the Gary policy:

> Republican and race majorities can be overcome everywhere as they were overcome two years ago in Edgefield, Abbeville, Aiken, and Barnwell. But the fight must be made as it was made in those counties. The straightout policy must be adopted, and a bold and aggressive campaign inaugurated. If this is done, the Republican vote in the present Legislature can be wholly eliminated from the next General Assembly.[62]

This determination to eliminate the Negro from politics rather than to assimilate him into the political activity of the state was a distinguishing feature of the Gary, and later, Tillman policy as opposed to Hampton's theory and practice.

Answering the Augusta paper, the *Register* asserted that Hampton's policy "won the victory two years ago. . . . If there is an 'aggressive policy' which does not approve the means hereby indicated, it is time that the fact was trumpeted in some quarter inside the State."[63] Gary, soon accommodated. At the Edgefield county convention he made what came to be known as a "straightout Edgefield speech." He told the story of 1876 with emphasis on intimidation and fraud, and he denounced what he called "Fusionists." "The only fear that I have for Democracy," he said, "has been created in the last Legislature by those who were formerly 'Fusionists,' and who now style themselves 'Conservative Democrats.' They have usually been found voting with the

---

[60]For a detailed account of the Abbeville convention, where such objections were raised, see Sheppard, *Red Shirts Remembered*, pp. 231ff. For Colonel William Wallace's dissent from unqualified endorsement because of "undue influence" by Hampton on the election of Chief Justice Willard and the Circuit judges, see the *Register*, March 25, 1878.

[61]Quoted in the *Register*, April 13, 1878.

[62]Quoted in *ibid.*, April 18, 1878.

[63]*Ibid.*, April 13.

Radicals."[64] Gary reiterated his stand throughout the canvass, with ever-growing emphasis and bitterness.[65]

This controversy soon developed into an argument of the who-won-the-war type. Since the victory of 1876 was won by Hampton's appeals for Negro support, the Hampton faction argued, obviously such an approach to the Negro was not only right, but also expedient. As General Hagood expressed it,

> ... while the federal ticket was defeated the state was redeemed. Our meed of success was due to the wise conservatism which framed the platform on which we fought. Without the Republican vote that was attracted to our state ticket, it ... would at that time have been assuredly defeated. ... to my mind there is but one solution to this question, and that is to mean what we say and do what we have promised. ... Obliterate the color line in politics.[66]

The Gary faction changed its line of attack from that in the Augusta *Chronicle and Sentinel* of January 10, 1877. At that time it was claimed that Hampton *lost* the state for Tilden by his "milk and cider, 'peace and prosperity,' conciliation of Radicals and flattery of negroes policy,

[64]Edgefield *Advertiser*, April 25, 1878, quoted at length by Sheppard, *Red Shirts Remembered*, pp. 247ff.

[65]See Sheppard, *Red Shirts Remembered*, pp. 259ff. See also reports in the state press of Gary's various speeches, particularly that at Greenville on August 17, "... time has proved the fusionists to be wrong and the straightouts to be right ... the Democracy of Edgefield ... should be the Democracy of South Carolina"; and at Aiken in August, "a Gary-[George] Tillman Edgefield speech, red hot and determined," The *Register*, September 5. As for Gary's bitterness, see particularly his interview in Edgefield *Advertiser*, October 17, 1878, quoted in the *Register*, October 18. Gary claimed that he had been "gagged" by the State Democratic Executive Committee. For the answer by the chairman of the committee, General Kennedy, see the *Register*, October 22.

[66]In speech at Barnwell, quoted in the *Register*, May 9, 1878. See also Newberry *News*, quoted in the *Register*, May 26; "If we set an example of pure steadfast integrity, he [the Negro] will give us little trouble ... white supremacy is essential, but ... when we assert our supremacy through brute force and lynch law we sink ourselves to the level of half-civilized people." See also Orangeburg *Times*, quoted in the *Register*, June 16; see General E. W. Moise, speech, *ibid.*, August 20. Sixteen thousand Negroes voted for Hampton; "... we must be conservative and secure the colored vote. We can only win it by kindness. ..." The *News and Courier* had many editorials on the subject; for example: "The [Democratic] platform makes it one of the gravest offences of the Radicals that they should have 'arrayed race against race,' and that is what General Gary contemplates. ... The condemnation of fusion and coalition with the Radicals has no bearing on the race question. The Democrats do not go to the negroes, but ask

instead of the bold and aggressive policy inaugurated by the straight-out leaders."[67] During the canvass of 1878, however, the Gary faction claimed that it had *won* the state for Hampton by its "aggressive" policy and that thereby it had demonstrated the only way to deal with the Negro vote.[68]

Thus began the tradition of a prideful telling of inordinate fraud and intimidation in the election of 1876. This practice, initiated by Gary and brilliantly carried on by Tillman, has had considerable influence on historians of the period. As Chamberlain said in 1901, "The historian here is no longer compelled to spell out his verdict [of an election won by violence] ... he needs only accept the assertions, even the vaunts, of many of the leading figures in the canvass since the canvass was closed."[69] What Chamberlain neglects to say, of course, is that these "assertions" were made with very definite political purpose, not just to air the truth. This constant reiteration of heroic extremes of fraud and violence, too, has strongly influenced the general attitude of whites in the state, not only towards the campaign of 1876, but also towards any participation of the Negro in politics. Characteristically Radical and Democratic extremists agreed in asserting excessive violence, extreme again meeting extreme.

The Democratic state convention in August renominated the entire state ticket and readopted the platform of 1876, with the addition of a

the negroes to come to them ... the rule of the Edgefield Democracy, excluding negroes from voting at the primary elections, is, as we conceive, a violation of the declared principles of the Democratic party." The *Register*, too, strongly supported Hampton's policy throughout the canvass.

[67]See above, pp. 155ff.

[68]For example, at Aiken, Gary said, "It has been found useless, owing to their [Negroes'] inferior intelligence, to appeal to their judgment...." *Register*, September 22, 1878. Hampton, of course, disputed Gary's claim that the policy of reasonable appeals to the negroes had been futile. "I believe that it was the conservative character of the last campaign, as contradistinguished from what he calls an 'aggressive' one, that enabled us to carry the state." The *Register*, September 20, 1878. Both methods, of course, played their parts; Gary's in Edgefield and, less so, in Aiken, Barnwell and Abbeville (or so the Gary faction claimed— see the *Register*, April 18, quoting Augusta *Chronicle and Constitutionalist*). Hampton's policy was followed throughout the state, with undoubted influence on the counties claimed by Gary. M. C. Butler, for example, was very active in Edgefield, and he followed Hampton's line after the August convention. General Hagood was the leader in Barnwell; he was one of Hampton's strongest supporters throughout the campaign, and he asserted (*Register*, May 9, 1878), "Our meed of success [in 1876] was due to the wise conservatism...."

[69]Chamberlain, "Reconstruction in S. C.," *op. cit.*, p. 480.

plank warning against "fusion" with Radicals. It was an all-out Hampton convention, but the Hampton-Gary feud continued. As the Augusta *Chronicle and Constitutionalist* said about the first of September:

> ... the Democrats of South Carolina will get into an ugly snarl among themselves if they do not have a care. It is not so much a matter of interest to them at present who saved the State as it is to keep the State safe.... Let each county ... fight out its own peculiar battle in its own way. What is good for Edgefield might not be profitable for Beaufort.... It is impolitic, therefore, for one county to force issues upon another.... At all events, bad blood and intemperate discussion are sure to follow these assaults and dictations. ...[70]

This shrewd suggestion of an evasion of central authority over the method of dealing with the Negro presages what was to happen in November.

Some further hint may be found, too, in a speech later in September at Barnwell by George Tillman, the older brother of Ben.

> ... most of the counties in the eastern and southern part of the state failed to carry the election of 1876, first, by the folly of adopting the North Carolina [meaning, of course, Hampton] plan of treating Radical speakers with Christian forbearance and Chesterfield politeness, and, second, by inflating the negroes with *entreaties* to vote the Democratic ticket.... In the coming contests the indications are that several of the eastern and lower counties are taking front on the Georgia line [meaning Gary] to do battle against Radicalism, and that they are done with the sociable, courteous, and Christian policy. ...[71]

Meanwhile, Hampton was pleading with the people of the state to hold his policy. The *Philadelphia Times* commented on one such plea by Hampton.

> There now comes a report of his speech at Greenville, S. C., before a Democratic meeting, in which he made one of the most eloquent and cogent pleas for justice to the negro that has ever been uttered, North or South. The occasion was a recently published card of General Gary, a fire-eater and a Democrat boasting a considerable following, who has taken ground in favor of what he calls the Mississippi plan.... Governor Hampton boldly takes issue with this doughty warrior, replying to him by denouncing any such policy as not only inconsistent, but contemptible. If General Gary meant to say that an effort should be made to carry the state by a "shot-gun policy," Governor Hampton wants it un-

---

[70]Quoted in the *Register*, September 3, 1878.
[71]Quoted in the *Register*, September 29, 1878.

derstood that he takes no stock in it. To use his own burning
words, "In the name of civilization and all that has been honorable
in South Carolina; in the name of our State and our God I protest
against any resort to violence or wrong or any adoption of the
shot-gun policy. We cannot do evil that good may come."[72]

Hampton, then, and the State Democratic Committee urged and
sought to enforce an obliteration of the color-line in politics; Gary
urged and sought to promote the obliteration of the Negro from politics. In seeking to spread his gospel, for example, he asked the state
committee to assign him speaking dates in the "lower and eastern
counties" (where Negroes were in large majority), but his request was
denied.[73] Undoubtedly, however, Gary-faction plans were made that
did not get into the papers or come to the ears of the state committee,
particularly in communities where large Negro majorities and sur-
viving Radical leadership threatened the continuation of white control.
As *The Nation* summarized the issue after the election in November:
"The Hampton policy proposes the political coalition of the whites
and blacks on equal terms and in good faith; the other the exclusion
of the blacks by force or fraud from all share in the government."[74]

6

The election, of course, was a Democratic landslide, as Clark had
predicted seven months before that it would be. Hampton was re-
elected by a vote of 169,550 to 213. The number of Republicans in
the state senate was reduced to five; in the house, to three. Twelve
Negroes were elected to the General Assembly in all, equally divided
between Republicans and Democrats.[75]

The Radical press took these results as adequate proof of a Negro
population terrorized and cheated into political impotence, as have
some historians.[76] The *New York Tribune*, for example, related on
November 29 that Dr. Cooke of Massachusetts, President of the State
College for Negroes, had been terrorized into voting Democratic. But
Dr. Cooke answered, denying that his vote had been influenced by
intimidation, but rather, that after watching Governor Hampton's
course for two years, he believed that the Governor was "a true friend

---

[72]*Ibid.*, September 28.
[73]*Ibid.*, October 18 and 22.
[74]Quoted in *The Nation*, XXVII (November 28, 1878), 325.
[75]Taylor, *op. cit.*, p. 292.
[76]*Ibid.*

of the colored man, and is doing vastly more for his elevation in this commonwealth than any Northern man could under bayonet rule."[77]

Undoubtedly, however, in the Gary faction's effort to eliminate the Negro from politics, there was a greater degree of fraud in 1878 than in 1876, when federal troops, federal marshals, and numerous special deputies, as well as Republican control of election machinery, made violence or fraud much more difficult and dangerous. Many tales of fraud that properly belong to 1878 and subsequent elections probably attached themselves to 1876, according to the normal tendency of legends to concentrate on a single point. Particularly the practice of stuffing the ballot boxes with "tissue ballots" probably was first followed by the Democrats in 1878, though many tales of their use are told of 1876. The trick of using these ballots depended on control of the count, and in 1876 that control was in the hands of the Republicans.[78].

Hampton's policy was the official program of the party, but Gary's advice was followed here and there where communities, probably with considerable justification, had little faith in the Negro majority's urge to vote for candidates satisfactory to the whites on the county tickets. On the other hand, it is also true that the great majority of Negro votes were cheerfully given to the Democrats, particularly on the state ticket, but also in many counties. The mass of Negroes in the state were probably well satisfied with the result, as their actions and words during the canvass would indicate.

The question arises, had Hampton kept his pledges to the Negroes? Taylor, in *The Negro in South Carolina*, says, "Hampton himself was presented as the clean man who guaranteed justice and equality to each race, but promises to the Negroes, many of whom voted for Hampton, soon turned out to be mere words."[79] Simkins and Woody,

---

[77]Quoted in *The Nation*, XXVIII (January 2, 1879), 1.

[78]The law required that if too many ballots were in a box, ballots should be drawn out blindly until the correct number was reached. Dropping in many extra tissue-thin ballots, those who controlled the count could add to their party vote by drawing out only those that were normally thick. For a detailed account of their use in 1878 see Edward Hogan, "South Carolina Today," *International Review*, VIII (February, 1880), 114f. For Hampton's discussion of their use in 1878, see *Congressional Record*, 46th Cong., 2nd Sess., Vol. X, Pt. 4, 3755. He said that they had been used in 1878 in eight out of thirty-three counties, which he regretted. They were introduced into South Carolina elections by Radical E. W. M. Mackey in 1870. There is no evidence at all that they were used by Democrats in 1876. The fact that Republicans then controlled the count indicates how wrong is the tradition of their widespread use in 1876.

[79]Taylor, *op. cit.*, p. 312.

in *South Carolina during Reconstruction,* say, "After 1877 there was no disposition to keep Hampton's promise that he would protect the political rights of the Negroes."[80] Contemporary reports, however, from white and black, North and South, Democrat and Republican, tell another story.[81]

It cannot be claimed, of course, that every single pledge in every single particular was kept absolutely during Hampton's administration. Rarely, however, have political pledges been better kept by a leader or kept under more difficult circumstances. It seems that a wiser course than a blanket indictment of Hampton would be to admit his effort to keep his pledges, and then to study closely wherein and why he succeeded and failed.

Too rarely has a political experiment such as his been tried for the nation to be able to afford ignoring its results and lessons. As *The Nation* summarized his accomplishment, "The State is, therefore, in a fair way to show by experience that its method of dealing with the negroes is the right one, and wiser than any plan followed in other states. . . . For these reasons South Carolina is today in a more promising, prosperous, and satisfactory condition than any other cotton state."[82] Dr. Cooke told a convention of Northerners in Charlotte, North Carolina, that "in no state at the North do the colored people enjoy superior rights to those enjoyed by them at present in South Carolina."[83] Despite ten years of Reconstruction with its heritage of fear, hatred, and suspicion, Hampton in two years accomplished more for both races and more nearly harmonized the two than has any other leader, North or South. But, as will be seen, he had not found a complete solution to the politico-racial problem of the state.

---

[80]Simkins and Woody, *op. cit.,* p. 547.

[81]See above, Chapter VI, *passim.,* particularly the testimony of such Republicans as ex-Governor Scott, ex-Associate Justice J. J. Wright, who was forced by Hampton to resign on charges of drunkenness, and the editor of the Springfield *Republican,* E. P. Clark, and the numerous state Republicans from whom he quotes. Note, too, the complaints of Democrats like Tom Woodward and Gary, and the resolutions of Republican clubs in the state. See also the public assertions and exhortations of state leaders like Hampton, Johnson, Hagood, and Moise. See also New York *World,* quoted in the *Register,* August 29, 1878, ". . . for the Governor cannot be accused of failing in the slightest degree to perform the pledges. . . ." See also *The Nation* throughout 1877 and 1878, particularly on education, XXV (August 16, 1877), 104f. and 388; XXVI (January 24, 1878), 49; XXVII (July 5, 1878), 48.

[82]*The Nation,* XXVII (September 5, 1878), 140.

[83]Quoted in *The Nation,* XXVIII (January 2, 1879), 1.

Chapter Seven

THE COURSE OF COUNTER-REVOLUTION
1878-1895

1

ON November 9, two days after the election, Hampton was hunting deer in the Wateree swamps a few miles from Columbia. He was riding alone on a young, badly broken mule when, according to one of many versions, the bridle broke and the animal, having become unmanageable, crushed the Governor's leg against a tree, breaking it in two places, the large bone protruding through the flesh. Unable to move and signaling for help with his rifle and horn, Hampton lay for hours before he was found, a road cut through the underbrush, and a wagon brought for carrying him to Columbia. Then came a long, agonizing ride over bumpy roads before he could be given the medical attention that he needed.[1]

The *New York Times*, perhaps having exhausted its credulity in accepting at face value the various tales of "outrages" purveyed by carpetbaggers in the South for a sympathetic Northern reading public, was not to be caught napping by the news of Hampton's accident. Under the caption "Mule Fraud" the *Times* explained that the report was a political trick designed to save Hampton from having to sign "fraudulent election certificates," though why he would ever be expected to sign any election certificates the *Times* did not explain.[2]

A thread of irony runs through Hampton's life. He had spent years and a fortune building a vast cotton-producing system only to have it swept away by war just as it was completed. After fighting for four years in Virginia, he had returned to South Carolina just in

---

[1] *News and Courier,* November 9, 1878; the *Register,* November 9, 1878.
[2] Quoted in *The Nation,* XXVII (December 5, 1878), 343.

151

time to see his city and home burned by Sherman. Following the war he had devoted his influence to racial and sectional conciliation, only to be selected in 1868 by the Northern press as the archetype of aristocratic fire-eater who threatened a new rebellion. He had been in the thickest part of the fighting throughout the war and had received several wounds, but not until 1878 did he lose a limb. By all accounts he was one of the finest horsemen in the South, yet the accident occurred as he rode a lowly mule. During his youth and young manhood he was accustomed to great wealth, but he ended his life in poverty. His hard-won policy of racial conciliation was completely repudiated by the state, and he himself was turned out of office; yet shortly after his death he was triumphantly chosen as one of the two South Carolinians for Statuary Hall. As happened to Lincoln, the man was honored but his policy was reversed. Most ironic of all, however, Hampton is best remembered in South Carolina as the man who led a slashing, fighting campaign to drive Negro-carpetbagger rule out of the state. He has been absorbed into the legend.

Perhaps, too, there is irony in the very timing of Hampton's accident. If he had honestly determined to lead an all-out fight for "a free election and a fair count," as he had solemnly asserted that he would, the crucial period was that immediately following the election of 1878; but for five months he lay helpless from his injury, his very life despaired of. His leg was not amputated at first; but serious infection set in; a month after the accident his leg was cut off just below the knee.

On the very day of this operation the legislature elected Hampton to the United States Senate to succeed "Honest" John Patterson. The day before the election Hampton had dictated a brief statement to a friend in the house, refusing to announce himself as a candidate for an office "which should neither be sought nor declined," but consenting to serve in whatever capacity the legislature should decide.[3]

How Hampton regarded his elevation to the Senate can only be conjectured. He must have known that his struggle for real political cooperation between the races was, under the circumstances, all but hopeless. He would not appeal to the Negro vote against his party, and the rank-and-file of that party, though they had more confidence in Hampton as a man, in their own convictions were probably closer to Gary. The ante-bellum leaders like General M. C. Butler, General Johnson Hagood, General James Conner, and Colonel A. C. Haskell,

---

[3]*News and Courier,* December 11, 1878.

of course, could be trusted to give him their loyal support. If he had remained as Governor, his high sense of moral duty and his conviction that his personal honor was pledged almost surely would have made him continue the fight — with what results no man can say.[4] The Gary-Tillman faction feared that he and his supporters would turn to the Negro vote if their power were threatened; but in 1890, when A. C. Haskell bolted and appealed to the Negro vote, he got little white support. Hampton repudiated Haskell and voted the party ticket for Tillman.[5] Consistently Hampton had since 1867 considered white solidarity an absolute requisite, though he must have understood the cost of such enforced conformity, being by nature an independent man himself.

Perhaps an honorable way out of the obligation was a relief to an old man worn with suffering and strife. Yet he did not seek that way out, nor did he entirely surrender his purpose; but, rather, he continued to use his influence against the "red-hot Straightouts." In 1880, for example, when for a time it seemed that Gary might be Democratic nominee for governor, Hampton was reported to have threatened to resign his seat in the Senate and run for governor himself unless a conservative like General Hagood were nominated.[6] Gary, who had violently attacked Hampton in an interview for the *New York Herald*, carried only ten delegates to the convention, and Hampton's candidate, Hagood, was unanimously nominated. Gary died in 1881, and his faction of the party was without notable leadership until Tillman recalled it to a very vigorous life a few years later, when Hampton's faction had become "the State House Ring."

Whether or not Hampton welcomed escape in his change of post, undoubtedly many of his party were relieved to see him safely away. Theirs was the extremely difficult task of maintaining white control in a state with a considerable Negro majority, a majority with a strong tendency to vote as a bloc. Moreover, for ten years the Negro had been accustomed to political supremacy, not only in the state government, but also in most counties and towns. Under these circumstances, to maintain white control without some restriction on the black vote —

---

[4] Two months after the election Hampton expressed the wish that a proposed Congressional investigation into the election would be thorough. "No good citizen," he said, "no wise man, no good patriot can afford to cloak and cover up fraud or corruption in elections." *News and Courier*, January 20, 1879.

[5] Frances Butler Simkins, *Pitchfork Ben Tillman* (Baton Rouge, La., 1944), pp. 163ff.

[6] Sheppard, *Red Shirts Remembered*, p. 279.

by fraud, intimidation, or law — was probably impossible for any length of time, no matter how much improved the Negro's lot might be under white government. Hampton had not solved the politico-racial problem of the state. Perhaps he could not do so because the Reconstruction Amendments and the temper of Congress at that time made difficult, if not impossible, the limitation of the Negro vote by law; yet some kind of limitation was essential if the disaster of Negro supremacy was not to be repeated.

On April 15, 1879, Hampton left Columbia for Washington. At Charlotte, North Carolina, where he received an ovation, he briefly stated his attitude towards his new job.

> I am going to Washington to represent my people in the National Council. I trust that while I shall never forget that I am a Southern man, I shall always recollect that I am an American Senator; that I shall always be able to subordinate a partisan spirit to the bringing about of that reconciliation which we all so ardently desire and need. Since I first laid aside my sword I have striven for peace between the lately contending sections of the Union, and I believed then, as I believe now, that such a state of feeling will bring prosperity and happiness to our land.[7]

Hampton had scarcely taken his seat in the Senate when he was attacked by a senator from Minnesota who had dug up the old newspaper charges of the campaign of 1868 to throw at the new senator from the South. Hampton patiently explained that he had not threatened a new civil war in 1868 and also that he had never participated in or approved of the Ku Klux Klan.[8] As late as 1880, too, John Sherman linked Hampton with the Klan in a nationally publicized address.[9] These attacks are typical of a failure of many Northerners to recognize the efforts of those Southerners most concerned for the Negro's welfare and of their refusal to differentiate between friends and enemies of the Negro in the South — a fruitful source of sectional misunderstanding and of political profit-taking. As The Nation observed in May of 1877, "The Negro has been made into a fetish for the worship of sentimentalists and impracticable idealists, who have too often sacrificed to it common sense and honesty alike."[10]

In spite of his inauspicious beginning, Hampton was soon warmly

---

[7]Register, April 17, 1879.

[8]Congressional Record, 46th Cong., 1st Sess., Vol. IX, Pt. 2, 1358.

[9]John Sherman, Recollections of Forty Years in the House, Senate, and Cabinet (New York, 1895), II, 780ff.

[10]The Nation, XXIV (May 24, 1877), 302f.

liked in the Senate. There was no occasion for the power of leadership that he had shown during the war and Reconstruction; but his generous nature and his earnest desire for understanding between North and South won him close friends on both sides of the aisle. Throughout his twelve years in the Senate, however, he strove against restrictive legislation directed against the South. One of his first speeches was against the "test oath" which in South Carolina virtually limited juries in federal courts to Negroes and carpetbaggers;[11] and his last speech was against a new "force bill" designed to control Southern elections. Indeed, the anti-Southern propaganda attending the agitation for this "force bill' of 1890, as so often before and since, strengthened the power of extremists in South Carolina and was an aid to Tillman in overthrowing Hampton's moderate supporters, extreme as usual begetting extreme.

2

From the time of his accident Hampton had little direct influence on policy towards the Negro in South Carolina; but with various modifications and a greatly diminished fervor, his policy rather than Gary's was followed by state administrations for a decade. To implement Hampton's policy, however, was more difficult for his successors than it had been for Hampton himself. In the first place, they did not have Hampton's deep, long-held convictions on the subject; nor did they, like Hampton, have the power over masses of men to lift them above their inclinations and immediate self interest. Moreover, as E. P. Clark had concluded in the spring of 1878, ". . . the majority of the Democrats have supported the man rather than the policy. . . . Hampton's work could [probably not] as yet be taken up and carried through by any other man." Whether or not two more years of Hampton, as Clark thought, would have established a permanent white policy towards the Negro and whether, as Hagood thought, it would have consolidated Negro confidence in white leadership must remain another unanswered *if* of history, but it seems unlikely.

Not only did the attitude of white men in the state make the problem more difficult, but also that of the Negroes. Their confidence even more than that of the whites was centered solely in Hampton, who more than any other man in the history of the state had caught their imagination and won their trust. As one ex-Radical Negro put it, he didn't "believe the Almighty made Hampton like He made other men.

---

[11]*Congressional Record*, 46th Cong., 1st Sess., Vol. IX, Pt. 2, 1779-1781.

He just dropped Hampton down from Heaven!"[12]   Since, therefore, the blacks had little confidence in the Democratic Party as such — nor did the activities of the Straightouts increase their feeling of security — soon the threat of the old Negro majority voting as a bloc began to reassert itself.   One Radical Negro preacher, for example, taught his congregation, "The Bible recognized only two political parties, the 'Publicans and the Sinners."   The political color-line had not been obliterated, only obscured.

Since Hampton's successful splitting of the Negro vote could not be maintained, after 1878 white men in the state were increasingly faced by the old dilemma: on one horn was the return of Negro supremacy; perched uncomfortably on the other horn were three possible ways of limiting the Negro majority — by law, by fraud, or by violence.   Against the return of Negro supremacy there was final and complete determination and unanimity; only thorough military occupation could have brought it about.   As for the three methods of limiting the Negro vote, all were tried in various ways and with varying degrees of success, though a hostile federal government watched all three suspiciously — a federal government that called the tune but did not have to pay the piper.

With an obviously Republican eye on the coming Presidential election, Edward Hogan, correspondent of the Boston *Herald,* published a rather inaccurate account of politics in South Carolina in the *International Review* for February, 1880, about a year after Hampton was elected to the Senate.   He recognized the difficulty faced by the state with its legally protected Negro majority.   "I doubt," he said, "if the men in the North, who ask the whites of this section so reproachfully and bitterly why they refuse the negro what the law has granted him, would obey the law themselves if they could come down here . . . or even know what the demand implies."[13]   He was, moreover, favorably impressed by Hampton personally; but he accepted a Gary-faction interpretation of state politics and rejected that of Hampton:

[12]*Register,* September 15, 1878.

[13]Edward Hogan, "South Carolina To-day," *International Review,* VIII (February, 1880), 112.   Said Chamberlain in this connection, "I do not know of so many as one white man, of good character and of responsible standing, who has lived at the South five years since 1876 and been identified with the interests of both races, who has not become and is not now a hearty supporter of the mass of the Southern whites in their relations to the Negro. . . ."   Letter to Springfield *Republican,* August 27, 1904, quoted in "Present Phases of Our So-Called Negro Problem," p. 27.

"With all his uprightness and integrity of character – and in my opinion he is, 'as men go,' one of the most perfect gentlemen in the North or South, – Wade Hampton's exposition of affairs is a lamentable defense of his party."[14]

Hogan, therefore, greatly overestimated the power of Gary's faction, asserting that it was virtually the party. As for Hampton, Hogan said further, his "views and the policy of his government have been so tinctured with moderation, and are in such marked contrast with the ideas of his party, that he is in a measure alienated from it. . . . It is doubtful if he would to-day receive the nomination for governor were he to become a candidate."[15] So sure was Hogan of the power of Gary's faction that like Clark he ventured a prophecy: "I think that if the Democrats are successful the future State government will be an extreme one. . . . Nearly all the candidates thus far mentioned are extremists as opposed to Hampton. . . ."[16]

Hogan was mistaken about the extent of Gary's power, and therefore, unlike Clark, very much mistaken in his prognostication. Gary was overwhelmingly defeated in the forthcoming convention, and the conservatives ruled the state for another decade. His estimate indicates, however, as compared with the better-informed one of E. P. Clark two years before, an increasing opposition among the whites to the policy of the conservatives, particularly in their political treatment of the Negro.

This article reveals, too, an increasing discontent among the Negroes.

> . . . [the Negroes] are disposed to be very friendly with Hampton . . . but they affect to believe that he was bulldozed by his party. It is said by them that he was sent to the United States Senate to get him out of the way of the extremists, and prevent his interference with their plans. . . . When it comes to an election or to any exercise of the rights of suffrage, the party steps in and takes charge of things. The negro is bulldozed and intimidated, and his vote is thrown out of the ballot-box after he has contrived to get it in. This done and the object obtained, the Butlers and Garys retire, and all is once more moderation and conciliation.[17]

A year after Hampton left the state, then, his policy of holding the whites in unity while he split the Negro vote was visibly failing; and ever present was the threat of the Negro majority, backed by the

---

[14]Hogan, op. cit., p. 107.
[51]Ibid., p. 108.
[16]Ibid., pp. 115f.
[17]Ibid., pp. 108f.

power of the federal government. Intimidation and fraud were obnoxious to many South Carolinians, and besides were not too successful. In the election of 1880, for example, George Tillman was denied a seat in Congress because of fraud and intimidation, a Negro, Robert Smalls, being seated.[18] White men in the state began to seek a means of limiting the Negro vote by law.

Such a reduction, of course, presented real difficulty since limitation on account of race was expressedly prohibited in both the federal and state constitutions. Moreover, to change the qualifications for voting required a change in the state constitution of 1868, which specifically provided universal manhood suffrage without material restrictions.[19] To get an amendment to the constitution contrary to the will of the Negro majority was virtually impossible since the Negro vote was at that time by no means so completely controlled as some writers have implied. A solution had to be found within the scope of legislative enactment.

The approach to a solution was suggested in 1881 by Edward Mc-Crady, Jr., later to gain distinction as an historian, in a small pamphlet "The Necessity of Raising the Standard of Citizenship." Having pointed out that the problem of an unrestricted Negro vote was forced on the state against the will and judgment of its white citizens, he gave a frank analysis of the *status quo.*

> In this condition of our people with race arrayed against race, under the name of political parties, and under our election law *as it now stands,* in order to secure the control of the government to ... the white people, but one of two courses is open to us, that of violence or fraud. It would be futile to rely on violence to secure a good government. ... But, by all means, let us hazard violence, be the consequences what they may, rather than rely upon fraud. Violence will, undoubtedly, lower us in our position as a civilized people. ... But violence will not degrade us as fraud will.[20]

McCrady's suggested solution was very simple — to require each voter to sign his name, an elementary educational qualification.[21] His suggestion soon was elaborated into the more complex "Eight-Box

[18]*Biographical Congressional Directory With an Outline History of the National Congress, 1774-1911* (Washington, 1913), p. 1002.

[19]Simkins and Woody, *op. cit.,* p. 97.

[20]Edward McCrady, Jr., "The Necessity of Raising the Standard of Citizenship" (Charleston, 1881), pp. 13ff.

[21]*Ibid.,* p. 17.

Law," which was enacted by the 1881-82 session of the legislature. A Negro historian of the period characterizes it as follows:

> By this law disfranchisement was accomplished in one of the several ways. The citizen was required to register under specified conditions, failure of which deprived him of suffrage. An elector was required to vote at the precinct designated by his certificate, failure of which prevented him from voting. No elector removing from one residence, precinct, parish, ward or county was permitted to register or vote without a transfer of registration. The law also provided separate ballots for the governor and lieutenant-governor, other state officers, circuit collectors, state senator, members of the House, county officers, representatives in Congress, and presidential electors. These ballots were to be cast in separate boxes. This was the eight box device which confused the less intelligent voters [i.e. illiterates]. According to the Republican State Convention of 1882, this law contemplated disfranchisement of the four-fifths of the Republicans in the State.[22]

After 1882 the threat of the Negro majority in the state ceased to exist, though in Beaufort County Negroes were still in political control and seven Negroes were elected to the legislature in 1884, one a Democrat; eight in 1886, two Democrats; five in 1888, two Democrats. Most of these Negroes were much superior to those who had represented their race during Reconstruction.[23]

Thus, from 1880 to 1890 the conservative faction in the state practiced a policy towards the Negro that was a compromise between that of Hampton and that of Gary. The "full vote" promised by Hampton was abandoned as it became evident that the color-line in politics could not be obliterated, but an honest effort was made to avoid the violence and fraud practiced by the Gary faction, and the conservatives did not seek to eliminate Negroes from all participation in politics, but only to eliminate the danger of a return of Negro supremacy. Throughout the period Negroes had representatives, although few in number, in the state legislature and in Congress to assert their point of view.

3

Revolutions and counter-revolutions rarely stop at a half-way point. As the decade of the eighties advanced, discontent with the ruling faction increased at the grass roots, though at first the death of Gary

---

[22]Taylor, *op. cit.*, p. 293.
[23]*Ibid.*, pp. 294ff.

and the success of the Eight-Box Law minimized surface manifestations. As D. D. Wallace put it,

> The economic distress of the '80's made agitation easy.... Ben Tillman was organizing a farmer's movement that could easily become a political machine. It was propelled by the hopes and indignation of men who had been taught by the Grange that government could relieve their ills, the brooding resentments of the devotees of Gary, the ambitions of a younger generation of shrewd politicians, and the passionate belief of many in the enthronement of the common man.[24]

Tillmanism was therefore the resultant of many component forces, not the least of which was the concentrated animosity and driving power of Martin W. Gary. "The Democracy of Edgefield," said Gary in 1878, "should be the Democracy of South Carolina."[25] The mind of Ben Tillman, a brilliant and intense young farmer of Edgefield County, was fertile ground for Gary's seed: animosity towards the old ruling families,[26] resentment towards the Low-country, distrust of the financial interests in Columbia and Charleston,[27] personal rancor against Hampton and his followers who had kept Gary from high office, and an abiding determination never to accept the Negro as a political equal[28] — even opposition to the University of South Carolina[29] and friendship with Thomas G. Clemson.[30] Under Tillman's leadership Edgefield did dominate the state.

The aspect of Tillmanism that has attracted most attention is Tillman's relationship to the populist movement throughout the South and

---

[24]Wallace, *History of South Carolina*, III, 337.

[25]In speech at Greenville, August 17, reported in the *Register*, August 20, 1878.

[26]See above, p. 126.   See also Simkins, *Pitchfork Ben Tillman*, p. 87.

[27]See above, p. 136.

[28]See above, *passim*, and Hogan, *loc. cit.*, "... General Martin Gary typifies this latent sentiment of opposition to the Negro in the following words: 'The North does not know what it asks of us.   No laws or regulations can overcome instinct allied to public opinion.   God never made the two races to unite on any ground of equality, and they never will.   The white man is the negro's superior, and as such he must remain.   The negro cannot be made my political or my social equal by any of your laws, and I will never acknowledge him as such. This is a white man's country, and I want it to remain so."

[29]See above, p. 126.

[30]Sheppard, *Red Shirts Remembered*, p. 260 and p. 318.   Clemson's will, leaving his estate for an agricultural college, was an important issue in Tillman's first campaign.   For Martin W. Gary's influence on Tillman and the Gary family's part in the Tillman movement, see Simkins, *Pitchfork Ben Tillman*, pp. 86f.   Said Tillman, "I was his staunch friend, conferred with him often, and was one of his lieutenants in Edgefield."   See also *ibid.*, pp. 188f., and Sheppard, *Red Shirts Remembered*, pp. 316ff., "... the new voice from Edgefield urged the reforms for which Gary fought."

West, though his heritage from Gary gave even that part of his movement an individual flavor. His influence on Negro-white relationships in South Carolina is more germane to this study. "Tillman," says his biographer in an article in the *Journal of Southern History*, "was dissatisfied with his predecessors' contradictory and unrealistic exposition of South Carolina's attitude towards its Negro majority. He cherished fervently the belief that the Negro should be held in subjugation...."[31]

Here again we find the demon of the absolute that rode Gary and Sumner, though in opposite directions. Each extremist was consistent, the one in asserting that the Negro, whatever his moral or intellectual equipment, was a full-fledged citizen; the other in asserting that whatever the Negro's moral or intellectual equipment, he was no citizen at all. Any middle road between these extremes can always be made to appear "contradictory and unrealistic." "It is believable, therefore," Simkins concludes, "that the modern reactionary attitude towards the Negro dates from Ben Tillman and represents one of the most significant ways in which he influenced American life."[32]

It seems unlikely that the federal government ever again can or will reassert Sumner's absolute in South Carolina — certainly not without a major blow at the American system of government. It seems equally unlikely that Tillman's absolute can be indefinitely maintained. However "contradictory," then, a workable middle road might be or seem, it is hardly so "unrealistic" as the absolute application of either extreme. The energies of both races, therefore, would be better spent in seeking such a way than in asserting either absolute.

Tillman was elected Governor of South Carolina in 1890. In his inaugural address he described his victory as the "triumph of democracy and white supremacy over mongrelism and anarchy, of civilization over barbarism...."[33] An important aspect of the Tillman movement was the fact that it was the last phase of the counter-revolution begun in 1876 — the elimination of the Negro from South Carolina politics.

Hampton and his supporters opposed Tillman in 1890 as they had Gary in 1878.[34] But in 1890 Hampton was no longer the idolized leader

[31]Francis Butler Simkins, "Ben Tillman's View of the Negro," *Journal of Southern History*, III (May, 1937), 161.

[32]*Ibid.*, p. 174.

[33]Simkins, *Pitchfork Ben Tillman*, p. 171.

[34]As late as 1895 Tillman estimated his "Conservative" opponents at 40,000. He urged the danger that they would unite with the Negroes against the "Reformers" as a justification for seeking to further cut down the number of Negro voters. *Journal of the Constitutional Convention, 1895* (Columbia, 1895), p. 464.

of seventy-six. In Aiken, for example, when he attempted to oppose Tillman's nomination, he was "howled down" and not allowed to speak.[35] Those doctrinaires who have tried to find in post-Civil War Southern politics a Marxian struggle between "Bourbons," on one side, and the lower classes, both black and white, on the other, should study Tillman's speeches. His appeals were consistently to the "wool-hat and one-gallus boys" and just as consistently against "aristocrats" and Negroes.[36] Nor was it surprising that a Tillman-dominated legislature refused to return Hampton to the Senate in 1890 and thus terminated his political influence in the state.

The official seal was placed on Tillman's policy towards the Negro by the constitutional convention of 1895, a convention fathered and dominated by Ben Tillman. While the entire constitution of 1868 was revamped, "the sole cause of our being here," as Tillman put it, was to so revise the election laws as to diminish the Negro vote.[37] The plan proposed by Tillman was adopted, and since 1895 it has functioned effectively, as he intended that it should.

This constitution completed one cycle of revolution and counter-revolution so far as Negro political activity in South Carolina was concerned. In the election of 1896, as in that of 1865, the black man was free, but few could vote. Just as the Negro-carpetbagger constitution of 1868 was the legal expression of Negro supremacy and marked the complete triumph of the revolution, so that of 1895 expressed white supremacy and marked the complete triumph of the counter-revolution. From 1876 to 1878 Hampton had tried to hold a middle road; from 1878 to 1890 Conservative Democrats, the "Bourbons," had preserved many of the Negro's political rights, as many as ten thousand Negroes registering to vote as late as 1894 in spite of stringent new registration laws.[38]

This thirty-year cycle of revolution and counter-revolution, this costly and futile swing from extreme to extreme, closed on a characteristically ironic note. The Negro delegates to the convention of 1895 offered as a substitute to Tillman's franchise proposal the plan

---

[35]Wallace, *History of South Carolina*, III, 348.

[36]Simkins, *Pitchfork Ben Tillman*, pp. 152ff.

[37]*Journal of the Constitutional Convention, 1895*, p. 443.

[38]Wallace, *History of South Carolina*, III, 373, states: "The Republican vote in the State [largely Negro] for the years indicated was as follows: 1884, 21,773; 1888, 13,736; 1892, 13,345; 1896 (though stimulated by a factional fight to control the party with a view to advantage in anticipated federal appointments, 9,313). It has since sunk ordinarily to two or three thousand."

urged by Hampton at the beginning of Reconstruction, a property or educational qualification applied to white and black alike.[39] But their proposal came too late. Hampton had pointed to the road, but it was the road rejected by black and white alike in their times of power.

---

[39]*Journal of the Constitutional Convention, 1895,* III, 373.

APPENDIXES

A

Correspondence between Wade Hampton and G. L. Park from the *Columbia Phoenix,* October 23, 1868.

General Wade Hampton:

Stevens Point, Wisconsin,
September 28, 1868.

Dear Sir: In view of the importance attached to everything spoken by you, and the great efforts made to present you as still adhering to and anticipating a renewal of the "lost cause" in a struggle with the Government, and because I believe you are greatly misrepresented, and therefore you, and through you the mass of the southern people, are wronged, I write this with a view to obtaining from you a statement as to the real opinions you entertain upon the issues of the war, its results and consequences, and also those of the people at large, whom you, to a great extent, represent. I need hardly add that this is intended for publication, and I truly hope you will not think it too much to comply with, if it can in any degree restore confidence between the people of the two sections, and so, ultimately, real peace and prosperity.

G. L. Park

Columbia, S. C.,
October 17.

My Dear Sir:

Absence from home and constant engagements have prevented an earlier reply to your letter, in which you ask me to give you "a statement of the real opinions you (I) entertain upon the issues of the war, its results and consequences, and those of the people at large, whom you, (I,) to a great extent, represent." If the mass of the Northern people have not been convinced of the pacific sentiments of the people of the South, by the authoritative actions of our conventions and legislatures; if the patriotic and truthful utterances of Robert E. Lee, indorsed, as they have been, by such entire unanimity by all the true men of the South, do not carry conviction, my words would, indeed, be powerless for good. But while I am profoundly impressed with this fact, it is due to you that I should respond to your inquiries in the same spirit that prompts them. This I shall do frankly, in the hope that all candid men among our opponents will grant me a fair hearing, and those who have so studiously perverted my sentiments and actions hitherto may at least give me credit for sincerity and honesty of purpose. First, then, as to "my real opinions as to the issues, results, and consequences of the war." The main issues involved in the war were secession and slavery; the first the primary one, the latter brought in at a later period. In regard to these, I adopt fully, and without reservation, the principles announced by the late National Democratic Convention in New York, and in the words of the platform promulgated there, I consider these "questions as settled forever." I accept this as the result accomplished by the war, and as its logical and legitimate consequence. This I have done from the day the war closed, and I have counseled our people to look upon it in the same light. I was strongly in favor of the action taken by this State, conferring on the negro equal civil rights with the white man, and, more than a year ago, I advocated the policy of giving him, as soon as we had the power to do so legitimately, suffrage based on qualification. The democratic convention held here in April last, recognized him as "an integral part of the body politic," and declared that it would, when our party came into power, grant him partial suffrage. The State Central Club has just reaffirmed this declaration, and I have no doubt but that this declaration is sustained by a vast majority of the white citizens of the State. We regard the reconstruction acts as unconstitutional, but we look for their overthrow not to violence, but, in the language unanimously adopted by the democratic party in convention assembled, "to constitutional agencies and peaceful remedies alone." We invoke a decision on the constitutionality of these acts from the only tribunal competent to pronounce on them — the Supreme Court of the United States; and we are prepared, in good faith, to abide by that decision. It may not be inappropriate here to correct a misrepresentation widely spread by radical papers touching these acts. In these I have been charged with having "dictated" that portion of the democratic platform relating to reconstruction. This charge I have more than once denied, and I do so again most emphatically. The sense in which I spoke of the words "unconstitutional, revolutionary, and void," as being my plank in the platform, referred to them as constituting the plank to which I, as well as any other southern man, clung to for safety. To place this matter beyond all question, I shall state, briefly, the action of the convention on this point, and my agency in it.

Several southern delegates offered resolutions upon these reconstruction measures, upon which a debate arose. Northern delegates asked us not to press our resolutions, but to trust to the democratic party, when successful, to give us all the relief in their power. A distinguished gentleman from one of the Northwestern States pronounced these acts "unconstitutional, revolutionary, and void," and urged us to leave this question to the democratic party for its proper solution. So anxious were the southern delegates to promote harmony — so solicitous were they to avoid any action that might endanger the success of that party, to which alone they could look for relief, that every one of them who had offered resolutions withdrew their resolutions at once. In withdrawing those I had the honor to submit, (and which, by the by, looked to the Supreme Court for the solution of this question of reconstruction,) I said the introduction of those three words into the platform would satisfy us entirely, and that we would trust to the democratic party to relieve us from measures that we knew must ruin our country. These words were subsequently introduced by a zealous and able delegate from that gallant New England State which has proved herself so ardent a supporter of the Constitution — brave little Connecticut. This is the precise history of this portion of the democratic platform. In alluding to it, as I did in an address to our people, my sole object was to show the spirit of conciliation that marked the action of the democratic convention, how sincere the North was in assuring us of relief, and how cordially the South confided in these assurances. How radical ingenuity could have perverted this into the charge of "dictation" on the part of any southern delegate, I should have been at a loss to conceive, had I not known, from experience, how skillful, and, I regret to say, how unscrupulous that party has proved itself to be in the use of their patent weapons of party warfare, misrepresentation and falsehood.

You do me the honor to say that "to a large extent, I represent the southern people." As I cannot flatter myself that this is the case, I do not venture to speak for them; but it is my honest and sincere conviction that they desire, above all things, *peace* — a just and honorable peace — a just and equitable settlement of all the questions that distract the country. They recognize that Constitution, as amended, abolishing slavery forever. They are willing to treat the negro with kindness, giving to him every civil right, and, I think, to accord him such political privilege as he is fitted to enjoy. They feel that their states should be restored to their old place in the Union, "with all their rights, dignity, and equality unimpaired." They would be unworthy of themselves, if they consented to resume their places as inferiors; they would be unfit associates for the freemen of the North. If the people of the North wish to build up a strong and lasting Union, let them be magnanimous and generous to the South; let them confide, more fully than they have done, to the honor of our people, and they will meet a cordial and heart-felt response. The future destiny of the republic is in the hands of the North, and upon their action it depends whether there is again to be a Union based on fraternal feelings, or one held together by the iron bands of military rule. We of the South are powerless to aid in the great struggle of constitutional liberty; but we cannot be indifferent spectators of a contest which is to fix our fate for all times to come. I pray earnestly that wisdom and justice may direct those who are called on to decide the momentous question, and that God will, in His infinite mercy, give peace to our distracted land.

Thanking you for the kind terms in which you have been pleased to express yourself, I have the honor to remain, very respectfully, your obedient servant,

Wade Hampton

G. L. Park, Esq.

B

The following account of the near-riot at Precinct Two in Edgefield is reasonably consistent with the testimony of General M. C. Butler and of the two army officers involved. It was printed under "Correspondence" in *The Nation* of June 14, 1877, and signed D. A. T. [Daniel Augustus Tompkins?]

To the Editor of The Nation:

Sir: In view of Mr. T. W. Higginson's argument about the bearing of the South Carolina election upon the question of woman suffrage, it may be of interest to you to know what were the actual duties required of a voter in that State on and about election-time. Therefore I offer to relate some actual events as by me observed in Edgefield County and at Edgefield Court-House on November 8th and 9th of last year.

But to make plain the necessity for some of the things done it will be of service to relate briefly the manner of previous elections since the war. At the first elections after the war, the whites and blacks met at the polls in a new relation, and under circumstances especially calculated to make any approach of the one by the other embarrassing and dangerous. The whites were humiliated by their late defeat, and felt uneasy and doubtful about what ought to be done. The negroes were elated and eager to test what extent of liberty their freedom embraced, most of them having a notion it was to be idle and to live as their former masters had lived. Therefore in the first election very many whites did not vote at all, some believing it to be best not to acknowledge, by voting with them, that it could be lawful for the negroes to vote; others from humiliation, and from various reasons; and the elections easily went for the negroes, under the management of a few soldiers and army followers — not of the best sort — who saw in the condition of things a field for their talents. Through these adventurers the forty-acres-and-a-mule promise was first made to the negroes.

Time, however, made the whites become more accustomed to the negro as a voter and citizen; and bad government, high taxes, and continually growing evidences of the permanence of the new regime made them see the need of putting aside sensitiveness, and at each succeeding election the white vote was better represented. But still there was never a full acknowledgment of the situation on their part, nor a decided concert of action, so that there was really never an organized opposition. The continually recurring local outbreaks show that there were neither leaders nor a plan. In Edgefield a thorough system of fraud had been established and carried out at each election by the negro leaders, as follows: The voters were never registered, although it was frequently urged by the whites. Neither was a man confined by law to a particular polling place. The negro leaders, being in charge of all arrangements, would put two boxes at the county-seat — one in the court-house, the other in an adjoining building — and would then order that the secret Union League clubs must each send a large delegation of negroes to the village, who should make a crowd to fill both rooms in which the boxes were placed. This crowd was directed to stay and keep these rooms full as long as possible — allowing themselves time enough in the afternoon to go home and vote at their respective county boxes. One of their leaders has since boasted of having voted squads of negroes over and over again in the crowd. The whites, until late in the afternoon, could never reach the boxes except by passing in this packed roomful of negroes, which was so disagreeable that many went home without trying it.

Now, at the last election the situation had become plain to every one, and it was seen that as long as this arrangement succeeded no salutary election laws could be enforced. Therefore a change in the result of the election must come from the energy of the opposition. The country was in no settled state. The Ellenton, Hamburgh, and Ned Tennant riots were only the conspicuous ones of a vast number of difficulties betwixt the two races. The negroes sullenly obeyed every order through the Union League with the accuracy that superstition prompts, and it was their purpose to fill the balloting rooms as usual at the village; and the whites were more resolved to have the boxes watched, and to have the space about them free from crowding. Clubs had been organized throughout the county, and fifteen members were sent from each club to vote at the village and watch the negroes from their respective sections, to prevent them from repeating, and to see that the boxes were not crowded in by them to the exclusion of the whites. To be sure of doing this peaceably it was necessary to be in the rooms before they were filled by the negroes. For this purpose, and to be ready to counteract any move the negro leaders might take, these delegations went to the court-house on Monday, the 8th — on horseback, and under a heavy, misty cloud, and over very muddy roads — most of them expecting to sleep upon the ground that night within the village limits. The negro leaders had been watchful, and knew of the design of the whites to be first in the court-house. On the 9th, therefore, they arranged for a magic-lantern show, and allowed the use of the court-house as a place for it, with the view of filling the room with negroes and have them remain all night. But the whites, understanding the trick, good-naturedly resolved to attend the show, and filled the room long before the hour it was to begin. The hour passed, but no showman came. The whites being now in possession of the room, it was thought best to remain all night — particularly since a drizzling rain was now falling, and the crowd could scarcely find a better place to sleep.

An hour before dawn, on Tuesday morning, a crowd of probably one thousand negroes came together in the rain, and were almost at the court-house door before they were discovered. They crowded upon the steps and close to the door, but found the room already full. Thus with the court-room full of whites, under the light of a single candle, and a crowd on the outside in a fast-falling rain, both sides waited for the morning. At six o'clock the officers of election ordered the room entirely cleared, and the voting commenced with allowing twelve at a time to enter. The whites refused to leave the room except on condition that twelve voters should enter it at once. Instead of putting the other box in the usual adjacent building, the managers announced, about 6 o'clock, that the location of it would be changed, and would not tell where it would be put, under the pretence that they had not decided. Immediately about two hundred men mounted their horses and said wherever it was located they intended to be present, and were determined it should not be left in possession of the negroes. Finally the box was taken to a negro school-house in the outskirts of the town, evidently by prearrangement, for a crowd of negroes were there. The whites rode close to the doors of the building and demanded that only a specified number of voters should go in at once. The negroes were much dissatisfied with this, but acquiescence or an open encounter was the only alternative. Soldiers were sent for, but were refused by the commandant of the garrison until about nine o'clock. About that time the negroes grew more clamorous to be admitted en masse into the school-house, and the crowd having increased to one thousand or twelve hundred against probably two hundred and fifty whites, who were keeping them out, the United States marshal, being unable to keep order, requested a company of soldiers. The soldiers came and stopped on the summit of the slope on which the school-house stood, and then the negroes were urged to crowd into the building with the assurance that the soldiers would help if they could not succeed alone. Then came the most critical moment of the day. Amid a deafening noise the horses of the few whites were crowded on all sides, and confusion and excitement were at the highest pitch when, a negro striking at a man's horse with a stick, struck the rider. Immediately a pistol was drawn, then another, and quicker than it can be told many pistols were in the air on both sides, ready to fire. Now the lieutenant on duty came with a squadron of four men, and climbed in the back window of the building and came out with a citizen, who demanded that all arms should be put up. Upon his promising to keep the room clear of all but a few voters at a time order was soon restored, the negroes were bayoneted back, and soon the voting was going regularly on, the voters being admitted at once. When night came, about 200 had not yet voted at this box, so large had been the crowd of negroes attracted by the presence of the soldiers.

On Tuesday night many of the voters had been up the night before, or slept in blankets on a stone floor in the court-house, had been in the saddle all day, and in many instances with one meal — some being even without breakfast or dinner — so watchful had they been about the boxes. . . .

C
Correspondence Between Wade Hampton
and
President Rutherford B. Hayes

(The originals of these letters and telegrams are in the Hayes Memorial Library, Fremont, Ohio. These copies are printed from typescripts generously provided by Mr. Watt P. Marchman, Director of Research.)

State of South Carolina
Executive Chamber
Columbia Dec 28 1876

My Dear Sir:

I have the honor to enclose a copy of my inaugural address on the occasion of my inauguration as the duly elected Governor of South Carolina.

In view of current events, and the official sanction given to gross misrepresentations of the acts and purposes of the majority of the good people of this commonwealth, I deem it proper to declare that profound peace prevails throughout this State; that the course of judicial proceeding is obstructed by no combination of citizens thereof; and that the laws for the protection of its inhabitants in all their rights of person, property and citizenship are being enforced in our Courts.

While the people of this State are not wanting either in the Spirit or the means to maintain their rights of citizenship against the usurped power which now defies the Supreme Judicial authority of the State, they have such full faith in the justice of their cause that they propose to leave its vindication to the proper legal tribunals, appealing at the same time to the patriotism and public sentiments of the whole country.

The inflammatory utterances of a portion of the public press render it, perhaps, not inopportune for me to state, that although the people of South Carolina view with grave concern the present critical conjunction in the affairs of our country, which threatens to subject to an extreme test the Republican system of government itself, it is their firm and deliberate purpose to condemn any solution of existing political problems that involves the exhibition of armed force, or that moves through any other channel than the prescribed forms of the Constitution, or the peaceful agencies of law. Trusting that a solution may be had, which, while maintaining the peace of the country, shall do no violence to the Constitutional safeguards of popular rights, and will tend still more firmly to unite the people of all the States in an earnest effort to preserve the peace, to sustain the laws, and to obey the Constitution.

I am, Very Respy
Your Obt Servt
Wade Hampton
Governor of So Ca.

His Excelly
  R. B. Hayes
    Governor of Ohio

P.S. As the settlement of the vexed political questions which have agitated the public mind must ultimately depend on yourself, or upon your distinguished competitor for the Presidency, I have addressed a letter, similar to this, to His Excelly Governor Tilden

Very Respy Yrs
Wade Hampton

State of South Carolina,
Executive Chamber
Columbia March 26th 1877

Sir

I have the honor to acknowledge your communication of the 23rd inst. addressed to me by your Private Secty. As you express a desire for a personal conference with myself I accept through motives of proper courtesy to yourself, the invitation you have extended, though I can not hope by doing so to throw additional light on questions which have already been so ably and throughly [sic] presented and the solution of which is so obvious and simple. But understanding from the communication I have received that the object contemplated by the proposed conference is solely that I might place before you my "views of the impediments to the peaceful and orderly organization of a single and undisputed State Government in South Carolina and of the best methods of removing them," I shall avail myself of your invitation, so that I may reiterate in person what I have had the honor to submit in writing that in my judgment, all impediments to the objects so earnestly desired by yourself and so anxiously expected by the people of this State can at once be removed by the withdrawal of the Federal Troops from our State House. This action on the part of the Commander in Chief of the United States forces would not only be hailed by our people as an evidence that civil authority is no longer to be subordinated to the Military power, in our country, but it would establish law, insure domestic tranquility, revive our wasted industries and give an assurance that this State is to be restored to her just rights under the Constitution. Whatever grievances exist, whatever wrongs we suffer, we propose to redress them not by a resort to force, but by legal and Constitutional agencies — In seeking such redress, I feel sure that I represent fully the determination of the thoughtful and conservative portion of our whole people, when I give the assurance that no prescription shall be exercised here on account of political opinions: that no discrimination shall be made in the administration of justice; and that all citizens of both parties and both races shall be regarded as fully protected by, and amenable to, the laws. Joining most heartily with you in the earnest desire you express that you "may be able to put an end as speedily as possible to all appearance of intervention of the Military authority of the United States in the political derangements which affect the Government and afflict the people of South Carolina, and fervently trusting that this auspicious result may soon be reached

> I have the honor to be
> Very Respectfully
> Your Obdt. Servant
> Wade Hampton
> Governor of So Ca.

To His Excellency
R. B. Hayes
President of the United States
    Washington, D. C.

                                        Willard's Hotel
                            Washington, Mch 29, 1877

To The President:
Sir:

    In compliance with your invitation I am here for the purpose of uniting my efforts with yours, to the end of composing the political differences which now unhappily distract the people of South Carolina. I beg you to believe that my anxiety to bring about the permanent pacification of that State — a pacification in which the rights of all shall be safe and the interests of all shall be protected — is as sincere as I feel assured is your own for the accomplishment of the same ends.

My position for years past in reference to the political rights of colored citizens and my solemn pledges given during the late canvass in So Ca., that under my administration all these rights should be absolutely secure, should furnish a sufficient guarantee of my sincerity on those points, which appear to be the subject of special anxiety.

I have the honor to ask at what hour it will be your pleasure to receive me and

I am Sir

Very respectfully

Your obt sevt

Wade Hampton

Governor of So.Ca.

To The President
    My Dear Sir
    Several telegraphic communications have come to me today from Columbia demanding immediate answer, but I can give none until I can have a conference with yourself. I should be very glad to call at any hour you may appoint, if it will be agreeable to you to see me. Both parties in S. C. are represented in my T/Ds and both seem anxious that matters may be arranged

I am, Sir

Friday 7 P. M.   Very   respy and truly Yrs
J. F. Cake   Wade Hampton

WILLARD'S HOTEL

Mar 31st 1877
Washington, D. C.

To The President
    Sir
    The result of the conference to which you did me the honor to invite me, has been to leave on my mind the conviction that you sincerely desire to see a peaceful and just settlement of the questions which are distracting our people and injuring so seriously the material interests of our State and I trust that you are equally convinced of my earnest wish to aid in accomplishing this happy end. As I may not have the pleasure of seeing you again on this subject, it may be proper to put before you in the fullest and most definite form, the assurance given to you verbally. I repeat therefore, that if the Federal Troops are withdrawn from the State House, there shall be on my part, or that of my friends no resort to violence, to assert our

claims, but that we shall look for their maintenance solely to such peaceful remedies as the Constitution and laws of the State provide. I shall use all my authority to repress the use or the exhibition of force, in the settlement of all disputed questions, and this authority shall be exercised in such a manner that the peace shall be preserved. We only desire the establishment in our State of a Government, which will secure to every citizen, the lowest as well as the highest, black as well as white, full and equal protection in the enjoyment of all his rights under the Constitution of the United States. No one can be more deeply impressed than myself with the imperative necessity of establishing cordial relations between all classes and both races in So.Ca. for it is only by these means, that the true and enduring welfare of the State can be secured. With the recognition of the perfect equality of every citizen before the law, with a just and impartial administration of the laws: with a practical secure exercise of the right of suffrage: with a system of public education which will open the services of knowledge to all classes, we may hope to see our State soon take the position to which she is entitled. It was the patriotic hope to aid in the accomplishment of these high aims, that called me from my retirement to become a candidate for the office of Governor of So.Ca. It was through the confidence of the people of that State that I would honestly and faithfully carry out all these purposes, that I was elected their Chief Magistrate: and I feel profoundly that peace can be surely preserved there, and prosperity restored, by assuring our people, that the right of "local self-government" so prominently brought forward in your Inaugural and so favorably received by the whole country, is to be promptly carried out as the rule of your Administration. I anticipate the ready fulfilment of the just and reasonable hopes inspired by the announcement of the policy you have unfolded, — a policy which found a responsive echo in every patriotic heart as indicating a purpose to administer the government in the true spirit of the Constitution. In conclusion, permit me to assure you that I feel the strongest confidence that the wise and patriotic policy announced in your Inaugural, will, as soon as it takes shape in action produce such fruits, that the whole country will enjoy the blessings of peace, prosperity and harmony. Thanking you, Sir, for the courtesy you have extended to me and with my good wishes, I am

Very Respy Yr. obt Sevt
Wade Hampton
Governor of So Ca

Columbia Apr. 22nd 1877

The President.
Sir

It gives me great pleasure to present to you, Col. F. W. McMaster, a prominent citizen and lawyer of this place, and to commend him to your consideration. He goes on to consult as to the appointment of Ex. Gov. Scott, to the place of U.S. Revenue Collector and while I do not propose to embarrass your Administration by any recommendations for office, I can consistently say that the removal of the present incumbent, would meet the hearty approval of our people.

I congratulate you on the results of your Southern policy and I have every assurance that it will, if steadily pursued, tend to solve the vexed Southern problem.

The papers have shown you what policy I have advocated here, and I am glad to say that it is strongly sustained by the people. You have seen too, that events have followed since the removal of the troops from the State House, precisely as I indicated to you, would be their course. I therefore hope, that we shall have now enduring peace and good government in the State.

I have the honor to be

Very Respy

Yr. obt Sevt

Wade Hampton

HALF RATE MESSAGES

THE WESTERN UNION TELEGRAPH COMPANY

2 – Ca

Dated Columbia.S.C. May 11 1877
Received at 6 50 P M
To The Pres't Washn D C

Sir, I beg to transmit concurrent resolution adopted by the general assembly and to ask your favorable and immediate action on it, the prosecution of these Cases will entail peculiar hardships on the people of Aiken County while the exercise of Executive clemency on the part of your Excellency will tend to promote harmony among all classes, as resolution provides abandonment of all prosecutions growing out of late political contest. I therefore earnestly urge your Concurrence with the recommendation of the legislature and I respectfully request an answer by telegraph as trials come off on fourteenth inst.

Concurrent resolution "invoking Executive clemency." Whereas in the opinion of this general assembly the people of this State earnestly and sincerely desire to cooperate with the good and virtuous citizens of all the States of this union to promote general reconciliation and good feeling and to harmonize the different States with the general government in every effort looking to that end, and Whereas there are now numbers of the citizens of this state of one political party under bonds to answer charges in the US Courts for alleged violation of law immediately preceding the last general Election Said offences arising perhaps from the heat and violence of a great political canvass most of these persons being poor and unable to meet the delay and expenses of Judicial trials, therefore resolved, "that his Excellency the governor be requested to communicate with the Pres't of the U S in reference to the particular cases alluded to above and to ask for such Executive clemency as the circumstances will warrant upon the assurance that the State of South Carolina will not prosecute any other person or persons of the other political party for any participation in the same offences for which clemency is now asked and the Atty Gen'l is hereby requested to "nol pros" all cases already commenced or that may be here after commenced" W D Simpson Pres't of the Senate" W H Wallace Speaker House of Rep's — Attest. Clerk of Senate — Clerk House Rep's —

Wade Hampton
Governor

Executive Mansion
May 12th 1877.

Gov. Wade Hampton
　　Columbia
　　S. C.

I am informed by the Attorney General that he has instructed the District Attorney of South Carolina to prepare for trials only three indictments in the Ellenton Cases and to notify the parties in all other cases that they need not prepare for trial.

It is possible that only one case will be tried. The fact that the indictments were found by Grand Juries composed of both political parties seems to justify the assumption that the prosecutions are not partisan.

I agree with you that a general amnesty should extend to all political offenses except those which are of the gravest character

R. B. Hayes

New York June 24th 1877

My Dear Sir

The enclosed letter explains itself, and I beg most earnestly to ask your favorable action on it. Mr Pillsbury voluntarily requested that these men should be released and he told me that their conduct had been admirable, I feel very sure that the exercise of Executive clemency on your part, is not only fully justified, but that it would exert a most happy effect. Amnesty for all their past political offences, is the best policy and I trust that you will let me have the pleasure of assisting in restoring these unfortunate men to liberty. I hope that such events, as led to their conviction, will be impossible in the future.

When in Auburn, the other day, it occurred to me that you had it in your power to pay a graceful and deserved compliment to Gen. Shields by sending him to Mexico. His command contributed greatly to the success and glory of our arms on that soil and he is very anxious to revisit the scenes which possess such interest to him. As he commanded then, the troops of So. Ca., I feel that I can, without impropriety, bring his name

to your attention. Hoping, that you may be able to pardon the men in whose behalf application is made
I have the honor to be

Very Respy
Yr. obt Sevt
Wade Hampton

His Excellency
   R. B. Hayes
      President

Columbia Sept 25th 1877

To The President
  Sir

     Sometime ago I made application for the exercise of executive clemency in behalf of three citizens of this State now confined in the Albany Penety. for offences committed during what was known as the Ku Klux excitement. I had the honor to forward at the same time a statement from the Supen't of the Penety. saying that these men had behaved well and recommending their pardon. One of them, at least, is in very bad health and I feel sure that a pardon to these men, would have a very wholesome effect just now. I have no sympathy with the offences with which they were charged, but I desire that good will should be firmly established between the races and nothing would tend more to this end than a general amnesty. The ends of justice have been satisfied by their punishment and I earnestly ask their release. They are the only three men left in prison and if you can pardon them on my request, it would strengthen my influence in preserving peace. Hoping that Mrs Hayes and yourself reached Washington safely and with my best wishes I have the honor to be

Very Respy and Truly Yrs
Wade Hampton

     The names of two of the men are John G. Wallace and Pinkney Caldwell. That of the third, I have forgotten.

Private
Columbia Jan 9th 1878

My Dear Sir

     Knowing how worried you must be, by a vast correspondence, I have been unwilling to add to your burthen, but as there are some matters recently brought to my attention which may prove of consequence to you, I venture to trespass on your time. It is only from a sense of duty and a personal regard for yourself that I do so. In July last I told Mr. Evarts in N. Y. that I had information which led me to believe that Mr. Conckling [sic] would assume a hostile attitude towards your Administration, and that then there would be an attempt to re-open the Presdtl question before

Congress. You may remember that I repeated this to you while we were coming from Louisville. Now Conckling [sic] has pursued the course indicated and my information of a recent date, is to the effect that he is disposed to push his hostility even so far as to attack your title to the Presdcy. I cannot vouch for the truth of this but there are various circumstances which tend to substantiate it. Our erratic friend Judge M. on his return from Washn. let drop various hints to this effect, and I have heard whispers from other quarters. Some time since I wrote to Gordon on this subject, and urged him to use all his influence to defeat any scheme of this sort. I expressed the hope that no Southern man would give any countenance to it and I gave it as my opinion that the Democrats in Congress should sustain your policy heartily. I think that they will do so and I am convinced that you are stronger than the Republican party. If you will steadily pursue the line you have marked out, appealing to the great patriotic heart of the country, the people will support you. You can crush the ambitious politicians who are trying to crush you, if you accept the gage of battle they have thrown down. Of course there are extreme men in the Democratic party who seek to keep up agitation, but they are powerless. I honestly think that you will receive the almost unanimous support of the South in your present line of action. I regretted much that Butler in a recent speech here, placed himself in opposition to you. He was under the impression that you had used your influence in behalf of Corbin, and was thus led to express himself with some warmth. I told him, that I thought he was mistaken in his opinion as to your course, for it seems that his only reason for judging so, was that Senator Matthews voted against his admission to the Senate. The Legislature here, would sustain you heartily, if any test question of that nature was made. I feel a profound solicitude to see the policy you have inaugurated, made a complete success and I am now as I have been from the first, in full accord with your patriotic efforts to restore harmony, and to secure the rights of all citizens, and of all States. This is my reason for writing to you so fully and I hope that you will appreciate the motive. To avoid troubling you again, let me say a word as to the reported violence used towards some Revenue Officers in Union Co. the other day. I took prompt steps to ascertain the truth of the matter, notifying the Sheriff that the laws must be enforced. If any Militia Co. was engaged in unlawful proceedings, it shall be disbanded, and if the trial Justice acted improperly he shall be dismissed. The parties have all been notified of my determination and I am only waiting for a full report. I wrote also to the Revenue Officer assuring him of all necessary aid, and I can safely promise that all parties implicated shall be arrested. You may remember that some months ago a man named Ledford was brutally murdered in Spartanburg Co. on account of some Revenue difficulty. Rewards were offered for the murderers, and I have just arrested one in N. C. placing him in jail in Spartanburg. I will use all my authority to stop these lawless acts, but I must say to you that the conduct and character of the Revenue Officers, in many instances, provoke these outbreaks. There should be a reform in this system and it can best be brought about by the appointment of good men whom the people respect. In this connection I venture to beg you to have Northrop confirmed for as he has resigned his Judgeship the loss of his present place, would be ruinous to him. He has the highest testimonials and his conduct has given satisfaction to the Court. One other of your appointees has appealed to me most earnestly to say a word in his behalf, and as he is really deserving, I hope that I may do so without impropriety. He is Geo. C. Tanner, U. S. Consul at Leipz. He is devoting himself to his duties and I trust that he can be retained in his position. Pray pardon me for the length of this letter, and with my best wishes for Mrs. Hayes and yourself, I am

Very Respy and truly Yrs.
Wade Hampton

His Excelly
   R. B. Hayes
     President

Personal   Columbia March 25th 1878
To The President
    My Dear Sir

        Among the last acts of the General Assembly was the almost unanimous adoption of a Resolution authorizing me to direct the Atty Genl. to "*Nol pros*" any of the cases which are regarded as political. I suggested the passage of this Resolution and my action in this matter gives full assurance as to my views on this subject. It is very desirable that all agitation should cease in the State and to this end I desire as full amnesty as can be granted. You may have noticed that Carpenter has been pardoned, and I have taken no action in the other cases — those of Cardozo and Smalls — because they are now pending before the Sup. Court. Mr. Milton the counsel for Cardozo knows my views in this case and approves my action. There have been but three trials of cases of this sort, though there is evidence sufficient for two hundred. I do not wish to see those who are minor offenders, tried, nor do I desire to have any cases brought up except two or three of the most important. None shall come up except on the most conclusive evidence of sufficient guilt, and every precaution shall be taken to secure impartial trials. You can strengthen my hands in carrying out this policy of amnesty greatly by the exercise of executive clemency in behalf of those who are charged with the violation of the U. S. laws and I appeal to you to do so. There are but three men from this State now in the Albany Penty. on the Ku Klux charges and I have already asked you to pardon them, in a former communication. Let me renew this request, and ask you to issue a Proclamation of pardon to those who were charged with complicity in the Ku Klux cases. Several of these men have left the State and they are anxious to return and I feel sure that you could do nothing which would be more grateful to our people, than to end at once all this irritating source of anxiety. The other, and more recent cases, could be disposed of afterwards, and we should then have peace and quiet in the

State. Pubic [*sic*] opinion would then sustain me in the course I wish to pursue here and all political causes of dissention, would be removed. My position here has been a very difficult one, for besides the opposition to me from political opponents, I have had to meet and control that of the extreme men of my own party. That this latter has been bitter, the enclosed article published here, will show you, but I can crush out all opposition, if you can grant amnesty to our citizens. It is very gratifying to me to learn that I have gained the confidence of the Republicans here, by my adminis- tration of the government, for this proves that justice has been done. A Republican Senator offered resolutions endorsing the course I have pursued, saying that I had redeemed every pledge made, and every Republican in the Legislature voted for them. The colored people urge me to be a candidate for the next term, and assure me that there shall be no opposition if I will run. We have peace throughout the State, and goodwill between the races is growing up. As you have seen, the people and the volunteer troops respond readily to my orders to assist the Revenue officers, and the laws are enforced everywhere. You have been largely instrumental in bringing about these happy results, by your policy to the South, and I feel therefore that I can approach you in full confidence that you will sympa- thize with my objects. We have in this, a common end in view, and if you will trust my judgment in the matter, you can accomplish a great work, one that will do much towards pacification. I shall be happy to go on to consult with you if you think it desirable to do so. My only excuse for the length of my letter, is the deep interest that I feel in the subject of it. Asking your thoughtful consideration of this matter, I am, My dear Sir,

Very respy and truly Yrs
Wade Hampton

P. S.

Atty. Genl. Youmans who will hand this letter to you can give full infor- mation as to the condition of things here and he can also express my views. You can speak to him with perfect freedom

Very truly Yrs
Wade Hampton

Private

State of South Carolina,
Executive Chamber
Columbia June 14th 1878

To the President
  My Dear Sir

        Enclosed you will find copy of a letter addressed to Col. Bratton, in reference to the subject of our recent consultation. I submit this to show you what course I have taken.

I regret to say that great excitement prevails in Pickens Co. in conse- quence of the killing of a citizen by the Revenue officers a few days ago.

The facts in this case have not yet been brought out, and I know that in many cases, the conduct of the officials provokes violence and retaliation and I think there is great room for reform in this service. I am firmly convinced that a force could be put on duty, which while enforcing the laws, could collect a larger revenue for the Government, and could preserve the peace of the country. Men should be assigned to this service, who possess the confidence of the people and whose characters would insure a ready obedience to the laws. Knowing your views on this subject, I venture to call your attention to it, assuring you of my hearty co-operation, in any movement, which could afford a satisfactory solution to this perplexing problem.

I am,

Very Respy and Truly Yrs
Wade Hampton

State of South Carolina
Executive Chamber
Columbia June 14th 1878

My dear Sir:

Your letter met me here, on my return from Washn., and I am happy in being able to convey to you, the assurance of the President, that your brother and all others connected with the Ku-Klux troubles, can return to the State, with perfect safety. Mr. Hayes promises that no action shall be taken against any of these parties, and that should any case be brought up, it shall at once be *noll prosd.* I should be glad that this information should reach all the parties concerned in this matter, and I hope soon to know that they are no longer exiles. It is not desirable to make any public announcement as to the action of the Presdt, just at this time, but he has done all that was necessary, and he has placed the people of the State, under additional obligations to him. Hoping that your brother will soon be at home I am

Very truly Yrs
Wade Hampton

Col Bratton

Personal

Columbia July 15th 1878

To The President
    My Dear Sir

On the 30th May Mr. Earle, of Greenville addressed you on the subject of the Revenue difficulties in this State, and made suggestions as to a mode of settling them. His letter has recently been shown to me and I concur fully in the views expressed. Since that letter was written, a citizen has been shot in his own house by the Revenue Officers, and this has created great excitement in Pickens Co. where this outrage was committed. Unless this unhappy condition of things can be changed, grave results may follow, and it is to ask your co-operation in restoring quiet, peace and a full obedience to the laws, that I now write. That the Revenue laws have been violated I have no doubt, but this violation has been brought about in a great measure by the conduct of the officers engaged in the Revenue service. I feel assured that the laws can be enforced more fully than they ever have been; that the tax on spirits can be more largely collected, and that all this can be done without violence or harshness, if the proper men are put on duty. I care not whether they be Republicans or Democrats, but I do urge a complete change among the present officials. If you will place the proper men on duty, I guarantee that there will be no farther trouble, and that the returns of taxes to the Dept. will be larger than heretofore. If you can carry out the suggestion of Mr. Earle, as to amnesty for past offences, you will be giving the strongest assurances of peace for the future. Armed with this amnesty, I would go among these mountain men, and I would call on them to yield full obedience to the laws. I could make them aid me in suppressing illicit distilling and supported by the moral influence of all the best citizens, I could put a stop to this traffic. When Congress meets some law might be passed which would not bear so hard on this class of men, who cannot bring their grain to market save in the shape of spirits. I have the assurance from all quarters that the illicit distilling will be stopped if past offences are forgiven, and I appeal to you earnestly to take action in that direction. This is the sole disturbing element now in the State, and I write to see this removed. It will give me great satisfaction to co-operate with you, in any manner, that will secure this desirable result; a result which I know that you have at heart. If you can take any action, I would suggest that it should be done promptly. Asking your favorable consideration of this subject,

I am

Very Respy and Truly Yrs
Wade Hampton

State of South Carolina
Executive Chamber
Columbia July 31st 1878

To the President
    Sir

        The enclosed communication is from the pen of one of the ablest lawyers in this State, and the spirit of it is so admirable, that I beg of you to read it carefully. It reflects my views, as I deprecate anything like a conflict of jurisdiction between the Federal and the State Courts.

Such a conflict can only result in evil consequences, and I trust that everything will be done to avoid even the appearance of a difference of opinion on the question now before the Federal Government.

I have the honor to be
Very Respy
Yr. obt Sevt
Wade Hampton

State of South Carolina,
Executive Chamber
Columbia Aug 5th 1878

To The President
Sir

Sometime since a communication addressed by Mr Corbin to Your Excellency in behalf of Mr. Kimpton, was forwarded to me, and it has been fully considered by the Atty Genl. of the State. The conclusion to which he has arrived. — in which I concur — is that if Mr. Kimpton will come here prepared to show all that he knows of the financial affairs of the State. bringing his books. with witnesses to prove and verify the entries in them, he shall have full immunity, if the Atty Genl chooses to use him as a witness. If he is not used as a witness, he shall be entirely free to return to the North, without any interference from the State authorities, and everything shall revert to the present condition of affairs, as far as he is concerned. If the Atty Genl. concludes after consultation with him, to take his evidence before the court of Claims, all proceedings on the part of the State against him, shall be discharged. As this court will meet tomorrow, Mr. Kimpton should be here by the 15th inst. at the latest. He has been notified of this communication, and advised to see Your Excellency at once.

I have the honor to be
Very Respy Yrs
Wade Hampton

The State of South Carolina
Executive Chamber
Columbia, S. C. Aug 7th 1878

Mr President
Sir

It is proper that I should inform you, in view of my recent letter in relation to Mr. Kimpton, that a T/D, just received, notifies me of his arrest in Mass. This changes the condition of affairs in so far that my duty impels me to send a requisition for him. The course to be pursued hereafter towards him, will depend largely on his own conduct. He had the opportunity offered him to come safely, to testify, if he chose to do so voluntarily, but he would not avail himself of it.

I have the honor to be
Very Respy Yrs
Wade Hampton
Governor

Washington, D. C.
August 13, 1878.

To His Excellency
    Wade Hampton, Governor:
Sir,
    Your response to my letter addressed to the President in behalf of Mr. H. H. Kimpton has been shown me by the President and I have had conversation with him about the subject-matter thereof, and he suggests that I communicate with you direct in reply. I therefore do so, showing him, the President, my letter and leaving a copy thereof with him. Mr. Kimpton thinks your proposition is not quite fair to him and suggests the following, which is a modification of your own, viz:
    Mr. Kimpton will go to Columbia, S. C., and take his books and book-keeper, prepared to testify himself as to what he knows, and to show whatever his books and book-keeper can prove as to the affairs of his Financial Agency before your Bond Court, if he and his book-keeper can be assured in advance of immunity from arrest under civil or criminal process, and that all proceedings of a criminal nature and all claims on behalf of the State against him, shall thereby be discontinued settled and ended.
    Mr. Kimpton regards it as unfair to him to require him to go to South Carolina and subject himself, his books and his book-keeper to examination and then be used as a witness or not as may be deemed advisable and in the event of not being used as a witness then to be remanded to his former state. If Mr. Kimpton's proposition hereby communicated is accepted he will be able to appear with his books and book-keeper in Columbia by the 21st or 22nd of this month.

Very Respectfully
D. T. Corbin
P. S. A reply to this letter will reach me at No. 243. Broadway New York City.

D. T. C.

State of South Carolina
Executive Chamber
Columbia, Aug 13th 1878

    To The President
Mr President
    I have the honor to submit the following Resolutions, which I have been requested to forward to Your Excellency. The clemency which you

have exercised has produced the most favorable results, and I feel sure that good will come of it. May I ask you to place Redmond on the same footing as the other illicit distillers in the Mts. He is anxious to surrender to stand his trial for the killing of Duckworth in N. C. and he has had nothing to do with traffic in whiskey for a year. Clemency to him will have more effect than the pardon of fifty other men, as he has great influence in the Mts. Though he has resisted the officers, he has himself been shot at by them 26 times. He has killed no one but Duckworth and as he wishes to stand his trial, without interference from the Revenue officials, the opportunity should be granted him. I propose to visit the disaffected counties in a few days, and the action of the Government in its generous treatment of the distillers will enable me to impress on the citizens the necessity of obeying the laws

I am

Very Respy Yrs
Wade Hampton

To his Excellency, Wade Hampton, Governor of South Carolina.

At a meeting of the Spartanburg, (S. C.) County Club, held on the 20th instant, the following resolutions offered by J. B. Cleveland, Esq., unanimously prevailed:

"Resolved

That the people of Spartanburg have heard with pleasure the pardon of all persons under prosecution in the United States Courts, as Ku-Klux, and regard this action, on the part of the Federal Government as conciliatory, and calculated in the highest degree to restore full and perfect harmony between the two great sections of the Union.

Resolved,

That the people of Spartanburg, in convention assembled, invite all her persecuted children to return to her, assuring them of her sympathy, and that under home rule and Hampton, the days of misrule and oppression are forever at an end.

Resolved,

That at this time when hundreds are outlawed, when many homes are deserted and fields uncultivated by those who are now ready, willing, and anxious to become Law-abiding citizens, we most urgently, but respectfully invite the attention of the Federal Government to this state of affairs; and would ask for the violators of Internal Revenue laws the same clemency that has been shown the Ku Klux, and the same general amnesty, which has been extended to the people of Georgia; and we express entire confidence in the belief that by such a course the United States Government will not only do an act of mercy towards many of its citizens, but will do much to promote respect for such of its Laws as have been regarded with disfavor by many of our citizens.

Resolved,

That a copy of these resolutions be forwarded to Governor Hampton with the request that he submit them to his Excellency, R. B. Hayes, President of the United States.

E H [?]
Chairman

Chas. P. Wofford,
      Secretary
July 26th, 1878,——

United States Senate Chamber
Columbia July 2nd 1880

To The President
      My Dear Sir

Since my return home, I have heard that an effort has been made to remove Mr. Northrop and to put Mr Corbin in his place. You were kind enough to assure me that this should not be done and I so informed Northrop. I hope that you will not allow his enemies to break him down for a change in that office would have a most disastrous effect here, by opening anew all the cases which we desire settled. Northrop has acted with firmness and moderation, and he is so familiar with these questions, that he can deal with them better than anyone else. I trust that you may be able to bring them all to a satisfactory conclusion before your retirement for I should regard that result as one of the happiest achievements of your Administration. I am told that Mr. Cockran has some very strong recommendations to present to you, and I beg to ask your favorable consideration of his application. He certainly has strong claims on the Republican party, and he is sorely reduced in circumstances. When I had the pleasure of travelling with you through Tenn. and urged the appointment of a democrat as Dist. Atty, you gave most satisfactory reasons why you should appoint a Republican to that office, but you did me the honor to say that for any other position, you would take my recommendation. I have never availed myself of your offer, but I should be much gratified if you will appoint this Republican who has always opposed me. He has always stood manfully to his colors, and I respect him for doing so, while I have great sympathy with his wife who is in great need.

With my kind regards to Mrs Hayes and good wishes for yourself, I am

Respy and truly Yrs
Wade Hampton

Washn Apr 27th 1881

My Dear Sir

Major [mayor?] Courtenay, fearing that his first invitation failed to reach you, has asked me to forward the present one. Let me express the hope that you will accept it for our people would be very glad to welcome you, and it would give me special pleasure to see Mrs. Hayes and yourself, in So. Ca.   Hoping that you may be with us, and with my best wishes, I am,

Very truly Yrs
Wade Hampton

Ex-Presdt Hayes

BIBLIOGRAPHY

This bibliography contains only the works cited in this study. For more extensive bibliographies see Simkins and Woody, *South Carolina during Reconstruction,* and Simkins, *Pitchfork Ben Tillman.*

BOOKS AND PAMPHLETS

Acts and Joint Resolutions of the General Assembly of the State of South Carolina. Columbia, 1868.

Allen, Walter. *Governor Chamberlain's Administration in South Carolina: A Chapter of Reconstruction in the Southern States.* New York, 1888.

Ball, W. W. *The State that Forgot: South Carolina's Surrender to Democracy.* Indianapolis, 1932.

Biographical Congressional Directory with an Outline History of the National Congress, 1774-1911. Washington, 1913.

Bowers, Claude G. *The Tragic Era: The Revolution after Lincoln.* Boston, 1929.

Chamberlain, Daniel H. "Present Phases of Our So-Called Negro Problem." An open letter to James Bryce, M. P. of England, 1904. *News and Courier* (Charleston), August 1, 1904, and reprinted with letters by Chamberlain on the subject to various newspapers.

———. "The Political Issues of 1892." A speech at the Academy of Music. Philadelphia, 1892.

Childs, Arney R. (ed.). *The Private Journal of Henry William Ravenel: 1859-1887.* Columbia, 1947.

De Forest, John William. *A Union Officer in the Reconstruction,* ed. James H. Croushore and David M. Potter. New Haven, 1948.

Dictionary of American Biography, ed. Allen Johnson and Dumas Malone. New York, 1929.

Dunning, William A. *Reconstruction, Political and Economic. American Nation Series.* New York, 1905.

Eckenrode, H. J. *Rutherford B. Hayes: Statesman of Reunion.* New York, 1930.

Field, Carter. *Bernard Baruch: Park Bench Statesman.* New York, 1944.

Gary, Martin Witherspoon. Address delivered in the Senate of South Carolina, May 2, 1877, on Bill to Regulate Rate of Interest. Columbia, 1877.

———. "Finance and Taxation." Speech delivered in the Senate, May 25, 1877. Columbia, 1877.

———. "On the Public Debt of the State of South Carolina." Speech delivered in the Senate. Columbia, 1878.

———. Speech before the Taxpayers' Convention of South Carolina at Columbia, February 19, 1874. n.p. n.d.

Heyward, Duncan Clinch. Seed from Madagascar. Chapel Hill, 1937.

Hollis, John Porter. The Early Period of Reconstruction in South Carolina. Johns Hopkins University Studies, Series XXIII. Baltimore, 1905.

Journal of the Constitutional Convention of the People of South Carolina, Held in Columbia, South Carolina, Beginning September 10th and Ending December 4th, 1895. Columbia, 1895.

Journal of the House of Representatives of the State of South Carolina. Columbia.

Kibler, Lillian A. Benjamin F. Perry, South Carolina Unionist. Durham, 1946.

LeConte, Joseph. Autobiography, ed. William Dallam Armes. New York, 1903.

Lee, Alfred M. Race Riot. New York, 1943.

Leland, John A. A Voice from South Carolina. Charleston, 1879.

McCrady, Edward. The Necessity of Raising the Standard of Citizenship. Charleston, 1881.

Pearson, Elizabeth Ware (ed.). Letters from Port Royal written at the Time of the Civil War. Boston, 1906.

Perry, Benjamin Franklin. Biographical Sketches of Eminent American Statesmen. Philadelphia, 1887.

———. Reminiscences of Public Men, with Speeches and Addresses second series. Greenville, S. C., 1889.

Pike, James Shepherd. The Prostrate State: South Carolina under Negro Government. New York, 1874.

Porter, A. Toomer. Led on! Step by Step. Scenes from Clerical, Military, Educational, and Plantation Life in the South, 1828-1898. An Autobiography. New York, 1899.

Powers, Stephen. Afoot and Alone: A Walk from Sea to Sea by the Southern Route, etc. Hartford, Conn., 1872.

Report of the Joint Investigating Committee on Public Frauds and Election of Hon. J. J. Patterson to the U. S. Senate made to the General Assembly of S. C. at the regular session of 1877-78. Columbia, 1878.

Reynolds, John S. Reconstruction in South Carolina, 1865-1877. Columbia, 1905.

Sanborn, Alvin F. Reminiscences of Richard Lathers. New York, 1907.

Sheppard, William A. An Open Letter to David Duncan Wallace, A. M., Ph. D., Litl. D. L. L. D., Concerning Certain Source Material on the History of the Reconstruction Period. Spartantanburg, S. C., 1943.

———. Red Shirts Remembered: Southern Brigadiers of the Reconstruction Period. Spartanburg, S. C., 1940.

———. Some Reasons Why Red Shirts Remembered. Spartanburg, S. C., 1940.

Sherman, John. Recollections of Forty Years in the House, Senate and Cabinet. 2 vols. New York, 1895.

Simkins, Francis Butler. Pitchfork Ben Tillman: South Carolinian. Baton Rouge, La., 1944.

Simkins, Francis Butler and Woody, Robert Hilliard. South Carolina during Reconstruction. Chapel Hill, 1932.

South Carolina: Resources and Population, Institutions and Industries, ed. Harry Hammond. Charleston: State Board of Agriculture of South Carolina, 1883. Cited as South Carolina Handbook, 1883.

South Carolina Women in the Confederacy. 2 vols. Columbia, 1903-7.

Taylor, Alrutheus A. The Negro in South Carolina during the Reconstruction. Washington, 1924.

Thompson, Henry T. Ousting the Carpetbagger from South Carolina. Columbia, 1926.

Tillman, Benjamin R. "The Struggle of '76." Speech at Anderson, S. C., 1909, n.p. n.d.

U. S. Congress, Senate and House. Ku Klux Conspiracy, The Reports of the Joint Select Committee to inquire into the condition of affairs in the late insurrectionary States, Vol. I. Senate Report 41, 42nd Cong., 2nd Sess. Washington, 1872. Cited as Committee Reports, Ku Klux Conspiracy, S. C.

U. S. Congress, Senate and House. *Ku Klux Conspiracy, The Testimony taken by the Joint Select Committee to enquire into the condition of affairs in the late insurrectionary States,* Vols. III, IV, and V. Cited as *Ku Klux Conspiracy, S. C.*

U. S. Congress, House. *Recent Election in South Carolina, The Testimony taken by the Select Committee on Recent Election in South Carolina.* House Misc. Doc. 41. 44th Cong., 2nd Sess. Washington, 1877.

Wallace, David D. *The History of South Carolina.* 4 vols. New York, 1934.

Webster, Laura Josephine. "The Operation of the Freedmen's Bureau in South Carolina." Smith College Studies in History. Vol. I. Northampton, Mass., 1916.

Wells, Edward L. *Hampton and Reconstruction.* Columbia, 1907.

Williams, Alfred B. *Hampton and His Red Shirts: South Carolina's Deliverance in 1876.* Charleston, 1935.

Williams, Charles R. *The Life of Rutherford Birchard Hayes.* 2 vols. Boston, 1914.

NEWSPAPERS

Chronicle and Sentinel (Augusta, Ga.), January 10, 1877.

Courier (Charleston), November 26, 1860.

Daily News (Charleston), November 1, 1867; November 9, 1867.

Daily Phoenix (Columbia), July 31, 1867; August 28, 1867; April 4, 1868; July 26, 1868; October 18 and 23, 1868.

Daily Register (Columbia), August 2 and 28, September 1, 13, and 19, 1877; January 4, March 3, 6, 12, 15, 16, 22, 25, 27, and 29, April 4, 6, 13, 18, and 19, May 9, 26, and 30, June 16, July 7 and 11, August 4, 17, and 21, September 3, 5, 7, 15, 20, 22, 28, and 29, October 1, 2, 3, 5, 16, 18, and 22, November 9, 1878. Cited as *Register*.[1]

News and Courier (Charleston), May 8, 1876; April 27, 1877; September 18, 1877; August 5 and 15, 1878; December 11, 1878; January 20, 1879.

OTHER PERIODICALS

Chamberlain, Daniel H. "Reconstruction in South Carolina." *Atlantic Monthly,* LXXXVII (April, 1901).

---

[1]This publication has a dual title. In the nameplate on Page One of each issue, it is rendered *Daily Register,* whereas the official masthead on the editorial page bears the title *Columbia Register.*

Congressional Record, 46th Cong., 1st Sess., Vol. IX, Pt. 2, 1352.

Congressional Record, 46th Cong., 2nd Sess., Vol. X, Pt. 4, 3755.

Harper's Weekly, XII, XIV, XV.

Hogan, Edward. "South Carolina To-day." *International Review*, VIII (February, 1880).

Maxwell, E. J. "Hampton's Campaign in South Carolina." *South Atlantic Magazine*, a series of seven articles from February-August, 1878.

The Nation, VII, VIII, IX, X, XI, XII, XXII, XXIII, XXIV, XXV, XXVI, XXVII, XXVIII.

Post, Louis, "A 'Carpetbagger' in South Carolina." *Journal of Negro History*, X (January, 1925).

Simkins, Francis B. "Ben Tillman's View of the Negro." *Journal of Southern History*, III (May, 1937).

[Townsend, Belton O'Neall.] "The Political Condition of South Carolina." *Atlantic Monthly*, XXIX (February, 1877).

——. "South Carolina Morals." *ibid.*, (April, 1877).

——. "South Carolina Society." *ibid.*, (June, 1877).

Trescot, William Henry. "Letters on Reconstruction in South Carolina." *American Historical Review*, XV (April, 1910).

Wallace, D. D. "The Question of the Withdrawal of the Democratic Presidential Electors in South Carolina in 1876." *Journal of Southern History*, VIII (August, 1942).

Wilson, Woodrow. "The Reconstruction of the Southern States." *Atlantic Monthly*, LXXXVII (January, 1901).

Woody, R. H. "Behind the Scenes in the Reconstruction Legislature of South Carolina: Diary of Josephus Woodruff." *Journal of Southern History*, II (February, 1936).

INDEX

Abbeville, 115 n, 144 n, 146 n; dividing time at, 67; Democratic victory, 75; election in, 92

Adams, John Quincy II, defends Hampton, 31

Aiken, 48, 82, 146 n; Hampton "howled down," 162

Aldrich, Robert, seconds Hampton's nomination, 52

American Bank Note Company, 38

Anderson, 133 n; Hampton speaks, 1876, 64; Hampton speaks, 1878, 136; first to adopt county primary, 140

Augusta *Chronicle and Constitutionalist*, on Negro support of Hampton, 139; warns against Hampton's Negro policy, 144; advocates Gary's Negro policy, 144; on Gary-Hampton feud, 147. *See also* Augusta *Chronicle and Sentinel*.

Augusta, Ga., *Chronicle and Sentinel*, publishes letter accusing Hampton, 115-116. *See also* Augusta *Chronicle and Constitutionalist*.

Ball, W. W., on Hampton and Gary, 60; on "preference, not proscription," 70; on cheering for Hampton, 72

Barker, Major Theodore, on Democratic split, 142

Barnhart, Lt. F. H., election Abbeville County, 92

Barnwell, 123 n, 140 n, 143, 145 n, 146 n; Negroes pay voluntary tax, 113

Baruch, Bernard, effect of Reconstruction on, 4 n

Bater, Lt. R. F., election in Newberry, 92

Beaufort, Hampton's speech, 83-85; Negro control of, 159

Blackville, Hampton speaks, 141, 142-143

"Black Code," 12-14

Blair, F. P., II, 29; Hampton seconds nomination, 28

Board of canvassers. *See* Dual government.

Boseman [B. A. ?], Negro postmaster, confidence in Hampton, 130

Bourbons, 57, 86, 120, 130, 162

Bowen, C. C., 121; record of, 39 n; rules Radical convention, 140; attacks pro-Hampton resolution, 140

Bowers, Claude G., on Hampton's efforts at national harmony, 31; on Hayes-Tilden election, 86

Brannan, Gen., at election in Edgefield, 93-95

Butler, Gen. M. C., 152, 157; effort at "fusion," 1870, 34-35; for straighout Democracy, 47; withdraws and nominates Hampton, 51-52; "dividing time," 67; attacks Chamberlain, 67; at election in Edgefield, 93, 97-98; becomes Senator, 127; for Hampton's policy, 146 n

Cainhoy, violence at, 69

Carolina Rifle Battalion, at Charleston riot, 66-67

Carpenter, Judge R. B., testifies on charges by Negroes, 35; on high taxes, 38 n; prodded by Chamberlain, 49; on election law, 88

Carpetbaggers, aid Radicals and themselves, 4; described by De Forest, 4 n; in constitutional convention, 1868, 22; described by Greeley, 22-23; described by Powers, 23 n; *The Nation* justifies hatred of, 40 n; on federal juries, 135-136. *See also* Radical government, S. C.

Census, federal, of 1870 and 1880, 91, 98-101

Census, state, 1875, 91, 98-101

Chamberlain, D. W., on racial equality, 11 n; on Democrats' cooperation, 37 n, 43 n; on Radical failure to support education, 39 n; record of to 1876, 41-44; defense of, 41 n, 42 n; accusations against, 42-43; printing ring, 42-43; state